THE ROAD TO EVERGREEN

The Road to Evergreen

*Adoption, Attachment Therapy,
and the Promise of Family*

RACHAEL STRYKER

Cornell University Press
Ithaca and London

Copyright © 2010 by Cornell University

All rights reserved. Except for brief quotations in a review, this book, or parts thereof, must not be reproduced in any form without permission in writing from the publisher. For information, address Cornell University Press, Sage House, 512 East State Street, Ithaca, New York 14850.

First published 2010 by Cornell University Press
First printing, Cornell Paperbacks, 2010

Printed in the United States of America

Library of Congress Cataloging-in-Publication Data
Stryker, Rachael, 1972–
   The road to Evergreen : adoption, attachment therapy, and the promise of family / Rachael Stryker.
      p. cm.
   Includes bibliographical references and index.
   ISBN 978-0-8014-4687-0 (cloth : alk. paper)
   ISBN 978-0-8014-7686-0 (pbk. : alk. paper)
   1. Attachment disorder in children—United States.   2. Adoption—United States—Psychological aspects.   3. Families—United States—Psychological aspects.   4. Parenting—United States—Psychological aspects.   I. Title.
   RJ507.A77S77   2010
   618.92'8588—dcs22   2009053488

Cornell University Press strives to use environmentally responsible suppliers and materials to the fullest extent possible in the publishing of its books. Such materials include vegetable-based, low-VOC inks and acid-free papers that are recycled, totally chlorine-free, or partly composed of nonwood fibers. For further information, visit our website at www.cornellpress.cornell.edu.

Cloth printing   10 9 8 7 6 5 4 3 2 1
Paperback printing   10 9 8 7 6 5 4 3 2 1

For Elias

Contents

ACKNOWLEDGMENTS

Publishing maven William Germano has written: "Books are like photographs, possible only because the camera and the eye were fortunate enough to be somewhere at the very moment when the clouds held their shape long enough." During the eight years that this book has been in progress, the shape of the politics surrounding the Evergreen model of attachment therapy has been at times as ephemeral as Germano's clouds. To know when, where, and how to watch the sky has required the help and support of many colleagues and friends. My gratitude to them is deep and heartfelt.

The research on which this book was based was made possible by a three-year National Science Foundation fellowship and a Henry Simpson fellowship from the Institute for International Studies at the University of California at Berkeley.

Of individuals, I thank first the many adopted children, adoptive families, adoption workers, and attachment therapists included in this book for allowing me into their lives. I owe them a great deal for their involvement, investment, and faith in my vision. It is not always easy to open up to a stranger, particularly about the personal project of growing up, or helping others to grow up, and I am grateful to all for their interest and participation. I hope they find that their words have been used to gain a deeper understanding of families and children, one that helps us make better choices about how we will engage them as members and creators of our society.

The following colleagues must also be thanked. Without their guidance and support, I could not have nurtured the on-the-page connections that were necessary to complete this project. As always, I thank Laura Nader for her expertise and faith in my work and David McCurdy, who always has been, and always will be, an inspiration to me. Gerald Berreman, Paula Fass, Nelson Graburn, Kristen Luker, and Nancy Scheper-Hughes provided challenging comments and suggestions during the early stages of my research and writing. In later stages, research assistant Joy Wheeler spent hours and hours in libraries and on the computer so that I could better enjoy my first pregnancy and the birth of my child. My colleagues in the Department of Anthropology and Sociology at Mills College were always available to talk about ways to improve the manuscript. Barbara Yngvesson and Beth Miller offered advice and encouragement throughout the writing and editing phases.

The following people are especially appreciated—without them, there simply would be no book: Elizabeth Dunn, whose indomitable optimism and energy fueled this project at every stage; Peter Wissoker and Fran Benson at Cornell University Press, who provided clear, forthright, and patient direction through the editorial process; Emily Zoss and Karen Laun, who answered countless questions before I turned in my final manuscript; Katy Meigs, whose attention to my manuscript went above and beyond that of most copy editors; two anonymous reviewers whose insightful comments improved the book's coherence and appeal; Karen Sobel, for impromptu photography; Jeff Bontrager at Colorado Health Institute for important data; and Sue Wilson, whose valuable contributions in the final stages are multiple and who I will always warmly remember. My dear friends Hilary Altman, Nancy Cardona, Linda Di Raimondo, Gillian Donahey, Maggie Hopkins, David Kojan, Kate McNear, Sarah McGee, Jennifer Soss, and Molly Thorsen-Connolly had unflagging faith in my ability to see this project through. To them I say thank you for many years of good talks, good walks, and the amazing ability to lift my spirits in the worst of times. I am also grateful to my Bay Area friends for their brilliant insights on trauma, attachment, and the brain.

Finally, I thank my husband, Bradley Rowe, who put in countless hours of reading, editing, discussion, and parenting while I wrote this book. He has my deep love and appreciation, not only for seeing me through what has been an incredible journey, but for simply seeing me. It has made all the difference.

THE ROAD TO EVERGREEN

Chapter One

The Evergreen Model of Attachment Therapy

Emotional Salvation or Economic Exploitation?

Evergreen, Colorado, the undisputed capital of attachment therapy in the United States, is a flourishing suburb thirty miles west of Denver. Best known as the pristine mountain town on which the animated comedy *South Park* is based, it is for most people simply one of a hundred exits that SUVs whip by while navigating Interstate 70 from Denver International Airport to ski areas at Aspen or Vail. Its borders begin inauspiciously with a stretch of newly paved four-lane highway that is dotted with strip malls, extending from Route 70 east until it dramatically reveals its heart, a self-consciously rustic downtown nestled between a set of terraced buttes and picturesque Evergreen Lake.

Beneath Evergreen's sleepy exterior, however, lies a complex history involving children, adoption, pathology, and power. First populated in 1859, Evergreen long enjoyed a reputation as a thriving logging and ranching community and as the site of several popular summer resorts. In the latter half of the twentieth century, the town's beautiful mountain setting and forgiving commute to Denver also began to draw a large number of mental health professionals, many of whom found that the area's isolated feel and tranquility made it an especially attractive site in which to conduct family and child therapies that included a retreat-like setting. By 2000, Evergreen's Jefferson County had 1.2 active licensed non-physician mental health

Fig. 1 Evergreen, Colorado, photograph by Karen Sobel

Fig. 2 Downtown Evergreen, photograph by the author

providers per 1,000 inhabitants (Colorado Health Institute 2009). Among these professionals are the employees of over a dozen treatment facilities specializing in attachment disorders (Bowers 2000).

Indeed, for thirty years, parents have traveled to Evergreen to seek help for their emotionally disturbed children from attachment therapists who practice the controversial "Evergreen method"—a form of attachment therapy characterized by a combination of intense psychotherapy, confrontation therapies most often referred to as "holding therapy," and therapeutic-parenting training. Most children who come to be treated in Evergreen have been given the diagnosis of reactive attachment disorder (RAD), which describes children who are considered to be unable or unwilling to bond with a parental (most often maternal) figure. The disorder, itself the object of some controversy,[1] is thought by psychologists and psychiatrists to result when a serious interruption occurs in the bonding between mother and child during the child's first twenty-six months of life (Reber 1996; Richters and Volkmar 1994). Attachment therapists often refer to children diagnosed with reactive attachment disorder as "RAD kids."

Until the twenty-first century, mention of the Evergreen model of attachment therapy might, at best, have elicited a puzzled look. However, in April 2000 after the highly publicized tragic death by suffocation of Candace Newmaker, a ten-year-old girl placed for treatment with an attachment therapist named Connell Watkins, the town's clinics became the center of a media frenzy that effectively incriminated all attachment disorder clinics in the area. To this day, the clinics continue to be lightning rods of controversy. On one side sit the attachment therapists and frustrated parents of emotionally disturbed children who swear by the Evergreen model and method. On the other side are medical practitioners who question the professionalism and morality of attachment therapists who follow the Evergreen model.

Despite professional and ethical concerns, attachment therapies of all stripes are increasingly popular with American parents. It is difficult to obtain reliable statistics regarding the exact numbers who are turning to attachment therapies each year. Nevertheless, it is widely recognized by pediatric psychologists that there has been both an increase in the number of children diagnosed with reactive attachment disorder in the United States (Hanson and Spratt 2000) and that more professionals are using attachment therapies, including those based on the Evergreen model, than they

---

[1] While this book has as its main focus one particular modality for treating children diagnosed with RAD, the vague nature of the RAD diagnosis and the contested understanding of the sources of RAD are considered in chapter 4.

did a decade ago (Chaffin et al. 2006). In addition, the number of therapists associated with the Evergreen model who are registering with the Association for Treatment and Training in the Attachment of Children (ATTACh), the professional organization for attachment therapists in the United States, continues to grow each year (ATTACh 2005, 2008).

If the Evergreen model of attachment therapy is so controversial, why does it persist as a method for treating emotionally disturbed children? One argument is that the Evergreen model, with its hybrid of talk, confrontation, and therapeutic parenting, is an absolutely necessary alternative to ineffective traditional therapies. For example, in this view, classical psychotherapy and play therapy are ineffective because they fail to recognize the severity of the core damage done to the psyche of RAD kids—their lack of trust, which precludes their developing a conscience (Cline 1979, 1991; Magid and McKelvey 1989; Randolph 1994, 2002). Proponents of the Evergreen model also argue that, without it, such children will grow up without a chance at emotional recovery (Levy and Orlans 1998) and will possibly even become "kids who kill" (Thomas n. d.; Thomas, Thomas, and Thomas 2002). They are also thought to be so severely damaged that Evergreen therapy is a last resort, the only intervention that can save them (Thomas 2005). These accounts also often portray the parents of RAD kids as long-suffering potential victims of the children's murderous behaviors, which only the intervention of the Evergreen method can help.

A contrary, more widely circulated argument, however, characterizes the Evergreen model as, at best, a fringe therapy and, at worst, quackery, fraud, or child abuse. The attachment therapy–related deaths during the last fifteen years of at least five children in the United States in addition to Candace Newmaker (Auge 2000; Bowers 2000) have increased skepticism about the Evergreen model in child psychology circles. Critics focus on questions of whether or not attachment therapists are adopting, and adapting, attachment theory in therapeutically and ethically appropriate ways (Mercer, Sarner, and Rosa 2003; Zilberstein 2006). The critiques most often characterize the therapeutic modalities as scientifically unsound (Speltz 2002). They also challenge the efficacy of attachment therapies (Bakermans-Kranenburg, van Ijzendoorn, and Juffer 2003). In these accounts, it is both the parents *and* the children who are portrayed as unsuspecting victims. In the most extreme form of this critique, attachment therapists are understood to be confidence artists intent on subjecting children to torturous pseudoscientific practices for the purpose of bilking their desperate parents (Mercer n.d.).

The controversy surrounding the use of the Evergreen method is obviously emotionally charged. The intense vulnerabilities of those involved compel both critical and supportive authors to use a virtue model to frame their positions—one in which individuals' innate characters are thought to drive social phenomena. Therapists are presented as either heroes or con artists, parents are understood to be either dedicated or delusional, and children are portrayed either as innocent victims or uncontrollable monsters. These emotions are compounded by the pressing situation of large numbers of formerly institutionalized domestic and foreign adoptees in the United States who, once adopted, are determined to be in need of post-placement interventions, including a wide range of psychological therapies (Barth and Miller 2000). For example, it has been estimated that approximately 1 percent of *all* children in the United States have RAD (Richters and Volkmar 1994, in Hall and Geher 2003) and that 80 percent of abused or neglected children in the United States demonstrate some behaviors associated with RAD (Reber 1996, in Hall and Geher 2003). This said, it is notoriously difficult to determine the prevalence of children with RAD due to a lack of a universally accepted diagnostic protocol (Newman and Mares 2007; Zilberstein 2006). Most longitudinal or meta-analytical studies available on *domestic* adoptions estimate that between 9 and 15 percent of them disrupt (terminate before finalization) and 3 to 12 percent dissolve (legally annul) sometimes due to children's difficult behaviors typical of RAD (Festinger 2002, 2005; George, Howard, Yu, and Radomsky 1997).[2] With regard to *foreign* adoptions, there are not yet reliable studies on the number that dissolve due to children's behaviors associated with RAD; however, there is strong anecdotal evidence that the rate may be higher than those for domestic adoptions (Lash, 2000; Miller 2004). According to the United States Department of Health and Human Services (2008), between 2002 and 2007, an average of 51,000 children per year were adopted into permanent homes in the United States.[3] With regard to internationally adopted

---

[2] Exact numbers vary depending on the population of children sampled. It has been noted, for example, that studies that include a larger number of children who were adopted at older ages or who have spent more time in foster care have higher rates of disruption and dissolution (see Barth, Gibbs, and Siebenaler 2001; Festinger 2002, 2005).

[3] To properly contextualize this figure, between 2002 and 2008, foster care systems served over 4.7 million children nationwide. Of these numbers, an average of 500,000 children per year were actually in foster care at any given time. Approximately 130,000 of these children per year were designated as "waiting" for a family outcome (waiting for reunification with parents or for termination of parental rights), and of *these* children,

children, the United States has received approximately 216,000 foreign adoptees between 1998 and 2008 (United States Department of State 2008). If studies and increasing anecdotal information on disruption and dissolution rates due to children's negative postplacement behaviors from these two groups are accurate, this indicates that between 7,000 and 17,000 new children per year may be candidates for attachment therapies and other postplacement interventions.[4]

While using a virtue model to explain the growing popularity of the Evergreen method of attachment therapy is understandable, the truth remains that individuals' actions can never be divorced from the social conditions that produce them (Kirmayer and Young 1999; Kleinman, Wang, and Li 1995; Simon 1999). Medical practices, in particular, are a rich source of cultural analysis, exposing the power relations of societies at the same time that they reinforce them (Farmer 2001; Porter 1987). It is therefore compelling to transcend an understanding of the Evergreen model as either a form of salvation or exploitation. A more anthropological approach to understanding the rise of the Evergreen model uses a social constructivist lens to examine the complex ways that the therapy functions to reproduce particular social relationships. This work is characterized by an interest in what medical anthropologist Allan Young (1995, 5) has called "the practices, technologies, and narratives" with which illness is diagnosed, studied, treated, and represented, and by the various interests, institutions, and moral arguments that mobilize these efforts and resources (Nader and González 2000). Only by moving away from a virtue model and taking this nuanced anthropological approach to the topic of the Evergreen method of attachment therapy can we understand why parents continue to turn to this controversial form of treatment for their children in the United States.

With this goal in mind, I explore some of the cultural factors that have contributed to the rise of the Evergreen model of attachment therapy in the

---

an average of 76,000 per year had their parents terminate parental rights, making them "adoptable." The 51,000 children adopted into permanent homes per year during this five-year period came from this pool (United States Department of Health and Human Services 2008).

[4] The numbers discussed here reflect only those adoptions that have been officially reported as disrupted or as having undergone dissolution. When the numbers of adoptions that have not been disrupted or undergone dissolution but are described by adoptive parents as having serious problems that have led them to consider disruption and/ or dissolution are also considered, the number of children in the United States who are candidates for attachment therapies may prove even higher (see Evan B. Donaldson Institute, 2004; Goerge et al. 1997; Groza 1996).

United States, with an ethnographic focus on the paths that families take that lead them to undergo the therapy. A central argument is that the emergence of the Evergreen model must be understood in relation to the simultaneous broader cultural move during the 1990s toward child adoption as a mode of family building in the United States. The Evergreen model initially had a short, unsuccessful life in the 1970s as a treatment for severely autistic children (Siegel 1996). It was not until it was embraced by an increasing number of American adoptive parents who were experiencing great frustration with formerly institutionalized children that the therapies began to enjoy the kind of popularity that we witness today. Indeed, contemporary studies indicate that children who are treated for RAD are more likely to be adopted than not (Hall and Geher 2003).[5] It is also well documented that children who have been severely abused or neglected and/or who have been formerly institutionalized for long periods of time or who have been adopted at older ages often have several difficulties in transitioning to nuclear family life (Brodzinsky, Smith, and Brodzinsky 1998; Groza and Rosenberg 1998). I argue that adoptive families that include formerly institutionalized children are attracted to the Evergreen model because it invigorates and legitimizes the same ideas about families, children, and domesticity that are socially reproduced by the adoption process itself. In other words, attachment therapy did not change to fit a new market—a new market found the therapies.

In 1999 I conducted an ethnographic analysis of the Evergreen model that began with nine months of participant observation at an attachment clinic in Evergreen. Throughout the book, I refer to this field site as "the clinic."[6] During my field research at the clinic, I conducted reciprocal research while doing light clerical work, archival research, and writing to aid the clinic in its state accreditation process in exchange for access to fifteen adoptive families that completed two-week intensive therapy sessions during my time there. With families' permission, I also took part in two role-plays during two different families' treatment periods and underwent one session of holding therapy to better understand what families and attachment therapists experience. Each family agreed in writing to be interviewed as part of their intake and exit procedure and to be observed through a

---

[5] However, studies also demonstrate that RAD behaviors are present in the general population and may be associated with "harsh or negative parenting behavior" (Minnis et al. 2007, 494).

[6] For the purposes of this book, the name of this clinic has been changed, as have the names and identifying information of all individuals.

two-way mirror during their therapy sessions. Clinic staff also provided access to copies of client files that had been altered to assure anonymity—approximately 114 additional families—dating back to 1995. Members of 59 of these families allowed me to interview them in some manner during my time at the clinic. Most of the ethnographic information presented here is based either on my direct observations, ethnographic interviews, and/ or familiarity with the case files of the 129 families in these two samples.[7] In addition, I interviewed the members of 14 other adoptive families in the Denver area between October 1999 and April 2000, all of whom included children diagnosed with RAD who later were treated following the Evergreen model at other U.S. clinics and 4 families whose children were diagnosed with RAD but who never sought the Evergreen method of treatment. Between 1996 and 1999, prior to my research at the clinic, I also interviewed 24 sets of adoptive parents recruited through contact with transnational adoption Internet support groups. For these interviews I used convenience and snowball sampling. Of these parent sets, 7 choose to go on to use the Evergreen model of attachment therapy. I have also used the ethnographic data from interviews with these 7 families.

To structure these interviews and organize the information I gathered during my participation observation at the clinic, I utilized the ethnosemantic method (Spradley, McCurdy, and Shandy 2005). This methodology is based on the premise that cultural themes can be elicited through language and that these themes are best elicited through a combination of structured ethnographic interviewing and participant observation. Using this methodology during my nine months of participant observation at the clinic yielded much valuable information about the experiences of the families who had brought their children there for treatment. It also yielded a clear understanding of the practices, rituals, and philosophies of attachment therapists who follow the Evergreen model. This methodology confirmed that the vast majority of families that follow the Evergreen model have formerly institutionalized adoptees.

Such confirmation suggested a strong and immediate need for me to move beyond the boundaries of the clinic to begin vertically integrated research (see Nader 1980) on the various pathways by which formerly institutionalized adoptees came to be treated there. For example, since domestically and internationally adopted children were both represented as clients at the clinic, I chose to conduct 27 ethnosemantic interviews with the employees of

---

[7] See appendix for a breakdown of the demographics of the two samples.

twelve international adoption agencies and eight domestic foster care agencies in the Denver metro area during spring 2000. As a result, I was better able to connect the similarities and differences in outcome with the processes by which these two groups of formerly institutionalized children are adopted. Because, at the time of this fieldwork, popular media created through omission the impression that Russian and Romanian adoptees were more likely than other adoptees to display disturbing behavior, and thus to be diagnosed with RAD and treated with attachment therapies,[8] I spent four months conducting participant observation and ethnographic interviews with adoptive parents in Russian orphanages between April and July, 2000. Data collected, analyzed, and offered for consideration here with regard to internationally adopted children and attachment therapy is only representative of Russian adoptees and cannot be generalized for children adopted from other countries. Data and analysis stemming from this phase of my research has been discussed elsewhere (Stryker 2000, 2002; Tunina and Stryker 2001).

Forging Family, Fixing Family: The Evergreen Model and the Preservation of Domesticity

In a lively essay titled "The Family Spirit" (1998), sociologist Pierre Bourdieu considers the trend in ethnomethodology to discount the sociological power of the family by presenting it as a mere semantic construction. Citing the work of ethnomethodologists who point to the emergence of alternate forms of family as well as to rising rates of cohabitation without marriage in the United States as evidence of the family's imminent demise, he asks what consequences arise from such ethnography that casts a cynical "radical doubt" on the social reality of the family (e.g., Gubrium and Holstein 1990). He critiques the notion that the family is mostly "constructed...by the *vocabulary* that the social world provides us with in order to describe it" (Bourdieu 1998, 64; emphasis mine). He also counters the assertion that families, and particularly the nuclear family, are best understood as either a hegemonic imposition or a discursive fiction. He then calls for investigation into the social history of family in more radical ways.

---

[8] See, for example, Greene (2000), Horn (1997), and Talbot (1998). In addition, the erroneous perception throughout the 1990s in the United States that Russian adoptees as a general group, were more likely than other formerly institutionalized adoptees to display behaviors that might lead to a RAD diagnosis has since been remedied by scientific studies (see, e.g., McGuinness, Ryan, and Robinson 2005; McGuinness and Pallansch 2007).

According to Bourdieu, four suppositions would categorize a more radical social scientific interrogation of family. First, "family" would be understood not as a word but more as a "watchword," one that—no matter
what word one actually uses to describe it—always connotes "a category"
or "a collective principle of construction of collective reality" (66) that
is both organized by, and organizes, human relationships. Second, language about the family would be investigated so as to make clear the ways
in which "family discourse" or "the language that family uses about the
family" (65) both describes and *prescribes* the reality of family. Third, family discourse would be understood to be "made real" through the tracking
of a series of practices that represent the family as "immanent" or enacted
(i.e., the practices that members of families engage in to solidify themselves as part of family, such as the transfer of property to blood relatives
through wills and surnaming) as well as practices that represent the family as "transcendent" or observed, that is, those practices that members of
families encounter in the form of objectivity in others, making the family
appear to be a natural, "transcendent" category that existed a priori its social construction. And fourth, the best "way in" to understanding the ways
in which family is presented as imminent is to investigate the rites and rituals of family; while the best way to understand the family as transcendent
is to investigate the relationship between family members and "licensed
state operators," or state agents. Such an approach anticipates the need to
investigate the family as a social construction, but it also identifies and
interrogates the social acts—both symbolic and institutional—that shape
actors' proclivity to invoke, and play out, family. It also begins to identify
the stakes for individuals in the construction—and protection—of family
as a social category.

While my *practical* goal in this book is to engage the compelling question
of why adoptive parents bring their children to Evergreen, despite the Evergreen model's controversial nature, my main *theoretical* imperative is to test
Bourdieu's prescriptions for a more radical investigation of the family as a
principle of construction of social reality. The second central argument of
this book, then, is that parents bring their children to Evergreen because attachment therapy operates not only as an important component of a logic
for preserving adoptive families as bodies, but also to preserve the social
category of family more generally.

With these practical and theoretical objectives in mind, in the first half
of the book I identify and interrogate the typical pathways by which adoptive parents make their way to attachment clinics in Evergreen. Chapter 2,
for example, which is based on ethnographic interviews conducted with 74
families of various compositions who adopted formerly institutionalized

children between 1995 and 2000 and who later entered their children in treatment programs at attachment clinics in Evergreen, introduces readers to the empirical experiences of parents who attempt to define and navigate the path toward family stability after adopting. Specifically, I ask: Why did parents choose to adopt institutionalized children and children from foster care rather than from other venues? What roles and behaviors did they originally expect from the children? Chapter 2 investigates the elements that make up the particular types of folk wisdom, or *doxa* (Bourdieu 1977 [1972]), about family, children, and domesticity that parents use to frame their preadoption choices and postplacement expectations. It reveals the negotiation of symbols, as well as the practices and rituals in which parents engage to represent the family as imminent and as an internalized collective.

While chapter 2 interrogates the folk categories that adoptive parents use to form their own representations of family, chapter 3 reveals both a potent source of these categories, as well as a site where they are socially reproduced: adoption agencies. Adoption agencies play a large part in representing the family as transcendent. They prescribe the parameters of "normal" family, children, and domesticity through several practices, including publicizing agency-founding stories, adoption testimonials, and promoting the iconography of "adoptable" children. Agencies also enact several disciplinary techniques such as parent fitness tests and postplacement reporting procedures that prescribe state-inspired definitions of family throughout the process. The exploration of parents' relationships with adoption agencies in this chapter provides a clear understanding of the ways in which adoption agencies' language and practice contribute to the ritual and technical institutionalization of the family. It also demonstrates an example of governmentality in the intimate realm of the family (Foucault 1991). In addition, when taken together, chapters 2 and 3 demonstrate that the successful movement of children through adoption processes as experienced by the parents who eventually brought their children to Evergreen is dependent on a particular type of social reproduction of attachment, in which adoptive parents and adoption agency workers portray it as a form of *social contract* between children and adults. Attachment is first "denatured"—represented as reproducible and negotiable—but it is also "re-natured" as commonsensical and inevitable. This model of attachment, which adoption agency workers construct to affirm adopted parents' hope of building a family unit that mirrors the biological nuclear family, is similar to the model used by attachment therapists in Evergreen to reanimate parents' hopes for family once problems arise after adoption.

Despite adoptive parents' and adoption agencies' firm faith in the family as an a priori social category, however, parents' initial hopes for the new family do not always materialize after placement. Children who are eventually brought to Evergreen to undergo attachment therapy exhibit behaviors that puzzle, frustrate, and sometimes terrify adoptive parents. Such behaviors may be so severe that parents feel they can no longer live in the same home as the children. While some parents attempt to keep children living in the home, others institutionalize them in group homes or boarding schools. Enter attachment therapy, which promises to emotionally rehabilitate adoptees and prevent their eventual exile from families. Chapter 4 outlines the specific ways in which adoptees' behaviors often come to contradict and challenge both adoptive parents' *doxa* and the institutionalized representation of the family. These children do not conform to parents' conceptualizations of family behaviors, rituals, and roles. In fact, they typically undermine the very practical and symbolic work of parents that is expected to oblige adoptees to love them. Parents, having already established for themselves (and having adoption experts reiterate for them) the field of "normal" versus "abnormal" family compositions, roles, and rituals, are often ill-equipped to respond to these behaviors. In addition, their initial turn to traditional therapies often proves ineffective. However, on discovering the Evergreen model of attachment therapy, parents believe they have found a treatment that can not only preserve the physical family but legitimate and reanimate their original expectations for the postplacement period. Initially, the most alluring component of the Evergreen model for parents is the firm assertion that children's postplacement behaviors are pathological, with the reactive attachment disorder diagnosis confirming this pathology. In this way, biomedical discourse legitimizes the category of family. Yet it also keeps the notion of attachment as a negotiable social contract alive.

In the first half of the book I suggest some of the ontological preconditions for the popularity of the Evergreen model. But why are parents drawn to the Evergreen model, specifically, over other models of attachment therapy? In the second half of the book I use case studies to demonstrate how the Evergreen model works and what its typical outcomes reveal. The model's unique and unapologetic operation as a form of emotional management promises that children can be *disciplined* to become emotional assets in the home. Chapters 5 and 6 discuss the Evergreen model's central axiom that broken attachment may be repaired through a series of exercises that break children of the habit of controlling others. This type of rehabilitation of feelings associated with the family promises to succeed where previous attempts have failed. Chapter 5 focuses on the ways in which attachment therapists at Evergreen use confrontation therapy (a modality of which holding therapy is the centerpiece) to physically and mentally condition children to comply with parents' expectations regarding family and domesticity. Chapter 6 outlines the ways in which therapists train *parents* to turn their houses into "therapeutic homes" that provide constant emotional discipline to children after the end of attachment therapy. Both chapters exemplify a particular clinical philosophy and methodology that reflects the belief that children can be *trained* to attach to adoptive parents. Attachment therapists in Evergreen socially reproduce attachment much as parents and adoption agencies did during the adoption process—attachment therapists both denature and re-nature attachment as being natural yet reproducible and negotiable, and this social reproduction of child love is the basis for a series of exercises, routines, and practices that promise to endow each member of the family with, as Bourdieu (1998) has offered, "a 'family feeling' that generates devotion, generosity, and solidarity" (68).

The popularity of the Evergreen model is not only sustained by its promise to physically preserve adoptive families. It is also sustained by its particular framework that preserves the *idea* of family more generally, even when adoptive family units disintegrate after treatment. The Evergreen model of attachment therapy has been shown to successfully reunite emotionally disturbed children with their families about as often as it fails to do so. Those children who are not reunited with their adoptive families are (re)institutionalized in long-term care in the clinic, or elsewhere, such as in group homes, military schools, or boarding schools. Attachment therapists at Evergreen call this outcome "loving each other from a distance." Implicit in this framework is an understanding that the exiling of the child from the adoptive family is a result of either the child's inability to perform as "family material" or the child's conscious *choice* to live outside of families, in a situation where attachment is not demanded. This framing allows children to have agency where once there had curiously and explicitly been none and allows both adoptive parents and clinicians to own some of the therapy's successes while disowning failure. It provides an opportunity for adoptive parents to transform "family" from a physical to a metaphorical collective without diminishing it as a social category. In other words, the family is preserved in spirit, if not in actual body.

As a whole, I demonstrate that the Evergreen model of attachment therapy, despite its controversial nature (and, in fact, perhaps *because* of it), is actually an important component of a cultural logic for preserving not just adoptive families but the social category of "family" more generally in the United States. It also illuminates the central role that the social reproduction of attachment, or "child love," plays in the maintenance of the family as a social principle on which we base, organize, and interpret this category. Romantic or marital love (Inden and Nicholas 2005; May 1988), parental love (Hamabata 1991; Trawick 1992), and mother love (Scheper-Hughes 1993; Seymour 1999) have been the subjects of previous ethnomethodological investigation, but the specific nature of child love, and the particular types of social reproduction it undergoes to make families, has yet to be explored in great detail. Finally, I ask how further phenomenological understandings of the workings of attachment might inform and reform both adoption practice and pediatric psychology.

How the Evergreen Model Works: From Attachment Theory to Attachment Therapy

Before tracing the paths that lead families to attachment clinics in Evergreen, it is helpful to describe what families find once there. The history and the basic workings of the Evergreen model of attachment therapy rest on a particular variation of attachment theory. Attachment theory, a combination of developmental psychology, psychoanalysis, and ethology (the study of animal behavior in a natural environment), posits that in infancy children form attachments with primary caregivers based on their need for protection, comfort, and nurturance. Such attachments are essential to all aspects of infant development and lay the groundwork for development throughout life. As early as the mid-twentieth century, psychiatrist and psychoanalyst John Bowlby (1944, 1952, 1965) and psychiatrist and psychoanalyst René Spitz (1945, 1962, 1965) investigated the importance of mother-infant attachment in child development and studied what became of infants separated from their mothers for various periods of time. Bowlby focused on infants hospitalized in mainstream hospitals, and Spitz observed babies hospitalized in foundling homes. The results of their studies demonstrated that babies who were not held or shown affection over time began to exhibit life-threatening apathy and depression, a condition that Spitz dually referred to as "anaclitic depression" or "hospitalism," with a difference being that hospitalism was more likely to snowball into a more lethal form of despair. Both Bowlby and Spitz also speculated that the longer such infants experienced emotional deprivation, the more likely that they would grow into emotionally detached, unloving, untrusting, and withdrawn children and adults. Along with D. W. Winnicott and Walter Goldfarb, Bowlby and Spitz were the first scholars to deeply investigate the impact of relationships during infancy on human behavior throughout the lifespan.

In the mid-twentieth century, Bowlby's work in particular was met with much suspicion, and even derision. Bowlby theorized that it was relationships, and specifically the mother-infant relationship, that determined the nature and quality of human behavior across the lifespan. This theory of relatedness ran counter to two of the most popular schools of human behavior of the day—classical Freudian psychoanalysis, which held that the unconscious workings of the individual psyche determined behavior, and behaviorism, which viewed behaviors almost solely in terms of adult environment and conditioning (Karen 1990). Beginning in the 1960s, however, other theorists began to study the possible impact of early relationships on human behavior, including interpersonal and social theorists, family-systems theorists, and object-relations theorists (Bretherton 1992). Researchers such as Mary Ainsworth (Ainsworth et al. 1978), Mary Main (Main, Kaplan, and Cassidy 1985), and Alan Sroufe (Waters, Matas, and Sroufe 1975) conducted studies from the 1960s through the 1990s that supported and nuanced Bowlby's theories. The most famous of these studies was Mary Ainsworth's "strange situation" experiment, in which she observed the behavior of infants who were separated from their mothers, introduced to a stranger for a short time, and then reunited with their mothers. Results indicated that infants had three different responses when their mother returned: (1) smiling, (2) ignoring her, or (3) crying angrily. Attachment, Ainsworth concluded, could be categorized in at least three different ways: as secure, ambivalent, or avoidant. This research became the basis for attachment theory for forty years, and practitioners who use attachment theory develop and modify their modalities to either aid secure attachments or repair insecure ones in infants and children.

An attachment as it is defined in attachment theory thus has a specific meaning, both in terms of its nature and the person to whom it applies (Prior and Glaser 2006):

According to attachment theory, an attachment is a bond or tie between an individual and an attachment figure. In adult relationships, people may be mutual and reciprocal attachment figures, but in the relationship between the child and parent, this is not the case. The reason for this clear distinction is inherent in the theory. In attachment theory, an attachment is a tie based on the need for safety, security, and protection. This need is paramount in infancy and childhood, when the developing individual is immature and vulnerable. Thus, infants instinctively attach to their caregivers. In this sense, attachment serves the specific biological function of promoting protection, survival and, ultimately, genetic replication. In the relationship between the child and the parent, the term "attachment" applies to the infant or child, and the term "attachment figure" invariably refers to their primary caregiver. In the terms of attachment theory then, it is incorrect to refer to a parent's "attachment" or "attachment" *between* parents and children. Attachment, therefore, is not synonymous with parental love or affection; it is also not an overall descriptor of the relationship between the parent and child which includes other parent-child interactions such as feeding, stimulation, play, or problem solving. A more appropriate term to describe the attachment figure's equivalent tie to the child is the "caregiving bond." (9)

Today, child psychologists primarily use three types of interventions to address child disregulation: social-learning (behavioral) modalities, family therapy or family-systems therapy, and attachment therapies. Of these three modalities, attachment therapies claim to most clearly utilize attachment theory as a foundation for practice (Barth and Miller 2000). Traditional attachment therapy claims that caregiver qualities such as environmental stability, parental sensitivity, and responsiveness to children's physical and emotional needs, consistency, and a safe and predictable environment support the development of healthy attachment. Attachment therapy as it is most commonly practiced today thus focuses on improving positive caretaker and environmental qualities to aid attachment (Bakermans-Kranenburg, van Ijzendoorn, and Juffer 2003). Such therapies use age-appropriate techniques, such as modified psychoanalysis and play therapy, to provide a stable environment and a calm, sensitive, nonintrusive, nonthreatening, patient, predictable, and nurturing approach toward children (Haugaard 2004; Nichols, Lacher, and May 2004). In these types of interventions, the focus is on the parent-child relationship and teaching positive parenting skills rather than on the child's pathology. Such parent-child relationship therapy usually favors maintaining children in their homes rather than removing them to institutional care (Chaffin et al. 2006).

While the Evergreen model can be likened to more traditional forms of attachment therapy in that it utilizes attachment theory as a foundation for practice, the similarities end there. Whereas traditional schools of attachment therapy are populated by direct descendents of Bowlby, Ainsworth, or Spitz, the central figures involved with the Evergreen model trace their intellectual lineage to more controversial forms of "feeling therapy" popular in the 1960s, such as Primal Scream Therapy, Gestalt, est, and Bioenergetics. And unlike more traditional forms of attachment therapy, the Evergreen model is marked by two additional components: confrontation therapy and therapeutic-parenting training.

Confrontation Therapy in the Evergreen Model

The Evergreen model emerged on the scene of pediatric psychology in the mid-1970s, when Foster Cline, an MD in child psychiatry, posited that psychoanalytical and behavioral models were not adequate to manage or improve behaviors associated with severely emotionally disturbed children. Cline claimed that children with character disorders differed from the merely neurotic child in that they had not internalized a mother object and, thus, felt no conflict regarding right and wrong. This lack of an internalized object resulted from the failure of the primary caregiver to adequately and lovingly respond to the child's needs during the first year of life, as well as her (or his) failure to teach the child to tolerate appropriate levels of frustration during the second year of life. The combination of infant deprivation and improper responses to, or neglect of, toddlers' desires, argued Cline, eventually led the child to have a severe lack of trust. The child would also become unattached, in that he or she would feel no desire or ability to form mutually reciprocal emotional relationships with others. Finally, such children would become unable to allow others to control their external environment. Breaking tradition with the prominent attachment theorists of the time, who argued that there was no known therapy that could help such children, Foster Cline argued that there was hope. This hope came in the form of an "armamentarium of specialized techniques" (1979, 27) including confrontational therapies.

The most controversial and well-known aspect of Cline's ideas was his belief in the efficacy of a confrontation therapy called the "Z-process," which was created by psychologist Robert Zaslow in the early 1970s to treat infantile autism (Zaslow and Menta 1975). Zaslow's rage-reduction methods involved physically holding a child patient to confront and work through rage and motor resistance in order to create a positive relationship with the therapist. In Z-process therapy, the therapist incites rage in the child to teach the child to work through intense emotions and to learn to express them healthily and at appropriate times. Zaslow believed that rage within holdings was the last resistance of negativism and also the beginning of positive behavior. Such methods were common in modes of "feeling therapy" popular in the 1960s and 1970s, all of which posited that early childhood trauma led to neurosis that could only be successfully healed by a client's reexperiencing the trauma in order to resolve it in the present (Eisner 2000). Z-process therapy was contemporary with other experimental therapies such as Wilhelm Reich's orgone therapy, the primary goal of which is to release libidinal energy, and Jacqui Schiff's interpretation of Eric Berne's transactional analysis (TA) and reparenting model, which focuses on regressing clients to their child ego state to purge them of emotions associated with early trauma (Schiff 1970). Zaslow's rage-reduction methods were intentionally intrusive, confrontational, physical, and lengthy, as he believed in the need to push through the resistance to gain a "capitulation" on the part of the child prior to gaining trust. Perhaps the most helpful reference to understand this approach is the climactic scene from the 1981 film *An Officer and a Gentleman* in which a defiant young army recruit in boot camp, played by Richard Gere, comes to trust his squad leader only after the two face off in a fistfight.

In 1972 the State of California revoked Robert Zaslow's therapy license on the grounds he was conducting "dangerous and reckless" therapy that caused severe physical injury to a patient (KidsComeFirst.info). Zaslow quickly disappeared from the landscape of American pediatric psychology, and is thought never to have published or practiced again. However, several years later, Foster Cline, adapted Z-process therapy, combining it with elements of psychoanalysis, to treat rageful character-disordered children, citing Zaslow's unappreciated genius (Cline 1979). Cline also argued that there were some children who had been so emotionally damaged that they not only lacked the ability to form attachments but they actively sought control *rather* than attach. In 1971 Cline, along with psychologist and colleague Russ Colburn, founded Evergreen Consultants in Human Behavior in the town of Evergreen, Colorado. By the end of the 1970s and for almost twenty years thereafter, Cline refined the theory and practice of Z-process therapy, with the program later renamed the Youth Behavior Program and later still the Attachment Center at Evergreen (ACE). He and his team of therapists eventually treated hundreds of severely emotionally disturbed children there.

According to Cline (1979), a typical rage-reduction therapy session would be conducted as follows:

> I lay the child across my lap so that his head is on my left with his body stretching out to the right. The child's head is cradled in my left arm. I may hold the child's left arm up and around the top of his head. Thus his own left arm forms a cradle for his head and restrains it, and this position leaves my right hand free to play "spider" or lovingly poke and tickle him around his ribs and tummy. One way or another,

the child's legs have to be restrained so that they cannot kick the therapist or other furniture in the room. This may take other people, or sometimes we can restrain their legs with one of our own. With my free right hand I can also open the child's eyelids, to force eye contact, or close his mouth when I don't like what he is saying....Essentially, the therapist controls the placement and quantity of tactile stimulation with his free right hand, varying it from a fun little "spider" burrowing into the navel or subclavicular space, to a somewhat abrasive, rubbing stimulation on the rib cage. When the child is not being worked with intensively through touch, his labyrinthian [inner ear] mechanisms may be stimulated by sitting him up, turning his head, etc. All of this varied, high-intensity stimulation is necessary to break up the child's habitually rigid and stereotyped responses. He is not allowed to use his usual repetitive auto-stimulatory mechanisms such as rubbing his lips, scratching himself, hitting himself, making repetitive vocalizations, etc. (171–72)

Cline and his staff operated primarily under the radar of general pediatric psychology throughout the 1980s, and those who did pay attention to

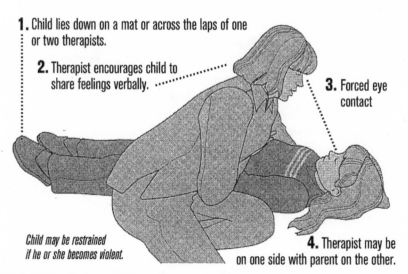

1. Child lies down on a mat or across the laps of one or two therapists.

2. Therapist encourages child to share feelings verbally.

3. Forced eye contact

Child may be restrained if he or she becomes violent.

4. Therapist may be on one side with parent on the other.

Fig. 3 Holding Therapy at Work
Source: www.autism-ppd.net; *Deseret Morning News* archives

his operation lauded his ideas and techniques as part of a courageous try-anything-to-see-if-it-works approach for an untreatable population that seemed to have nothing to lose. The popularity of attachment therapy began to increase through word of mouth, training videotapes, privately published books, adoption agencies, and the Internet. Parents heard about Cline's methods through seminars, conferences, and parent-support groups. In 1993, however, Colorado state regulators began to pay closer attention to Cline's methods after Andrea Swenson, a thirteen-year-old adopted girl undergoing attachment therapy at the Attachment Center at Evergreen, was found dead of an aspirin overdose at the home of therapeutic foster parents employed by ACE. She was violently ill and incoherent during the night, breathing heavily and still vomiting the next morning. However, her foster parents went bowling, leaving her alone. A visitor later found her dead in the hallway. The suit was settled out of court (Auge 2000).

In 1996 Cline voluntarily surrendered his license to practice medicine in Colorado soon after the state's Board of Medical Examiners disciplined him for a separate attachment therapy–related incident at the Attachment Center at Evergreen. He retired to Idaho, where he coauthored with Jim Fay several popular books published by Love and Logic Press, which publishes books that teach consequence-based parenting techniques to biological and adoptive frustrated with their children's behavior. In recent years, Cline and Fay's books have found a particular following among evangelical parents and within Christian schools (Buttner and Fridley 2007). Some of Cline's books are now published by NavPress in Colorado Springs, Colorado. The press, which also publishes the work of James Dobson, founder and former chairman of the organization Focus on the Family, is committed to serving people by facilitating spiritual growth through products that are "biblically rooted, culturally relevant, and practical" (NavPress 2009).

Foster Cline's transformation from defamed child therapist to parenting guru, however, did not mark the end of attachment therapies among professional therapists. The Attachment Center at Evergreen, which in 2002 changed its name once again to The Institute for Attachment and Child Development, continues to operate, and the new attachment therapists who work there have treated hundreds more children since the 1990s. And while Cline's Love and Logic series sold thousands of copies during this time, a new figure soon arrived on the scene to reinvigorate professionals' interest in attachment therapies: Dr. Martha Welch. Psychiatrist Welch first gained notice by claiming that a form of compression therapy that she introduced in the 1970s while at the Albert Einstein College of Medicine in New York and which she called Welch Method Regulatory Bonding was an effective treatment for autism. The ideas presented in her 1989 book *Holding Time,* particularly with regard to a practice that is now known as holding therapy, became the new textbook for incorporating rage-reduction methods into attachment therapies:

> In her book, Welch instructed mothers to take hold of their children during defiant periods, holding them tightly to the point of inducing anger. Therapists told mothers to expect that the child may spit, scream, swear, attempt to get free, bite, and try to cause alarm by saying that he is in pain, cannot breathe, will vomit, is going to die, or needs to urinate. With Welch's approach, parents were encouraged to accept these behaviors calmly and silently. Welch described a subsequent stage (marked by the child's weeping and wailing) in which parents were encouraged to resist the temptation to feel sorry for the child or to feel guilty about what they were doing. Therapists told mothers that if they could successfully resist these temptations, the child would enter an acceptance state in which the child would fight less and become relaxed and tired. The therapist then instructed the mother to loosen her hold on the child, at which point a bonding process was believed to begin, in which the child would find comfort from the mother in this relaxed state. (Speltz 2002, 5)

As holding therapy began to wane as an autism treatment, primarily because it could not be empirically demonstrated to work on that population, Welch continued to promote it for attachment between parent and child more generally. In the last thirty years, Welch's methods have gone by several names, including Compression Therapy, Direct Synchronous Bonding (DSB), and Prolonged Parent Child Embrace (PPCE). Since the late 1980s, Welch's book has served as an important part of attachment therapies to varying degrees. While Foster Cline's form of confrontation therapy is most often used to gain compliance from children during therapy, Welch's particular model of compression therapy is more sparingly used on children whom therapists want to restrain during holding therapy.

Just as Foster Cline's work had operated under the radar of mainstream pediatric psychology until the 1990s, so did Welch's. But the use of certain elements of Welch's particular form of holding therapy came under fire in April 2000 when Candace Newmaker, the ten-year-old from North Carolina, was suffocated during a therapy session under the supervision of an Evergreen therapist named Connell Watkins. By 2000 Welch's model of holding therapy had been taken up and modified in several ways by different clinics in Evergreen. Watkins, a former employee of Foster Cline's Attachment Center at Evergreen, had left the clinic in the early 1990s to start her own practice. One of the specific modifications Connell Watkins made to Welch's method of holding therapy was the addition of a practice called "rebirthing." While rebirthing, as a therapeutic method, takes several forms and is used to achieve several different therapeutic goals, in the practice used by Watkins, therapists tightly wrap a child in a flannel sheet symbolizing the birth canal and encourage the child to push his or her way out of the blanket "into the world" to be "reborn." In this case, therapists use rebirthing as a kinetic metaphor for the child being "reborn" to new parents (Gillian 2001). In the case of Candace Newmaker, Connell Watkins used rebirthing to encourage Candace to attach to her adoptive mother, Jeane Newmaker. This attempt went tragically wrong when Candace suffocated inside the blanket in which she was wrapped for seventy minutes. During this time, Candace repeatedly called for help, but neither Watkins nor Jeane Newmaker came to the child's aid. In 2001 Connell Watkins and an associate were tried for reckless child abuse resulting in death and sentenced to sixteen years in prison. All others who were employed by Watkins and associated with Candace's death were given probation and community service for criminally negligent child abuse. Since Candace's death, both the states of Colorado and North Carolina have passed "Candace's Law," which makes dangerous reenactments of the birth experience during child therapy illegal. Watkins became eligible for parole in March 2007 and was released on parole, after serving a fraction of her sentence, in June 2008 (Nicholson 2008).

Therapeutic Parenting in the Evergreen Model

It is important to note that another controversial element in the Welch model is the transformation of the role of the therapist and the parents during therapy. Whereas the therapist was once the one who did the holding during sessions, in her version the therapist supervised holding sessions while parents carried out the work. Welch was also among the first to encourage parents to use these techniques frequently at home to prevent problems, as well as to treat a host of conditions such as ADHD and various learning disorders. Welch's emphasis on the therapeutic role of the parent dovetailed in the 1990s with a similar practice encouraged by Foster Cline called "therapeutic parenting." As described in the treatment protocol for The Institute for Attachment and Child Development in 2009:

> Therapeutic parenting is an approach to treating children and training parents of children with severe emotional disorders. The therapeutic parent is a highly skilled and trained individual who works in conjunction with the treatment team to treat the child in the therapeutic milieu of a family. The expertise and involvement of the therapeutic parent are the foundation of this unique approach. The therapeutic parent creates a therapeutic environment in which [a] team treatment plan is implemented on a 24-hour basis.
>
> During [attachment therapy based on the Evergreen model], the child usually stays with a therapeutic family. The parents have the opportunity to stay at [hotels or local accommodations]. The child usually does not stay with his parents. Instead the child receives 24 hours per day therapeutic care at the treatment home of the therapeutic foster parents. Parenting techniques that have been found to work for children with attachment disorder are used in the treatment home and throughout the [therapy] are taught to the placing parents. The placing parents spend time in the therapeutic home observing and learning the new parenting techniques. The placing parents thereafter take the child on "practice visits" to their lodgings, local restaurants and other appropriate places to practice using these new techniques with their child. These newly learned parenting techniques teach the child to think through and make appropriate choices, to accept responsibility for their actions, and to develop an "inner voice" (conscience). These newly learned techniques allow the placing parents to be empathic in dealing with the child, but at the same time allow the child to learn from his/her own experiences. As the child learns to trust and love, the child's beliefs change. The child no longer believes that he/she is worthless and the world is hostile. Instead, the child now believes that he/she is worthwhile and capable and the world can help him/her to grow. (The Institute for Attachment and Child Development n.d.)

Just as mainstream therapists view confrontation therapies with suspicion, so do they typically view therapeutic-parenting techniques as questionable. And just as with confrontation therapies, the reason why therapeutic parenting techniques are held with such suspicion largely has to do with highly publicized cases in which they have been associated with the deaths of children (Boris 2003; Reed 2008). Perhaps the most highly publicized case is that of David Polreis.

On February 10, 1996, Renee Polreis, a Greeley, Colorado, mother of two adopted boys who had undergone some training in the Evergreen model of therapeutic parenting, placed a call to 911. Her three-year-old son David was lying unconscious on the bathroom floor of her home and he appeared to be choking to death. Emergency personnel found him dead when they arrived. Emergency personnel originally assumed that David suffered a fatal heart attack. However, it was later discovered that he suffered acute blunt trauma to the head. In addition, over 90 percent of his body was found to be covered with bruises. Coroners later determined that David suffered brain complications from a severe beating that caused him to stop breathing. Further police investigation revealed a broken wooden spoon and bloodied diapers in a trash can in the Polreis house and that Renee Polreis had suspiciously placed a call to her attorney prior to making the call to 911. Within days, police gathered enough evidence to link her to the murder and she was arrested for the beating death of her son. She was put on trial in March 1997 (Bowers 1996; Canellos 1997; Horn 1997).

The Renee Polreis trial made the national newspapers and quickly embedded itself in the cultural landscape. Many reports mined the case for gruesome details, while others bemoaned the Polreis case as an example of the ways in which family values were breaking down in America. The story took on legal significance, however, when, closer to Renee Polreis's trial date, her defense lawyers announced that they were to make an original defense for their client: Renee Polreis, they said, was not guilty, because David was not a "normal" child. He suffered from reactive attachment disorder (RAD).

Renee Polreis and a cadre of medical clinicians were called to the stand to describe young David's behavior: he was superficially charming, overly friendly with strangers, and indiscriminate in his attachments with family members. He threw tantrums and was continually obstinate. He also seemed to have no empathy for others or to feel remorse for anything he did wrong. Most disturbing, David displayed self-injurious behavior—banging his head against walls, punching himself, and pulling on his penis until it bled. David's severe emotional disturbance, the defense said, made him impervious to pain and thus made it not only possible for him to fatally inflict injury on himself, but likely. Renee Polreis had sought treatment for David from several therapists practicing the Evergreen model in Colorado to no avail. It was not Renee Polreis who beat David to death, but David himself.

Testimony about the nature of David's disturbance was provided by psychologists and clinicians, including Foster Cline and several others who practiced the Evergreen method. All claimed that David suffered from reactive attachment disorder and that it was likely that he had, indeed, beaten himself to death. Each also testified that the therapeutic-parenting techniques that Polreis had been taught and executed in her home had been sound. In the end, however, the jury decided that it was more likely the strain of trying to keep a full-time job and disciplining David, without any emotional reward for parenting him, ultimately caused an exhausted and frustrated Renee Polreis to kill David. On September 22, 1997, after only two hours of deliberation, a jury found Renee Polreis guilty of second-degree murder in the death of her adopted son. She was sentenced to twenty-two years in prison (Canellos 1997).

The Evergreen Controversy and Beyond

The Evergreen model of attachment therapy is both believed to save families and to hurt children. One can find it spoken of in the highest regard or with the strongest suspicion, and when one does hear of it, it is undoubtedly its controversial history that draws the most attention. In this view, the therapy might be studied as either a form of social control (see Nader 1997), a high-stakes "performative theater" designed to reinforce social roles between medical professionals and clients (Wenegrat 2001), or as the pseudoscientific result of a collective "hysteria" about children's negative behaviors toward parents (Showalter 1997). Indeed, an ethnographic analysis of the controversy itself is a vital social-scientific endeavor, one that is necessary to continue to draw attention to the need to improve the safety and efficacy of all forms of pediatric psychology treatment. At the same time it is just as vital to conduct an ethnographic analysis of the Evergreen model that illuminates the deeply coded terms and stakes associated with the social reproduction of child love in America. Amid the accusations and blame, behind the sensationalist accounts, real people are struggling to forge, fix, and redefine kinship. This—for better or worse—is what sets parents and children on the road to Evergreen. Thus, in this book I aim not only to tell a story about the inner workings of a controversial treatment modality; I also aim to show the lengths to which many will go to make, and preserve, the American family.

CHAPTER TWO

"LONG BEFORE WE HEARD OF EVERGREEN"

Adoptive Parents' Representations of Family

In September 1999, I arrived in Evergreen, Colorado, and immediately began conducting participant observation at the clinic. My initial observations at the clinic were of what attachment therapists there call the "two-week intensive." The two-week intensive is the basic level of therapeutic treatment that a child receives when accepted in the clinic's program. It typically includes ten weekday sessions of psychoanalysis and holding therapy. Children also receive two weeks of what therapists refer to as "family practice time" in a therapeutic-treatment home, while parents receive several sessions of parent-skills training. A psychiatrist affiliated with the clinic provides consultations, particularly on appropriate medical diagnosis and adjustment of drug type and dosage for children. At the time of my research, a two-week intensive cost seven thousand dollars; for most families the cost is not covered by insurance.

Over the course of my nine months at the clinic, I observed fifteen families in their two-week intensives. The first interaction between families and attachment therapists that I often observed was the discussion of their intake packets, a series of questionnaires, essays, and psychological tests that children and parents complete prior to their arrival. These discussions, as well as the intake packets themselves, provide an excellent source of information about the families who chose to use the Evergreen model.

One of the most immediate, interesting, and obvious themes that emerged from parents' intake packet essays was their surprise about the need for professional intervention. Many could not believe that in their quest to build family, they would need a place like Evergreen. It was, as one parent put it, a "heartshock." One of the first, and most memorable, families I observed during my nine months at the clinic was the Meschlers. The Meschler family comprised husband and wife, Harry and Bev, and their three adopted children—seventeen-year-old Horacio; thirteen-year-old Rayna; and twelve-year-old June. Bev and Harry, two no-nonsense and forthright high school teachers from Cherry Creek, Colorado, had adopted the children about five years earlier. They had seen the children featured on a program called *Wednesday's Child,* a weekly local public-service TV program that publicizes children who are ready for adoption through their local department of human services. After initial calls to their department, a few months of introspection about creating a racially diverse family (the Meschlers are Caucasian and the children are Hispanic), and a year and a half of sporadic supervised visits and a difficult drama involving the children's birth mother's attempts to reinstate her parental rights to the girls, Bev and Harry were allowed to adopt the children.

During the discussion of their intake packet, the Meschlers recounted the many weeks they had spent preparing for the children's arrival in 1995. They had first looked into enrolling them in the local elementary school and preschool, and they had registered them for swimming lessons at the local recreation center. They then began the paperwork to qualify for any state-subsidized health care that might be available to them as a newly adopting family. The two weeks prior to the children's arrival in their home was especially hectic with such tasks as child-proofing the house and setting up the girls' bedrooms. In addition, they were buzzing with excitement about the fortuitous timing of the children's arrival: their newly installed outdoor pool was about ready for swimming, which Bev thought would delight Horacio, and a cadre of painters had just finished painting the inside of their home. They discussed turning their hardly used office into a turquoise playroom—turquoise being Rayna's favorite color—and loading the toy chests with Barbie dolls and accoutrements, since Barbie, at the time, was June's favorite toy. According to Bev, she had never been more excited about anything in her life.

Two and a half years later, the Meschlers sat in the waiting room of an attachment clinic in Evergreen. June and Rayna sat opposite them. Horacio had been removed from their house to live in a group home two hours away. Rayna moped, while June sat silently staring at the ceiling. Said Harry: "If you had told me years ago, long ago, before we heard of Evergreen and what they do here, that we would be here, I would have called you a pessimist. We just didn't understand what we were getting into."

The Meschlers were one of seventy-four families I observed or interviewed who had their children treated at the clinic between 1995 and 2000. The story of how the Meschlers prepared for their adopted children's entrance into their homes is typical of the families I met, as were the hopes that they initially had for their new families. In this chapter, I introduce the preadoption experiences of the parents who ended up at the clinic. I investigated their choice to adopt formerly institutionalized children, the ways in which they prepared for the children's arrival, and their expectations for the postplacement period. I discovered that parents' attempts to define and navigate the path toward family stability prior to adopting are based on particular social representations of family, ones that reveal parents' expectations that the adoptive family will ultimately operate in ways analogous to biological families. I also discovered that certain forms of *doxa* influenced parents' representations of family, ones that children would challenge postplacement. Such representations served as generalizations about family that parents accepted as true and that they used as a basis for the construction of postplacement reality, despite their adopting formerly institutionalized children. Finally, conversations revealed the specific roles that parents expected children to play in the family and the ways in which the adoption of formerly institutionalized children resulted in parents' particular deep commitment to these representations.

The Gift of a Good Home: The Impulse to Adopt Formerly Institutionalized Children

While parents in the data set most often reported infertility as the reason why they initially chose to pursue adoption, they revealed a much wider range of reasons why they chose to adopt children specifically from *institutions* such as foster care or orphanages rather than from other sources.[1]

---

[1] While Mosher and Bachrach (1996) estimate that between 11% to 24% of couples in the United States who experience difficulty conceiving or carrying a pregnancy to term ultimately pursue adoption, Berry, Barth, and Needell (1996) report that infertility more often drives individuals toward private, independent adoptions (adoptions brokered privately through an attorney or some other form of facilitator) than towards agency-facilitated adoptions, which are much more likely to involve formerly institutionalized children. Their data supports the conclusion drawn from my own data set that infertility

These included being unable to afford the cost of hiring an attorney to broker a private, independent adoption with a birth mother,[2] wanting a racially matched family,[3] or simply not being "baby people" who could deal with the pain of labor or the needs of infants. These latter were more comfortable with adopting older children, who are characteristically available in orphanages abroad or through domestic foster care systems. By far, however, the largest number stated that they adopted formerly institutionalized children for altruistic reasons, namely, to provide a "good home" for a child in need.[4]

The theme of the "good home" as motivation, and sometimes justification, for adopting from institutions became the immediate centerpiece of my research with adoptive parents. The ubiquity and banality of the phrase immediately caught my attention.[5] For example, as Jesse Goldman, a Colorado mother who had adopted two children from an orphanage in St. Petersburg, Russia, stated:

> We felt funny about doing what would amount to, in essence, *buying* a child, but we're not really baby people.... Plus, we had a nice home, we had so much land, we live up in the mountains, and we thought

---

alone does not necessarily serve as a primary factor in one's choice to adopt formerly institutionalized children over other types of children.

[2] Costs of adopting from U.S. adoption agencies can range from free to $2,500. The cost of using a U.S. agency to facilitate foreign adoptions ranges from $7,000 to $25,000. Independent domestic adoptions can cost anywhere from $4,000 to $30,000 (North American Council on Adoptable Children 2009). Individuals who adopt from U.S. agencies generally have lower levels of education and income than independent adopters. According to Barth, Brooks, and Iyer (1995), public agencies are less likely to place children in families earning $50,000 a year or more, and more likely to place children in families earning $30,000 or less.

[3] Particularly among Caucasian parents, the choice to adopt internationally, and from Russia, was made based on the decision to adopt a white child. The "racialization" of adoption decisions has been discussed at length by Yngvesson (2002), Volkman (2005), Eng (2006), Howell (2007), and Jacobson (2008). Another strong motivation for adopting internationally was the decreased chance of adoptive parents' having interaction with adoptees' biological families, and thus more likelihood that they could assume full ownership of the children (see Modell 1994, 2002).

[4] In a study that investigated parents' self-reported motivations for adopting and fostering children in the United States, Tyejbee (2003) found that parents most often cited "making a difference in a child's life," "providing a child with a positive family experience," and providing aid to "children in need" (701) as reasons.

[5] Of the seventy-four parents surveyed in this research, an overwhelming 71% used a variant of the phrase "to give a child a good home" to answer the open-ended question "Why did you want to adopt?"

the kids would enjoy what we had. You know, it seemed *more* selfish to keep all that to ourselves.

Other parents echoed this sentiment: "We knew that there would be challenges to parenting a black child, but we also knew there were children out there with nothing, while we had everything" and "We wondered if it was God's plan for us to go without children; but it is a waste for a child to go without a home when we could give that to them. Now we think that it must have been God's plan for us to go in a different direction after all."

What, according to adoptive parents, are the components of a "good home"? Based on ethnographic interviews in which adoptive parents were asked to further define the term, we can see there are many components of the "good home" and that the "good home" can be understood to operate as a catch-all phrase, a sort of summarizing symbol (Ortner 1973) that succinctly communicates the expected composition, roles, and practice associated with the family, as well as the culturally sanctioned emotions that the family arouses (see table 1).

Breaking down the empirical data presented here, the "good home" can be seen to comprise both emotional and material elements. While 100 percent of parents indicated that "love" is a vital part of a good home, a significant number also indicated that a good home provides sufficient material goods. There are many reasons for this. Although one unmarried parent explained that she had been "running around buying stuff for [the child] because I was so nervous and excited, it's the only thing I could do...to keep myself sane," most parents linked providing material goods to filling a material void that they believed children raised in institutions or in foster care had. For example, the Meschlers believed that their outdoor pool,

Table 1. Components of the "good home"

Component	Subjects mentioning it
Love	100%
Shelter	98
Food	90
Safety	77
Clothing	76
Toys and recreation	56
Quality schooling	33
Child's own bedroom	24
Transmission of cultural values	12
Doctor or health care	9
Furniture	6

their newly constructed playroom, and special toys would please Horacio, Rayna, and June because they would make up for a lack of material wealth: "The kids [didn't] have this stuff where they came from. Their foster parents [couldn't] afford it with what they make." Parents also discussed the wardrobes they had purchased for the children, PlayStations or other video games, bathroom products, schoolbooks, eyeglasses, and medical supplies, just to name a few purchases. They also recounted that they often took great pains to prepare menus that inspired children to "eat differently" than they had before being adopted by including what one parent sardonically referred to as "cutting-edge kid food"—these included foods traditionally marketed to children such as fruit roll-ups, Pepperidge Farm Goldfish crackers, and snacks in bright packages or foods dyed bright colors. Parents' might also signify eating "differently" through the purchase of healthy food that they assumed was not available to children in their previous lives—organic, pesticide-free, and ecologically conscious meals. With regard to rituals of consumption, parents assumed—especially when they were adopting children from abroad—that the children had never experienced such material bounty before. Parents were proud of their consumer power and pleased to use it for what they understood to be altruistic purposes.

In addition to the actual provision of consumer goods *for* children, rituals that provided children with the opportunity to practice consumption and exhibit their own consumer choices was considered an expression of a good home. Parents often offered unsolicited narratives about taking children on shopping sprees and trips to the mall for a school wardrobe and letting them decide which clothes would make them "look cool." Parents also took great pleasure in the act of taking children to restaurants so they could learn to choose food for themselves. Many compared their exciting array of material offerings with the lack of choice they believed children received in institutions or foster care, as shown in this exchange with Margaret and John Perkins, a Parker, Colorado, couple who adopted a boy and a girl from Moscow. The couple was offering reasons why they thought it was important to introduce the children to new kinds of food:

MP: They didn't know about all the different kinds of fruits and vegetables. They didn't know about different breads. They didn't know what French fries were. I think all they had was the soup. The beet soup. What's it called? Oh my God, I'm so embarrassed. I can't remember the name of the soup.
RS: Borscht.

MP: Yes!...this thin soup with cabbage and you know, maybe some onions. The kids in the orphanage had this for lunch and dinner every day. And some black bread. When we went there, that's what we ate for a week. It's fine, but...every day? Can we have a little variety? Kids need variety.

While parents spoke about providing children with material goods, new experiences, and consumer choice, and understood their own consumer power as an important component of the good home, it is important to note that they rarely saw the provision of material goods as an end in itself. For example, parents equated the provision of clothing and toys with an unprecedented show of attention and affection, and they hoped that the children would read it that way. Parents also regularly expressed a belief in the correlation between more food and a healthy body and more toys and a healthy imagination. Most often, however, parents equated consumption and teaching consumer practices with children's *assimilation* into a new culture, neighborhood, and school, or peer group. For example, those parents who adopted from abroad often understood the act of consumption, and particularly the consumption of American goods with corporate logos, as important for Russian children's assimilation into American culture. As Paul DeMarco, the parent of a thirteen-year-old adoptee from Russia, stated regarding a recent purchase that Paul had made for the teen: "I hope he'll like the shirt. He should. He wanted 'American,' and that's what he gets. It's *very* American to wear basketball jerseys of your favorite team....You can't get more American than Nike either. He really wanted those Nikes!" Other parents I spoke with who had adopted children from orphanages in Russia frequently brought with them to Russia clothing, mugs, and toys with American iconography, such as flags and eagles, as well as goods emblazoned with quality "American" logos such as Baby Gap, Discovery Channel, and FAO Schwartz. In addition, parents frequently spoke with excitement about providing children with their first trip to McDonald's. It was not uncommon for parents to make a special trip to the McDonald's franchise in Moscow with their children prior to leaving for the United States from Sheremetyevo International Airport. Once home, parents continued to encourage children to embrace things American.

For those parents who adopted from foster care systems in the United States, consumption was not usually understood to be about assimilation into a new culture, but rather into a new class or income bracket. For many parents, it was vital that their children "fit in" aesthetically with their own social class. They wanted the children to be clean, dressed in the current trends "like other kids," as explained by Bev and Harry Meschler:

> BM: Oh, God. You should have seen the clothes the kids came with when we'd go for the supervised visits. Almost always the same clothes…holes in the knees, holes in the socks, shirts too tight, stains, sometimes safety pins on the pants. We wondered what the foster parents were spending their money on.
> HM: Urchins [laughs].
> BM: We'd take them to the store that very day. We'd see them again in a month, and they were wearing the old clothes again. I don't know what the foster parents did with the clothes. When we finally got the kids, they were wearing the old clothes and the new ones were packed up. We made them put the new ones on right away. We didn't want people to think that's how we dressed these kids.

As well as equating consumer practices with assimilation, parents equated their consumer power with the children's productive potential. They often equated the provision of material goods with the more abstract concepts of "opportunity" and a "better chance at success." For example, Marva Olson, who adopted a child from Omsk, Russia, in 1995 had this to say:

> [The orphanages] in Russia are terrible. You know. You've been there. There's a million kids; no one has their own things; they have to share all their toys and clothes. The people there don't have time to pay attention to the kids. How does a child grow up in that? How does he learn how to be his own person?"

Also telling is this interview excerpt from Shelley Herman, an adopting mother from Minneapolis:

> No one would adopt Rhonda because she's special needs [paraplegic]. It's too much work and people can't handle it. Her life in foster care was all about what was wrong with her. They didn't want to pay for her meds. She needed her wheelchair upgraded [and this was not considered important by Rhonda's foster family]. I believe that we're here to make the world a better place, and a family is strong with God's love. Rhonda's in a wheelchair; she doesn't talk, but she is a person. She deserves a place where she can do the best with the time she has with us.

Both Marva Olson and Shelley Herman understood their attempts to provide their children with "the better things in life" in more than financial terms. Providing children with a home, clothes, toys, and "their own things" was inextricably related to helping children reach their full potential.

While parents expected the "good home" to set up the preconditions for children's eventual productivity, they also expected their children's experience in the "good home" to be characterized by some degree of leisure. This became apparent to me when a parent who had adopted from Russia expressed surprise when he found out that it is common for very young children in state-run orphanages to help with institutional chores. James Bailey, a prospective parent from Miami, recounted that when he went to Ulyanovsk to meet and pick up his ten-month-old adopted son, Jonathan, he was "shocked" to find children as young as two years old helping to do household chores such as setting and clearing tables or making beds. According to James:

I kept thinking, "How old is that kid?" It [was] so weird to see one that little doing those things. We don't make Thom [his biological son] wipe dishes, and he's twelve! [Laughs.] I think it's kind of weird...they've got these kids running around like little marching soldiers!

Perhaps the most common association that parents made between leisure time and their adopted children occurred when parents offered stories about taking their children to Disney theme parks. The majority of parents I spoke with were either planning to take, or had already taken, their adopted children to Walt Disney World or Disneyland, or, if they could not afford the trips to California or Florida, they had made a pilgrimage to Hersheypark in Pennsylvania, a Six Flags amusement park, or some similar place. Carol Schenk, an unmarried adopting mother from San Luis Obispo, California, who adopted a little boy from Vladimir, Russia, even tailored her trip home from the orphanage to include a connecting stop in Paris, where she took her new son to Euro Disney. As Jeremy Bell, an adopting father from Orinda, California, remarked, "Every kid has to go to Disneyland, right? You haven't had your childhood 'til you get your chance." Parents equated these trips to amusement parks with providing children with a real childhood. By consuming childhood, adopted children would eventually embody normal childhood.

Love Conquers All: Parental Affection as a Curative Agent

In addition to believing that a "good home" would fill a material void for adopted children, parents assumed that their "good home" would fill an emotional void as well. Adopting parents assumed that children who were raised in foreign institutions or domestic bureaucratic systems failed to receive love or emotional support, and they believed that they could offer this to children. Parents also understood that in addition to the pain of losing their birth parents, many children were neglected or abused, and it was adopting parents' duty to heal these emotional wounds. Parents often referred to the sterile environment of foreign institutions and the practice of swaddling, which is common in Russian orphanages, as physical and emotional cruelty. They also cited the lack of staff attention to children, particularly infants, as puzzling, inhumane, and unnecessary. As Theresa Murray, an adoptive mother from Atlanta, stated:

Why do they wrap them up so damned tight? Why do they just leave them lying there? When we saw the pictures of what happens to kids [in orphanages in Russia], we felt like we had to help.

In the case of those adopting from social service systems in the United States, parents sympathized with children's "shuffling" from foster home to foster home, children's lack of stability and ability to feel safe. For example, according to Angela Walker, an adopting parent from Yuma, Arizona, who adopted three-year-old Mark from county services:

I think that where these kids are coming from can be bad places, emotionally. When we had to go on our supervised visits with Mark, we would talk to the caseworker, and she would tell us little bits and pieces of the puzzle [about Mark's early childhood history]. He was placed three times with three different foster parents in a year. He shared a room with two other kids. No consistency, no values, no...nothing. That's the saddest part of all...these are throw-away kids. Nobody to love them....You know, you can't see that and be in our position and not do anything.

Thus, although it was more common for parents to correlate material goods with the formation of a "good home" in the open-ended surveys I conducted, my more in-depth ethnographic interviews with them revealed that parents actually believed that it was not just material things, but "love," "safety," and "values" that ultimately would provide the building blocks of a "good home." As Jenny Lark, a single adoptive mother from Ardmore Park, Pennsylvania, told me, "I think...of course...a good home is a place where a kid feels safe, doesn't want for much, and is loved." Hector Mendes, an adopting father from Leadville, Colorado, said:

> A good home is when you give a kid a roof over their head, a direction in their life. They know that they can come to you for help no matter what. That's the way it was in my family. I think that's the way most people hope it will be.

Of particular interest in parents' comments is that the concepts of "love," "safety," and "values" are believed to operate as solutions to potential or actual problems the children might have. In this scenario, love is constructed as a curative agent or a failsafe measure should parents' attempts to assimilate children into a new culture or social class prove rocky:

> We thought love would be the safety valve. We thought any kid coming from that kind of background would have trouble adjusting for a while. There's a whole new environment to adjust to. And new people.

Others expressed confidence that if children had trouble, they would be able to "love it out of her," or that "over time, they would grow to love us." Parents also believed that adoptees were starved for love and acutely aware of an emotional void in their lives. Parents sometimes compared the children they adopted to the child protagonists in such movies as *Oliver!*, *An American Tale*, or *Like Mike*, and children's books such as *Stuart Little*, in which orphaned children (or mice) construct fantasies about being adopted by a good family and whose fantasies are ultimately satisfied. When I later mentioned this trend to Maureen Holden, a social worker I interviewed in Denver in 2000, she said that she was not surprised:

> Parents picture kids are sitting by the orphanage window, dreaming about getting a loving family who will never, never leave them. But it's just not true. Most of these kids don't even know what family is."

When we examine the data from adopting parents' thoughts regarding the "good home," we glean that parents understand the child's movement toward more material and emotional attention as innately progressive for them, unequivocally signaling a positive advancement in their life situation. Implicit in the rhetorical devices that parents used to explain what they offered their adopted children was salvation from disadvantaged backgrounds, whether by providing upward social mobility, by upgrading their national citizenship, or by helping them escape from a lower-class status. Parents also assumed that, with their help, children would be escaping from an emotionally impoverished environment, and many times, a dangerous environment. In the final analysis, parents constructed children raised in institutional settings as "children in need"—this was their primary distinguishing characteristic—and alleviating this need as a primary objective of their relationship with their formerly institutionalized adopted child.

Giving Family or Making Family? The Role of Adoptees as Emotional Assets

Since parents who eventually brought their children to the clinic saw formerly institutionalized children's childhoods as materially and emotionally lacking, they often concluded that *providing* or *giving* was their own primary role in the adoption process. In this view, parents first provide children with a "good home": a place to live, clothes on their back, a yard (or amusement park) to play in, toys to play with, safety through surveillance, a chance for success through structure and discipline, an education, and love. Perhaps even more important, parents saw themselves as providing adopted children, and particularly those raised in institutions, with *family*. When parents provided a family for adopted children, they envisioned a mutually agreeable, intimate environment that they were wholly responsible for shaping and controlling. This responsibility was often rhetorically framed as an altruistic gesture, a "gift" in the Aristotelian sense, in that it is voluntary or uncalculated, spontaneous and limitless in content and scope. As one parent put it, "We were willing to give her anything we could to make her life better. That's the truest gift a person can give in their life."

Rayna Rapp (1999) has referred to the phenomenon of "gifting discourse" among parents during the adoption process as a strategy for centering the child in what is invariably a complex, commodified relationship within a contractual market. Likewise, Barbara Yngvesson (2002) has noted that gifting rhetoric is often used to signify both a birth family's—and, in the case of transnational adoption, a home country's—offering of a child, as well as the beginning of an ongoing chain of reciprocity between adoptee and adoptive parent. Like Yngvesson, I observed such a duality in parents' framings of adoption: on the one hand, parents' used emic expressions such as "providing a good home" and "the truest gift one can give" that suggested their commitment to an altruistic offering of family with the sole objective of benefitting the adopted child. On the other hand, a close reading of their words reveals that providing children with "a good home" operates more frequently for them as a gift in the sociological sense (Mauss 1967)—in other words, adoption was a highly self-invested act that was expected to generate specific social returns. Put more simply, despite adoptive parents' seeing formerly institutionalized children as somehow different than other children in their early childhood experiences, they still expected that some-how the children would create a typical family. For parents at the clinic, then, adoption was not only a process by which a child receives family, it was a process by which children were expected, and required, to provide parents with family as well.

How, exactly, did adoptive parents expect children to provide them with family? According to some parents, family was implied by the mere physical presence of the adopted child in their home. For example, many parents described adopting their children as something that they had felt certain would make their families "full" or "complete." Similarly, another parent stated that he had felt that his family (which, prior to adoption, had consisted only of himself and his wife) wouldn't be a "true family" until there were kids "running around the house."

For others, however, it was not just the presence of children in the home that signified the provision of family, but also the presence of a parent-child bond, one characterized by many as more valuable than any other relationship. For example, as one parent stated, "Without kids we just had a marriage. With kids, we thought we'd have a family." Several other parents expressed their dissatisfaction with their lives before adoption as being "lonely," "boring," "apathetic," "disconnected," and "unfulfilled," and revealed that they had thought that adoption would remedy the condition by "creating some connections that really mean something." And as one parent eloquently expressed it: "We understood that [adoption] would give us a purpose. We wouldn't just be thinking of ourselves anymore. It's nice to be a person, but it's better to be a real human, part of the species."

For still others, adopting a child was an opportunity to practice the very rituals they used to define family. For example, parents animatedly discussed their original hopes for the beginning of holiday traditions, what their adopted children's first day of school would be like, and when and where they imagined they would attend their children's first sporting events. They also mentioned family rituals—such events as nightly dinners, taking family photos, annual vacation trips, and frequent visits to the homes of extended family members. Finally, parents discussed the hopes they had once had for their children as they approached and entered adulthood, often envisioning the children as upstanding citizens, college educated, with well-paying jobs, sometimes married with children.

A final way that parents expected adopted children to provide them with family was by creating an opportunity for parents to make a series of lifestyle changes that they associated with family. For example, parents had assumed that the children would help them restructure their time, slow down, and stop working so hard, while shifting their attention from work to household. According to Margaret Perkins, a woman who adopted a boy and girl from an orphanage in Moscow:

John [her husband] and I saw each other for about ten minutes a day. We were both working sixty-hour weeks. It sucked the energy right out of both of us. I can conceive, but we didn't want younger children. We talked and talked and thought that it would be a great idea to adopt. What I thought was that I would go part-time and come home from work and make dinner for them. We'd play games and do things together, tuck them into bed and read them stories. Doesn't that sound nice? Be a real family, not just two people running around like chickens with their heads cut off.

In each of these examples, we can see that for parents who came to the clinic, the visualization of a "real family" is marked by at least two representations. First, it is marked by the assumption of the family as a sort of emotional refuge. Second, it is marked by the centering of the *child* in the promotion of family as that emotional refuge. The role that the child plays in establishing the family and/or home as a sanctuary has a long social history, one that has been captured by many scholars (Anderson 1971; Anderson, Bechhofer, and Gershuny 1994; Aries 1960; De Mause 1974; Donzelot 1979; Engels 1999 [1884]; Shorter 1977; Wood 1968; May 1988; Zaretsky 1973). These authors have demonstrated the extent to which the separation of public and private spheres during the Industrial Revolution created discursive and empirical boundaries between home and workplace in the United States that realigned gender, class, and age-set roles and firmly fixed the child in the realm of the private domain. With this creation of the public and the private, the home became opposed to the workplace, a site where morality could not be shaken by the dictates of the market.

According to Christopher Lasch, the image of the home as a "haven in a heartless world" (1977, 1) was inspired by the socialization of production and reproduction in the United States, particularly the way capitalists took production out of the household and collectivized it under their own supervision in factories. Corporate executives and managers, with the help of advertising media (Aronson 1980), extended control over the private lives of workers by extolling the virtues of marriage and children, depicting the household as an emotional refuge in a hostile, industrializing landscape: "In a bureaucratic society...the individual cannot afford to have deep emotional ties outside the family circle." (Lasch 1977, 144). Corporations also offered incentives to reorganize family relationships within the household to create a private domain, a site not where production values are expressed, but for the reproduction of consumer values. The primacy of the emotional child-parent relationship was asserted as one early twentieth-century, modern ideal, which, combined with the concepts of romantic love and maternal love, would persist as the mortar and bricks of the stable home.

The normalized emotional roles and behaviors of *children* in the modern family are perhaps best brought into relief, however, by Viviana Zelizer, whose book *Pricing the Priceless Child* (1985) documents the cultural construction of the child as "emotional asset" (11) in twentieth-century America. Zelizer argues that simultaneous to corporate and state drives during and immediately after the Industrial Revolution to make children economically useful (e.g., through child labor), rising numbers of child injuries and deaths in urban areas also began to be framed as emotional losses. Such responses included practices of "sacralization"(3), that is, an investment of children with sentimental value, such as memorial acts of remembrance for children who had died, community initiatives to prevent child injury and death, and public education about child safety and health. In the process, children were expelled from the cash nexus at the turn of the twentieth century, and they began the rocky transition from the edge of the labor pool to the center of family consumption. Throughout the first half of the twentieth century, the home became the new site of this sacralization, and the child became, if not the head, then the figurehead of the household—the reason, in essence, to maintain the family as the site of socialization and consumerism (see also May 1988).

Cultural studies scholars (Kincheloe and Steinberg 1997) and anthropologists (Stephens 1995; Coco and Nader 1996) have concluded that the child in the United States is thus not necessarily considered to be an economic actor but an affective one. The power that children wield in capitalist societies is their successful operation not as producers, as they were once viewed by corporations and states, but as consumers—of material items, time, energy, and, especially, parental love. Implicit in their roles as consumers are certain collective assumptions about their personalities and abilities. As Paula Fass has noted, today, a "proper childhood" is free of labor, consists in large part of education, play, and recreation; and is free of sexuality (2007, 204). Children are understood not as fully formed cognizant or physical beings but rather are thought to be mere cultural repositories, always *in the process of cultural acquisition.* They are also semicognitive, semiculturally literate and unaware of the ways of the world. Children, in this view, are also useless. Perhaps the most widely held assumption about children, however, is that although childhood may be political, children *themselves* are not political actors. Children may ideally embody the eventual promise of capitalism as laborers-in-waiting, but during childhood, they are meaningful only because they have *affective* value.

The idea that children should operate as emotional assets was supported by the preadoption experiences of the parents I interviewed at the clinic. As we have seen, if parents originally understood their role as being providers of an emotional refuge, then the primary role that they envisioned for adopted children in the "good home" was to *accept* parental provisions. If parents' primary raison d'être was to *give* family to children in need, then adopted children's complementary role in the household was to *receive* the family that parents altruistically offered without question. In fact, many of the parents I spoke with not only expected adopted children to be pleased with the offering of family, but to be grateful:

It's not that I think they [adopted children] should be grateful....Well, I do, but I can't expect a child to be grateful when they're so young. Maybe when she's older though, she'll know what we did for her. That would be nice.

While studies suggest that it is common for both biological and adoptive parents to expect or assume emotional reciprocity from children (Englund 1983; Diener, Heim, and Mangelsdorf 1995; Delmore-Ko et al. 2000; Welsh et al. 2008), Sara Dorow (2006) has noted that adoptive parents may invest adopted children with a particular kind of meaning as symbolic capital because adoptive parents' power to establish family is not necessarily taken for granted. Indeed, in agreement with Dorow, my data suggests that the stakes associated with formerly institutionalized adopted children's performance as emotional assets may be even higher than with children of biological parents.[6] Child love not only completed the transaction begun by parents when they first chose to adopt, but it secured the family as a product of the transaction, and adopted children finally gave parents permission to perform long-awaited rituals that would fix the family firmly as a body in the future.

To sum up, by interpreting family discourse, that is, "the language that the family uses about the family" (Bourdieu 1998, 65), we find that parents who eventually go on to utilize the Evergreen model of attachment therapy had several reasons for adopting formerly institutionalized children rather than children from other settings. We also find that parents had several postplacement expectations. First, they expected their own primary role to be altruistic providers of what they called "a good home" that provides material goods and curative love. Parents talked openly about the "good home" as an offering or a gift that took a specific form and should be especially meaningful to formerly institutionalized children more than to children adopted from other backgrounds, because of parental perceptions that the children suffered from deep material and emotional deprivation in their early childhoods. They also envisioned the home as a permanent and transmissible space where material offerings, such as toys, clothing, food, and a physical residence, as well as more abstract ones, such as education, health, safety, and social values, would serve as the tools for the children to successfully realize their own potential and their potential within the adoptive family. In addition, a "good home" was a sacred and private space, a refuge characterized by a series of uncalculated exchanges between children and adults, in which parents gave all they could without expectation of any specific return.

However, further investigation of the ethnographic data reveals that parents did expect at least one important social return in exchange for their

---

[6] Parents were acutely aware that they, like biological parents, wanted to make families "real" but that unlike biological families there were often obstacles to doing so. It is worth noting here that parents at the clinic who identified themselves as infertile appeared all the more conscious and thoughtful about what returns adoptees would give them. As Strathern (1992) has noted, when families are placed in the position of challenging the immutability of kinship to create family, they especially come to appreciate the emotional returns that adoption offers. The ability to mimic biological constructions of the family may be especially desirable for infertile individuals or couples, whose very conception of personhood may depend on the act of adoption (Pfeffer 1987). Indeed, in my observations, those parents who identified as infertile often claimed that their infertility caused feelings of shame, frustration, incompleteness, and self-pity. Many claimed in interviews that adoption was, for them, a "last ditch effort" at family.

generosity: they expected children to perform as emotional assets who would provide child love to make families "real" through narrative, ritual, and practice. Parents hoped to center the loving child in a series of relationships and rituals designed to institute in each member of the family certain feelings that solidified the collective. For example, parents envisioned eventual gift exchanges, assistance, visits, attention, kindnesses, family occasions, and photograph opportunities that would become possible after children first displayed love, affection, and sometimes gratitude, for being adopted. Such narratives, rituals, and practices, as one adoptive parent expressed it, "*are* family." For parents, then, just as the successful postplacement experience relied on their provision of a good home to children, so did it rely on a foundation of child love.

The role of emotional asset that parents expected children to play in making the good home possible in this data set suggests that children and their expression of child love may be particularly essential for establishing *families* for adoptive parents. Adoptive parents expressed much hope that through the construction of various narratives, rituals, and practices, parents and children might work together to do "the practical and symbolic work that…tends to endow each member of the family with a 'family feeling' that generates devotion, generosity, and solidarity." (1998, 68)

While the families who ultimately bring their children to attachment therapy are prone to envision the home as a refuge and their adopted children as emotional assets, the adoption agencies through which children are circulated prescribe and legitimize these ideas. In the next chapter, ethnographic fieldwork I conducted in international adoption agencies and county social services in Denver confirms that adopting parents are not the only actors in the adoption process engaged with creating this vision of the family. Adoption agency staff and social service workers also have a stake in promoting adults as providers and children as emotional assets capable of doing certain symbolic work within a family. When the empirical data from adopting parents, adoption agencies, and social service workers are taken together, we see that parents' representations of family, children, and domesticity do not appear from thin air. Technocrats' language and practices often legitimate the folk wisdom that parents use for their pre-adoption choices and postplacement expectations.

Chapter Three

The Fuel That Drove Us to Care

Adoption Agencies' Institutionalization of Family

According to parents at the clinic, the process of adopting their formerly institutionalized children, which almost always meant working with an agency, was a double-edged sword. On the one hand, they were grateful to the agencies that had given them the chance to form families. But parents were also prone to decry the bureaucracy associated with their adoption experiences. Several pointed out what they perceived to be a discrepancy between the personality and behavioral history of their children as promised by the agencies that they had worked with and how their children had actually behaved and their adjustment postplacement. A few even went so far as to say they were victims of agencies' "false advertising" and that they had been "duped" into adopting children who were unadoptable. It gradually became obvious that adopting parents had much ambivalence about working with agencies. As one adoptive father put it, "Maybe it's the nature of the beast, but you develop a love-hate relationship with [agency] people."

I was curious why so many parents felt compelled to discuss their adoption experiences during a seemingly unrelated intake packet discussion at the clinic. In this chapter I investigate those adoption agency practices and techniques that parents most frequently identified as vital to their formation of their preadoption choices and postplacement expectations. In an effort to provide more depth, I also include results of several months of additional ethnosemantic interviewing with Denver-area adoption workers to include their own understandings of their work. I conducted this research in the Denver metro area at the two types of agencies from which the parents at the clinic had most often adopted their children: (1) nonprofit agencies that facilitated international adoptions; and (2) county service agencies that facilitated domestic adoptions from foster care systems. In this chapter I look at two sets of adoption agency operations that parents most uniformly listed in their interviews as influential. The first is what one parent eloquently called "the fuel that drove us to care." The set includes foundation stories (the ways that agencies present themselves); testimonials (the ways that agencies present former clients); and personality profiles (iconography through which agencies present available children) that are designed to draw potential clients to the agencies and build their confidence in the agency as their adoption processes progress. The second set of techniques is what parents referred to as the "mounds of paperwork," the "hoops to jump through," and the "dog and pony show," which included various home assessments, parent-fitness tests, and postplacement reporting procedures. In examining this data, we find that adoption agency workers must engage a series of workplace paradoxes regarding the nature of state intervention into their attempts to build families, and that ultimately, the narratives and representations of children and family do work to reinforce children's roles as emotional assets and position adoptive parents' roles as the provider of "the good home." Indeed, as licensed operators of official classifications, adoption agency workers are invested with the capacity to construct reality, and thus prescribe the category of "the family" for adoptive parents.

The Crapshoot: Parents' Initial Contact with Adoption Agencies

According to the majority of families I interviewed, when individuals or couples decided to adopt formerly institutionalized children, they often chose their agency based on word of mouth from friends and acquaintances or from the Internet. During these initial inquiries, they discovered that there were a lot more decisions to make about the process and many more steps involved in adopting than they had initially thought. Parents were faced with choosing between adopting domestically or internationally, and if domestically, then whether from statewide private adoption agencies or public county agencies. They had to decide whether to work through the initial stages of adoption with privately funded referral groups and to choose between adopting an infant or an older child, a single child or a sibling group. They had to choose a child to match their race or to adopt transracially. They had to decide whether they could manage adopting children with disabilities, medical problems, or histories of severe neglect or abuse. Parents also had to choose the proper agency based on the diversity of children available, how long it would take to adopt a child, and where children would be adopted from. The issue of cost also played a large role, particularly in international adoptions: whereas, at the time of my research in early 2000, it cost approximately $1,000 to adopt a child from domestic cultures of care, adopting a child from abroad could cost up to $30,000.

In addition to a dizzying array of decisions to make, parents found that adopting through international and domestic agencies is a highly bureaucratic process involving several state interventions. Once parents decide what kind of child they would like to parent and, thus, what agency to work with, they then had to fill out general information forms, pay nonrefundable application fees, and attend training seminars to learn about the adoption process of their particular agency. If they still wished to adopt after this session, they were informed of several more fees they needed to pay. The agency would assign a licensed adoption caseworker, who then assigned or conducted a home study to determine fitness for adoption. Once an agency declared the parents "fit" to adopt, caseworkers or agency staff would work with parents to find an available child or children.

In the case of international adoptions, the pool of children available is often limited. Parents usually do not choose the children they will adopt. Instead, they wait for adoption agency staff to contact them about available children. Once contacted, they may be given a file on the child's vitals and medical history and shown a video of the child. Parents are given a few days to decide whether they would like to adopt the child. If parents do not choose the child, they must wait until another suitable candidate for adoption passes through the agency's files, which can take months. If they do choose the child, parents await instructions for the "pick-up date" when they will fly to the child's country of origin, meet the child for the first time, and bring him or her to the United States. Adoption agency staff members may schedule the "pick-up date" as soon as a week after parents' agreement to adopt or as long as a year or two later. Once parents fly to the child's country of origin, they undergo a series of legal procedures such as court appearances and hearings, where parental rights are transferred from the state to the parents. After about ten days, parents are free to file paperwork with the U.S. embassy there declaring their intention to acquire the child's passport and to transfer the child's citizenship. Once home, parents must finalize the transfer of the child's citizenship with United States Immigration and Naturalization Services.

When faced with the checklist of things they needed to do to adopt formerly institutionalized children through adoption agencies, parents often recounted the dismay, frustration, and resigned determination they came to feel. On one hand, many were grateful to the agencies for their very existence. As Megan Wicke, an adoptive mother of a little girl from Moscow stated, "We actually loved the agency we worked with. We felt they supported us the whole time. They were the ones who took our phone calls, answered our questions, helped bring Katrina [to us]. It wouldn't have happened without them." Yet, in the same breath, Megan articulated what she thought to be double role of adoption agencies: "They're your 'way in' to adopting, it's like a gateway, but they're also the gatekeepers."

In the case of couples who self-identified as infertile, the frustrations and concerns associated with the dual and sometimes contradictory role of adoption agencies compounded those that they already had about the process of trying to conceive. As one parent put it:

> Oh yeah, we had *had* it. We wanted someone to give us a reason why we could be parents. Desperately wanted that. Everyone was telling us what the barriers were…and here were a million more.

In addition, many parents, while excited about the process of adopting, had trepidation about the risky nature of building a family through adoption:

> We saw it as a crapshoot. You can see a kid's picture and think, "Oh, that kid is so cute, let's bring him home," but you don't know what you're going to get. Who knows? And then you think, "I'm going to go through all this work." We just didn't have a clue if it was going to be worth it.

When speaking to agency staffers about parents' initial contact with agencies, they generally agreed that parents come with about as much reservation about adopting as they do excitement and joy. As one staffer put it, "In some ways, it's harder to adopt than to give birth to a child. It's like prolonged labor, sometimes for years and everybody's watching you. It can be intimidating." Agencies require that parents trust the organization's ability to assess the health of children being adopted from institutions. Adoption agencies also require parents to assume that agency staff is qualified to approve or reject family applicants. Parents are also asked to assume that agency staff has been deemed qualified by the state to choose appropriate children for every set of parents they accept.[1] With so many important decisions in the hands of agency staff, parents often found the process precarious. Said one parent: "The process of choosing an agency was stressful. The most important decision of our life [was] left up to strangers: you throw a dart and hope you hit a winner." Adoption agency staffers agreed that it is important to build trust with potential parents. According to one director of an agency in north Denver: "It's very important to build trust with our clients, to let them know that we want to work with them to create the family they envision for themselves." Likewise, a caseworker at the same agency told me: "We do our homework. We have to. And parents need to know that. So we spend a lot of time thinking about ways that we can help them understand that."

Inspiring Confidence in International Adoption Agencies

As mentioned previously, one of the most common types of agencies from which parents at the clinic typically adopted was a nonprofit, independently founded international adoption agency. My ethnographic research conducted in such agencies revealed that in staff members' efforts to build trust with adopting parents, the family becomes institutionalized as a social category. There are several ways that international agencies attempt to inspire trust. First, they design their advertisements to appear personalized and humanized, to appeal to parents' frustrations about adopting through impersonal, institutional means.

Their ads and websites often relate their *founding stories* that introduce potential clients to the personal stories associated with the roots of the organization. For example, Hope's Promise, a Christian, non-profit agency located in the Denver metro area introduced itself to potential clients this way in its brochure:

Paula founded Hope's Promise in 1990, after she and her husband adopted their son...from India. We have been serving both birth and

---

[1] Despite best efforts, is not always possible for agencies that facilitate adoptions, and particularly international adoptions, to know how, why, or from where the children that circulate through their agencies have come to be identified as "adoptable" (Babb 1999; Marre and Briggs 2009). Some adoptive parents in my data set, having read about this, expressed some anxiety about adoption agencies' ability to assess, as one parent discussed it, the "adoptability" of the children they would choose or be assigned.

adoptive families for over ten years. We accept applications from adoptive families who live throughout the United States and abroad, and provide counseling and support services to birth families who reside throughout Colorado.

The Staff of [the agency] has both personal and professional adoption experience. We understand your needs to maintain control over the decisions that intimately affect your lives; to have accurate, timely information; and to receive support and ongoing communication. (Hope's Promise 2000)

As we see here, adoption agency administrators highlight their unique positions as "just plain folks" who have already successfully navigated the rules, regulations, and practices associated with adopting through an agency. According to the staff member of a different agency in the Denver area: "They have to know that if our founder could do it, especially at a time when adopting kids from outside the U.S. wasn't so easy, then they can do it. And we'll help them however we can." By positioning administrators more as plain folks, staff members hope to appear less as intimidating professionals and more like friendly facilitators, or parents helping other parents achieve their dreams of family. The founders' primary motivation for creating the agency is empathy—staff understands the pure joy and importance of building families and want to help others to do so.

A second way that international adoption agencies attempt to build trust among parents is by providing *testimonials* on their websites and in their brochures. A lengthy example of a typical testimony used by international adoption agencies follows here from a couple who adopted a fourteen-month-old Russian boy in 1997 from a popular agency in Maryland that is devoted to facilitating international adoptions in the former Soviet Union:

Our story started in…1997, when we attended our first meeting on adoption. Cradle of Hope staff members and parents who adopted through the agency were at the meeting with their children. It was after this meeting when we knew who would be handling our adoption process. We were very impressed with the agency, and after the meeting spoke with some parents who adopted using the agency. They were very pleased and confident about the agency. We then started our paperwork and got the ball rolling. We were a little slow during our paperwork, due to some family situations that needed our attention first. Finally all paperwork was done and the call came about our son. We were so excited that we jumped in the car and drove to the agency to pick up the video, medical information and pictures. Our social worker was also excited, and asked if we wanted to watch the video in the office. Of course we said, "yes."

Finally a court date! After eleven years we were going to be parents …we had about three weeks notice. That gave us plenty of time to pack and get ready. We were so excited; we thought the day would never come. We chose to make two trips due to the ten-day wait in Moscow, and we also chose to stay with a host family. We were very happy with our decision. On our first trip we were able to visit our son every day, except for the first day in Moscow because we arrived too late. The rest of the time we were able to visit Alex every day, even on Saturday for one and a half hours. We were able to play with him and feed him during this time. After visiting with our son, we went sightseeing with our translator and driver. Moscow is really a beautiful city to see. We were able to go to the Kremlin one day, Red Square another day. Our translator also turned out to be an excellent tour guide. We could not get over how beautiful the buildings were. When we arrived back at our host family's apartment, she usually had our dinner waiting for us. After dinner we would go to our room and watch the video of our son that we had filmed earlier that day at the orphanage. Then we would go back into the kitchen to have tea and cookies with our host family and talk with them and play with their children.

Our court day was a day I will never forget. Everything went so smoothly, thanks to our coordinator. She really seemed so well organized and confident in her work. The court hearing lasted about 45 minutes. After our court hearing, we went back to the orphanage to visit with our son, take more videos of him and hold him for the first time as his real parents. What a feeling that was! After our visit, we took our coordinator and translator out to eat to celebrate our officially becoming…parents. We asked our coordinator to pick a special restaurant that she would like to go to. The restaurant was very nice and the food was delicious. When we arrived back at our host family's apartment, they had a cake for us to celebrate our adoption. We really felt so good about that. Having to leave…to go home and wait for our second trip was a little hard, but we knew Alex was being well cared for at the orphanage. We were very pleased with the orphanage and their staff.

Now for our second trip. The first day we did not get to take Alex out of the orphanage because we arrived too late, but the second day of the trip was the big day. It was a very happy and sad day. We were so happy to finally take [him] out of the orphanage, but we felt bad for the staff members who looked so sad as they said their good-byes....We think [he] might have been a favorite child in the orphanage due to his outgoing personality. Straight from the orphanage we took [him] for his medical exam; everything went well there. At the embassy were [*sic*] very pleased to have worked with the agency because before we left, they informed us about the employment verification letter that is now required by the American embassy. At the time we were upset about having more paperwork to do, but as it turned out, other parents there could not get their children's passports because they were missing this new form. Everyone was asking us how we knew to get it. Anyway, we were in and out in about an hour and a half.

Then came the big day that we left to come home. It was such a wonderful feeling when we arrived at JFK and saw our families there with flowers and balloons and signs all excited to meet [us]. Alex was 14 months old when we adopted him, and he has gained 9 lbs. in the four months he has been home with us. [He] is doing very well. [He] does receive speech therapy after his first six months evaluation is up. We are very thankful to the agency for helping make our dream come true. (Cradle of Hope 1997)

Again, as we can see, a defining feature of this testimonial is that it operates to allay parents' fears about the bureaucracy involved in adopting through a particular agency. As a hotline coordinator for an agency in Aurora, Colorado, commented:

We don't write [testimonials], let me make that clear, but we choose which testimonials we include on our sites very carefully. It's important that people have confidence in the agency...that they understand we know what we are doing.

Testimonials such as the one above provide narratives that address state interventions in the adoption process but do not dwell on the hassles of those interventions. Successful testimonials demonstrate that the agencies are able to conduct business with a personal touch, making adopting an enjoyable experience complete with sightseeing experiences and friends made along the way. Perhaps more important, though, is that families testify to agencies' excellent abilities to protect adopting parents from state interventions. This is most evident when the mother above describes her experience with the agency at the U.S. Embassy in Moscow. While other parents waited in lines or requests for their children's passports were outright rejected, this particular family was able to bypass the problem. This makes the agency an attractive one to parents, who wish to complete the process of adoption as quickly as possible. According to parents I interviewed at the clinic, testimonials particularly appealed to them because they believed that the less state intervention they would encounter during the process, the more control they would have over the process and over the creation of their family.

The third agency technique for building trust that parents at the clinic discussed was what one parent referred to as "the family catalogues." This is iconography of children that offers proof of the agency's ability to choose children who are, as one agency staffer put it, "good family material." This iconography is usually provided in the form of *photo listings* and *personality profiles* of children who are available for adoption. Sometimes presented in regularly published written bulletins or booklets, photo listings of adoptable children are also available on agency websites, where photos are connected to links such as "Waiting Children" and "Children Seeking Loving Families." Adoption agencies choose photos that portray children as happy and smiling and aesthetically pleasing in dress and personality. According to most caseworkers I interviewed, photo listings are the key to attracting parents to their agency. As one agency director stated:

> Especially today when people don't have a lot of time to investigate agencies, it's often how the kids look or seem that will help them determine which one they go with. We encourage the orphanages to try to capture the true personality of the child when they take their pictures... [the children] should look clean though. We want them [orphanage staff] to help them put some effort into their presentation.

Indeed, parents at the clinic whom I interviewed expressed that checking out photo listings was the most "exciting" or "fun" part of looking for agencies with which to work because it allowed them to fantasize about what their families would eventually look like. The photos provided the opportunity for what Sara Dorow (2006) has called the "paradoxical grounding" (108) of parents in the reality of adoption and the magnification of the hope for their future with children. Many of them stated that the way children looked in photographs also sometimes swayed them to work with one agency versus another and set them on a course of action with an agency, even before they officially contracted with that agency. This is evidenced in this exchange I had with the Meschlers:

RS: And what did you think when you saw the pictures of the kids?
BM: Oh, we thought they were so cute.
HM: Yeah, I actually had the picture from the site, and I downloaded it, and I was showing it to all the guys I played basketball with, saying, "These are gonna be my kids!"
BM: Just really cute. We couldn't wait.

In addition to providing images of children that allow adopting parents to project their family into the future, photo listings and personality profiles also construct accompanying narratives that claim to provide an accurate picture of the child's personality. The large majority of these photo listings and personality profiles include information that assures parents that, despite a child's experience in institutions, she or he has personality characteristics that would aid in the transition from institutional living to the nuclear family. Typical examples of personality profile text that accompanies the photo listings for adoptable children from Russia also assures parents that children adhere to typical gender roles—girls love to play dress-up, cook, and take care of younger siblings; boys like to fix things around the house, play sports, and take leadership roles:

Sibling Group of Three! Forever Family Found! Meet this darling sibling group! The eldest of this group has been like momma to the other two. She is a very compassionate child and loves her siblings very much. She dreams of dressing up like a princess with high heels and fancy dress and of course to have long hair! Although only 6 years old, she knows how to cook, clean, iron and sew. She is a very responsible child. She also dreams of being able to start school. Brother is lively and active. He is a leader among his peers. He is fond of sports and games. He loves to assist the adults in sweeping the leaves and cleaning off the snow from the paths. He loves to be read to. He can recite his favorite stories. The baby of the group is described as having a good personality and smile. She is lively, amusing and chubby. She loves to play with her dolls and pretend she is a nurse. The whole group loves to sing and dance. They are all friendly children and take care of each other, which is evidenced on their video. They play together and miss one another when apart. We have medicals and video

on these children. (www.littlemiracles.org/photolisting/photolisting.
html on May 18, 2002)

He seems to be very mature for his age. At eight years, he already
seems to have a grown-up, not boyish, air to him, with a courageous
heart, and a harsh realization that he lives in a world where he'll have
to take care of himself. When he smiles though, his childish spirit
is revealed and he becomes a kid again. When asked if he has any
dreams, the boy looses [sic] his smile, looks down shyly, and utters a
heartbreaking "No." But if he had one wish that could come true...he
says he would wish for a mom. His biological mother died. By the
Adoption Law, both parents must travel overseas to pick up the child.
(adoption-photolisting.net/childpages.asp?sID=310 on May 18, 2002)

Children are described as "compassionate," "having a good smile," "having a good personality," "responsible," and "friendly." Children's productive
potential is also emphasized—most often, personality profiles will include
information about what the child would like to be when he or she grows up.
Such iconography also appeals to parents' sense of altruism and desire, as
outlined in chapter 2, by highlighting and confirming *the child's* unequivo-
cal desire to find an adoptive family. In these cases, the children's public
status is accentuated along with their acute awareness of their orphaned or
abandoned status. These listings also imply that children raised in institutions understand the terms of private family life. In these scenarios, potential adopting parents are presented as the solution to a child's problems.

Inspiring Confidence in Social Service Agencies

Whereas parents at the clinic who adopted through agencies specializing in facilitating international adoptions discussed the tendencies of these
agencies to strengthen their representations of adoption as an altruistic
and emotionally fulfilling experience in which families would easily obtain needy children without much state intervention, those parents who
adopted through county social services more often discussed the ways in
which social workers legitimized family expectations at the same time as
they positioned themselves rhetorically and practically as *transparent* agents
of the state. For example, in the initial stages of adoption, most of the social
service caseworkers I interviewed during spring 2000 attempted to convey what several called a "comprehensive" view of social services through

mission statements and educational sessions about the social service agency itself. Instead of orienting parents to the agency by using founding stories that reflected the personal touch that the agency could offer, the sessions were designed to fully inform the parents as to the logic of the bureaucracy behind the process. According to one caseworker at the Denver Department of Human Services, for example, when prospective parents first come to their agency, caseworkers publicize the services that DDHS offers, introducing the mission statement right away so that they will understand where the Adoptions Unit fits in with the rest of the DDHS's Family and Children's Division. At the time of my research, the mission statement for DDHS's Child Welfare Division stated:

All Child Welfare services are consolidated within the Family and Children's Division of the Denver Department of Human Services. The Child Welfare League of America has accredited this Division since 1946.

The largest division of the Denver Department of Human Services, the Family and Children's Division, is responsible for the investigation of physical child abuse, sexual child abuse, and child neglect, as defined by the Colorado Children's Code.

Working in collaboration with the Denver Police Department and Denver Juvenile Court, all allegations of child maltreatment are addressed through various activities and services designed specifically to identify and to protect victims from further abuse.

These services may include temporary placement of a child out of the child's home; however, maximum effort is directed toward keeping families together whenever possible.

The Family and Children's Division is comprised of [sic] four major sub-divisions: Intake section, child protection section, youth services section, and resource section coordinating services such as foster care, kinship care, adoption, etc. (DDHS 2003a)

The mission statement continues to be an important introductory document because caseworkers want parents to understand the Adoptions Unit is only a small part of a larger social service system that serves displaced children in Colorado. The caseworker's job not only encompasses the facilitation of a successful adoption, but it aids in processing children through the many divisions of child services, sometimes over years at a time. Children begin their relationship with the county months, and often years, before they are passed on to the Adoptions Unit. They move through several other divisions first.

DDHS caseworkers tell this typical story to prospective adoptive parents: First, there is a citizen report of neglect or abuse. Immediately thereafter, an investigator is sent from Child Protective Services (CPS) to investigate the report. Family, neighbors, and employers are interviewed. The child is medically examined, and parents are psychiatrically evaluated. If there is a "matched report," that is if the cause of injury matches the claim of how the injury was caused ("He fell down" or "He burned himself on the stove"), then the child is returned to his or her parents with advice from the caseworker on how to prevent similar injuries in the future. If there is a "mismatched report," that is, if the cause of injury does not match the claim of how the injury was caused, then within seventy-two hours, a court date is set to have the parents charged with negligence or abuse so that the child may be taken from the parents and placed in the hands of CPS. During this time a foster placement is found for the children, and CPS investigators do a background check on the parents that includes an investigation into criminal records, residential histories (to see how long they live in one place), possessions (property, cars, etc.), employment, and finally, a family and child-care history.

Once the court date has been set and the parents are charged, caseworkers do what they call "the dance" between the CPS worker and the parents to see if the parents are willing to do what the CPS worker asks them to do in order to have their children returned to them. In general, CPS requires the following:

Parents must be willing to treat an existing medical problem with medication or therapy.

They must be willing to visit with their children regularly at DDHS.

They must meet with supervisors in charge of their family's case on a regular basis.

The must approach the placement of their children in foster care in a positive fashion—that is, they cannot "badmouth" or "put down" the CPS worker in front of the children.

They must take responsibility for why their child is in placement.

They must not blame the child for the placement.

If they are drug addicted, they must submit to urine analyses and agree to undergo rehabilitative treatment.

If they are violent, they must undergo an anger management/domestic violence prevention program.

If they are destitute or homeless, they must apply for and receive welfare, and they must apply for and receive low-income housing.

Child Protective Services workers are also trained to help parents through the completion of this checklist so they may get their children back. The caseworker documents the progress of the parents in monthly reviews and regularly scheduled court dates. Ideally, it is supposed to take approximately a year for CPS workers to determine whether a parent can get their lives back on track to properly care for their child. At the time of my research, this was especially encouraged by federal "permanency laws" such as the Multi-Ethnic Placement Act of 1994 and the Adoption and Safe Families Act of 1997 that prioritized a child's immediate placement in a permanent home over the rights of birth parents in such a situation. However, according to caseworkers, since the parent's rights are often represented by court-appointed attorneys—who can deftly defend a parent who has missed the last two scheduled visits or dropped out of rehab by pointing out the importance of "blood relationships"—the actual time it takes for CPS to transfer the case to adoptions is closer to two years. According to one caseworker: "As long as [the parents] aren't passed out, their lawyers will fight for them." According to Lisa Kelly, a social worker at a private foster placement facility in Denver, this was actually an improvement over five years earlier, when it would take on average three years for DDHS to begin to look for a permanent home for a child whose parents were unmotivated or unable to follow CPS dictates. In the DDHS if birth parents do not meet the conditions set by CPS within approximately two years, parental rights are terminated.

While birth parents and CPS staff members do "the dance," the children whose lives are on hold are placed and monitored in several sites. Their options are: preadoptive homes, a foster family home with their own relatives, or a foster family home. The average child spends forty-six months in continuous foster care before adoption. According to Mike Mitchell, a caseworker for Denver Area Youth Services (DAYS) program, the "lucky" children have the same foster home throughout the period and thus some stability. There are many, however, who pass from home to home because of a mismatch or because of external circumstances. According to most of the adoption workers I spoke with, a child is usually moved for one of two reasons: (1) The birth parent is considered by social service workers to be making headway on their list and so the child is returned to the birth parent; or (2) the caseworker makes the determination that it is a "mismatched" foster placement. If it is determined that parental rights should be terminated, the caseworker in the Adoptions Unit begins looking for a permanent home for the child.

One point that caseworkers believe is important to communicate to prospective adoptive parents is that even though it is a caseworker's objective to provide either reunification with birth parents or permanency in adoptive homes, the fact is that when children are raised in foster care systems, their lives are hectic. Just how hectic this can be is brought into relief by the case of Bev and Harry Meschlers' adopted children, Horacio, Rayna, and June. According to Harry Meschler, when they first met the children, all three resided in foster care through the DDHS. Horacio resided with one couple and the girls with another, about a mile from where Horacio was staying. Horacio shared his foster home with one other foster child and two birth sons. Rayna and June were the only foster children, but there were other birth children living in the home as well. The children had been taken into custody in the Denver area when a neighbor called Child Protective Services with a concern that there were children in the house not attending school. Caseworkers told the Meschlers that the police removed fourteen children from the home. They also told the Meschlers that they suspected that June had been sexually abused, but mostly, the birth parents had simply neglected the children—the home was filthy, and no one was designated to care for them. Their birth father was in prison on drug charges, and he had voluntarily terminated his rights once the children were in the custody of social services.

The Meschlers' caseworker also told them the children's birth mother had occasionally "resurfaced" while the children were in foster care and demanded to see the children. The social workers who had direct contact with the children told the Meschlers that many times foster parents had gotten the children ready for a visit and their birth mother failed to show up or call. Once, when she did arrive for a supervised visit at the courthouse, she behaved inappropriately with the children, putting her tongue in the mouth of one of them when they kissed. The county caseworker felt confident that there would be no problem terminating the mother's rights because she had failed to maintain regular contact with the children and there was the documented incident of inappropriate behavior. The Meschlers decided to begin preplacement visits, despite the possible risk of the children's birth mother reasserting her rights. This they did primarily because of the assurances the caseworkers gave them.

A second important point that caseworkers try to help parents understand is that children have varying reactions to being raised in foster care. In a minority of cases, children are able to maintain their hope and faith in others and welcome a family when they are placed in the Adoptions Unit. However, caseworkers frequently described cases where children expressed overt hostility to the foster parents and the caseworker, or a mixture of sadness and anger that caseworkers saw as depression (as one caseworker put it, they "simply die inside") along with lowered self-esteem—children "internalize the rejection" and blame themselves for the biological parent's abandonment. This, say caseworkers, makes it difficult for some children to believe in "family" and makes them apathetic about being adopted.

In addition to transmitting a comprehensive understanding of children's involvement with DDHS during their initial meetings and education sessions with prospective parents, caseworkers' desires to inform parents about children's histories is also reflected in the way they construct their own version of the photo listing or personality profiles of children waiting in foster care. DDHS photo listings are similar to those constructed by nonprofit agencies that specialize in international adoptions, in that children are presented as smiling, happy, and clean-cut. The narrative that accompanies the photo listing, however, focuses on children's early childhood background and alerts parents to what they call the "special needs" of children adopted through DDHS. In particular, caseworkers attempt to depict as accurately as they can the child's perceived ability to attach. For example:

> Kellye has a lengthy history of trauma, abuse and neglect. She has had multiple placements as a result. Kellye has multiple special needs and requires an experienced family who has the flexibility and availability to meet her needs. The ideal situation for Kellye would be to have a family that could begin involvement with her within her current therapeutic placement. This would allow her to develop a relationship slowly and to prepare for the future. Kellye's ultimate wish is to establish a permanent placement where she can grow up. (Denver Department of Human Services, Child Welfare Division 2003b)

According to caseworkers, this is a conscious strategy; because of their unique perspective on children's early histories, they say it is nearly impossible for them to romanticize that children will immediately perform as emotional assets. As one case manager for the State of Illinois told me, "It's false advertising. And, you know, it's really not what these kids need. It creates more problems down the road; we don't even try."

Still, most caseworkers I interviewed expressed optimism about the ability of the children they place to perform *eventually* as emotional assets. For example, said Lisa Kelly:

> The kids I work with have it so bad. They deal with so much. They've been through things that would send adults crying, and I have cried a river for the kids I work with. It [early childhood abuse] makes it

so hard for them to look forward to family. What has "family" meant for them up to that point? Heartache, sadness, abuse, exploitation. Almost dying? [And] some of them don't make it. They don't make it to the legal adoption, or they make it to the legal adoption but then disrupt [aren't finalized]. They can't do it. A lot of [caseworkers] I know have cause to give up, and I know a few who have just left [the job] altogether, but then you get some kids who do make it, and it keeps me going....I gave up long ago thinking I was here to save every child. But I have seen enough kids make it to feel that [the success of a child in an adoptive family] is a matter of me telling [adoptive parents] who these kids are, what has happened to them, what they really need, and then encouraging [adoptive parents] to be patient. Not to expect too much too fast or to try to turn the kids into something they can't be right away, and eventually, they can have the child they hoped for.

State Requirements of Adoption Agencies and Proving the Ability to Parent

As we see here, adoption agents, whether they are employed in international adoption agencies or domestic placement services, share the goal of presenting themselves as strong allies of adoptive parents, particularly in parents' efforts to incorporate formerly institutionalized children into their families. In addition to demonstrating expertise in facilitating the process of making families real, however, agencies must also expose parents to a rigorous process that begins with proving their ability to parent. The nuances of the process depend on whether parents adopt from abroad or from social services, and, if internationally, which country and region within that country they are adopting from. However, parents typically begin their adoption process by sending in a lengthy general application form that requires parents to disclose, among other things, their family, financial, and psychological status, for example:

Name	Contact info	Age/birthplace
Race/ethnicity	Citizenship	Passport number
Employer information	Income	Residential status
Credit history	Insurance status	Health information
Psychological status	Chemical dependency disclosure	Infertility history

Marital history	Current marital status	Family composition
Death of a child	Adoption/foster care history	Child abuse
Domestic violence	Criminal record	Motivations for adopting
Home study status	Adoption preferences	

In addition to the application, parents send a nonrefundable application fee and a photo. These and other seemingly mundane procedures are the result of several state requirements for adoption agencies, including accreditation postplacement standards.

According to agency staff, maintaining state accreditation, required for state funding, preoccupies them constantly. This is because accreditation serves many important purposes. As staff members from both international and domestic agencies told me, it provides an external, objective marker for "consumers" (adopting parents) and "stakeholders" (state agents), while disciplining the agencies to meet national standards of organizational strength and quality of service. According to the Family Service Association (2004), accreditation standards for adoption agencies are specifically designed to result "in a detailed analysis that charts specific strengths and weaknesses in areas of an organization's governance, operations, and services and that provides a framework for ongoing improvement" (FSA 2004). Accreditation standards are also designed to identify organizations in which consumers can have confidence.

According to the Family Service Association (2004), accreditation should do the following:

1. Provide evidence to the community that the organization providing service has met accepted standards of operation;
2. Identify for private and public funders organizations that are worthy of financial support;
3. Generate knowledge on which an effective organizational referral system can be built;
4. Establishes goals for organizational improvement; and
5. Protect the organization from pressures to lower standards.

Accredited organizations are notable for the following strengths: (1) the quality of their services; (2) a strengths-based focus on the person or family served; (3) a collaborative relationship with the community and with other organizations within the community; (4) a respect for diversity and the assumption of responsibility to provide service in a culturally competent way; (5) a commitment to producing positive outcomes and to accountability to those who purchase and use their services (http://www.fsasatx.org/coa.htm).

Among the adoption staff members I interviewed, I found that, across the board, they take the accreditation process seriously. From beginning to end, no matter how they may personally feel about state demands on their agency, their stated goal is to try to proceed "by the book." State demands seemed to particularly influence the thinking of international adoption agents in various ways. For example, adoption staffers perceive the application procedure as a vital part of the adoption process.

According to the director of one international agency in Denver, the application procedure is designed for two purposes. The first is to comply with rules set out by the Bureau of Citizen and Immigration Services (BCIS) in the Department of Homeland Security, the federal agency that handles the citizenship paperwork for children adopted from abroad and which requires certain disclosures from parents in order to approve citizenship for adopted children. Thus often simultaneously to filling out general agency forms, parents complete the BCIS application as well.

It is also important to note that at the time of my research, the United States had, in 1994, become a signatory of the Hague Convention on Protection of Children and Co-operation in Respect of Intercountry Adoption. International adoption agency staff members were thus anticipating an overwhelming number of changes to the way they interacted with the state with regard to accreditation compliance. The Hague Adoption Convention is an international treaty that aims to establish international standards of practices for intercountry adoptions to ensure that adoptions take place in the best interests of a child, and that the abduction, sale or traffic in children is prevented. In 2000, the United States Congress had passed the Intercountry Adoption Act (IAA), which provided the U. S. implementation of the Convention. Agency workers spent much time following the development of the federal and state bureaucracies associated with the enforcement of the Convention and learning how it would impact their organizations.[2]

---

[2] After over a decade of preparation, the United States began enforcing the rules of the Hague Convention on Intercountry Adoption in April, 2008. As expected, the Convention has had a tremendous impact on adoption agencies' accreditation requirements. The Convention, which is administered through the U.S. Department of State, is overseen at the state level by two accrediting bodies—the Council on Accreditation (COA), which oversees accreditation of international adoption agencies located in all

The second purpose of the general application form is to provide adoption staff information they need to determine applicants' fitness as parents. Although many staff commented that there really was no one factor other than certain types of criminal records that could preclude parents' acceptance, and that staff usually approved or disapproved applicants on a case-by-case basis, some individual staff members had strong feelings on the issue:

We have to be careful that we don't place children with families that are not prepared to provide them with the kind of home that the kids deserve. Parents have to be prepared to essentially give over their lives to this new person. It's a big deal to adopt, and they have to be financially and emotionally prepared. That's why the application forms are so long. We have to be able to assess to the best of our ability if they're going to make a good home for the child. For instance, we had some applicants just a few weeks ago who wanted to adopt a child from Sierra Leone, and this family disclosed that they had a lot of debt. I don't mean credit card debt, I mean a bankruptcy with no signs that it helped [their debt reduction] much. Other times, we've had applicants with criminal records, and there are some times, you know, not often, but a few times, there are people who have a history of domestic abuse somewhere in the family. That's not really acceptable. Other times we've got parents who want to adopt kids from other countries, and the adoptions will be transracial, and the parents don't really show any indications that they thought through the implications of that kind of match, so these might be grounds for rejection. It doesn't always mean that, but it's safe to say that we'd look twice.

Through the application process, the state shapes the thoughts and actions of the agencies, who, in turn, shape those of potential adoptive parents. The application is the first of many procedures that expose adopting

---

states except Colorado, and the Colorado Department of Human Services (CDHS), which oversees accreditation for agencies located within Colorado. The U.S. Department of State also increased the number and requirements for agencies' accreditation. By November, 2008, over 300 U.S. adoption agencies applied for accreditation and approximately 220 had received some form of accreditation (Council on Accreditation 2009; U.S. Department of State 2009). Studies demonstrate that the Hague Adoption Convention's regulation of intercountry adoption is also having a global impact on the numbers, types, and sources of children associated with international adoptions (Wingert 2008; Worthington 2009), leading to increasing debates about the advantages and disadvantages of the global regulation of intercountry adoptions.

parents to state-inspired definitions of family and train them to utilize these definitions themselves. Immediately on applying, parents are taught to think about their disclosures in terms of whether they can provide a "proper" family for adopted children: for example, whether they possess certain income levels and financial histories. Here one can begin to understand the ways in which adoption agencies institutionalize the core concepts of the "good home" that adoptive parents envisioned in chapter 2. In particular, their conceptualizations of the material and emotional aspects of the "good home" are both made and reinforced in the application process.

Simultaneous to filling out a general application form (and sometimes even before), parents are required to contact a licensed social worker, who conducts a home study. A social worker's recommendation of a family after doing a home study certifies them to the BCIS as appropriate for adopting. In fact, many regional BCIS offices will not process parental applications to adopt a child from overseas until their home study is submitted and approved. Similarly, a social worker's recommendation is needed before a family can adopt from a foreign country. As the director of an agency in Boulder, Colorado, told me, the home study is also an important aspect of the adoption process in that it is the basic "passport" to international adoption and provides proof that parents have filled out their initial application truthfully. The home study once again requires applicants to disclose family and individual backgrounds as well as information about parents' home environment, neighborhood, education, careers, health history, financial position, and motivations to adopt. When I asked one home-study consultant what agencies look for in home studies, he said:

> We look for a lot of things. We check out how many bedrooms the house has. Is the house clean—you know, not crazy clean but are there any health hazards there. What hours do the parents work? What kinds of things are they going to feed the kids? How far away is the school they're sending the kids to? What kind of education are they providing? Will the kids have access to health care? Are they going to childproof the house? How would they go about childproofing the house? We ask them questions like that. We ask them about their neighbors, their employer. We just need to get a picture of their lives and match up the people on the application form with the people in front of us.

A third way that adoption agencies train parents to take on state-inspired definitions of the family is through postplacement *reporting*. In order to make it possible for the state to create postplacement statistics, many adoption agencies are mandated to provide postplacement reporting and services for client families for a set amount of time "ranging from six months to three or more years" after the child has been placed. Postplacement reporting includes monthly surveys and evaluations to be completed by adopting parents. These agencies may also provide state-monitored counseling for the new family, observe the child's adjustment to the new home, and supply parents with information and referrals. Many foreign countries also require postplacement supervision for six months to two years to ensure the child has been well placed and is receiving adequate care. During this time, agencies often ask parents to furnish photographs, written reports, and medical reports which are kept in their files and sent to the child's country of origin. As part of the postplacement experience, many agencies also have organized support groups for new adoptive parents. These support groups introduce parents to one another and provide a time and place for them to meet to discuss postplacement issues. They also encourage parents to socialize outside the agency by sponsoring picnics, lectures, and cultural events.

While many agency staff speak about postplacement services as supportive services—or as one staffer put it, "the saving grace for parents," because they saw them as providing a support network for coping after placement—others provided insight into the more disciplinary aspects of the practice. For example, as one volunteer coordinator for a private adoption referral service in Aurora, Colorado, explained, postplacement monitoring, in addition to being an expression of the state's requirement that children be placed in a healthy environment, was needed by the agency to obtain needed state funding or licensing:

> Nonprofits like the ones you're working with have a ton of state requirements they have to meet, or else they get closed down. You've got to have positive postplacement reports, or they send licensing agents, inspectors, down. So yeah, there is an investment in those reports.

Other staff agreed that postplacement reports helped them keep tabs on parents, but they legitimated the reporting based on the health of the family:

> When you've done the paperwork and the home study, when you've got parents that fly halfway around the world to give a home to a kid, you know, that's dedication. That's a genuine desire to make that family. But you still don't know what's going to actually happen when the

kid gets there. Maybe there's stress or maybe there's something keeping that family from thriving. Maybe someone's lost their job...a death in the family...psychological problems maybe. It's real important that we keep on top of that so that we can take appropriate action.

Whether adoption staff members understand postplacement reporting as evidence of higher state intervention or necessary for the proper functioning of the family, one commonality is present. Adoption agency staff members believed that they were qualified to determine what makes a good family. They also saw postadoption placement services as having the potential to create a lasting relationship between an agency and families, which extends beyond the actual adoption process and ensures some much needed guidance from the agency to families during the challenging period immediately following children's placements.

Family Building versus Institution Building

When I first embarked on my interviews with adoption agency staff in the Denver area, I went with certain questions in mind. I wondered if staff attitudes toward adoption and expectations for children would match those of adopting parents. In particular, I wondered if agency staff members would invest adopted children with the same kind of power to make families real that parents at the clinic did, and if their speech would reveal the same motivations for taking part in the adoption process as those of parents. In other words, would agency policy and practice reflect a primary motivation for adoption agency staff "to provide good homes" for children? Indeed, during the first few weeks of my research at both types of agencies, when I read their advertisements and had preliminary interviews with directors and caseworkers it seemed that the needs of parents—and the desire to get children placed in good homes—determined an agency's attitudes, practice, and policy. As seen here, the series of "trust-building techniques" that agencies use to establish professional relationships with parents constructs the narratives that allow agencies to present themselves as allies of parents in their quest to make families real via adoption. Through these techniques, agencies also make their initial promises to incorporate a formerly institutionalized child into the private nuclear family. The ways the agency staff accomplishes this depends on the type of agency. International adoption agency staff seek to establish alliances with adopting parents through what they call "founding stories," "testimonials," and "photo listings" or "personality profiles" that deemphasize the role that state agencies will play in the adoption process. Adoption agents see these techniques and narratives as necessary and useful because they "buffer" parents from the hassles of state intervention. In the case of social service agencies, caseworkers use mission statements, "introductory scripts," and their own version of photo listings and personality profiles to make their relationship to the state as transparent as possible to parents, highlighting the bureaucracy associated with the process. Caseworkers say that by making state intervention transparent, they are hoping to comfort parents and educate them to the "realities" of what it takes to adopt formerly institutionalized children. Caseworkers also justify these strategies as part of their larger willingness to "go to the mat with the truth," even if it means initial conflict between themselves and adopting parents, because ultimately, it is for the good of the children and the right path to constructing families.

However, before long I realized that, in addition to adoption agencies constructing and producing several types of narratives and policies that help parents realize the power of children to help establish families, when it comes to day-to-day practice, both international and social service agencies have institutional needs that result in specific forms of agencies' management of adoptive parents. In other words, as explained in chapter 2, while parents at the clinic expected adopted children to make *families* real, the staff at the agencies where I conducted my research also invested formerly institutionalized children with the power to make *institutions* real. Particularly, staff invested the successful placement of formerly institutionalized children with what Bourdieu terms "institutionalized cultural capital," or the type of capital that makes it possible for institutions to profit from a collective belief in "officially recognized, guaranteed competence" (1998, 248). Through these institutions' rituals, which generally rely on and reiterate state-inspired definitions of family, as seen in the case of parent application questionnaires, international adoption agency staff encouraged parents to adopt from institutions as a means to assert the family as a body at the same time that they slowly and consistently worked on individuals to see it that way. Adoption staff reinforce the family as a field, a "network, or configuration, of objective relations between positions" (1998, 97) through which they exert their power as professional experts. Ultimately, through the prescription and legitimization of the family as emotional refuge and adoptees as emotional assets, adoption staffers establish bureaucratic permanency for themselves and their institutions. This creates an atmosphere in which adoption agency staff and adopting parents operate simultaneously as both allies and competitors for the power to construct the adoptive family, which results in an ambivalent relationship between adopting parents and staff members.

Attention to the ambivalent relationship between the adoptive parents of formerly institutionalized children and adoption staff members also serves as a way in for thinking about the changing political and economic conditions in which adoption workers are operating, particularly within the context of a transforming global order that is, in itself, reordering families. As Nybell, Shook, and Finn (2009) have noted, practitioners involved in the circulation of children have "historically been embedded in contradiction" (20); however, with the introduction of new adoption options and policy for both U.S. and foreign children, they face an even larger number of paradoxes. For example, they not only face competing claims concerning the rights and needs of children and youth, but they also confront contradictions between policy and practice. They are also often expected to fight for the best interests of children, even when financial support for children's welfare and education grows scarce. Finally, they are asked to save "children at risk," while, at the same time, they are urged to protect communities from "risky children," and they are encouraged to "leave no child behind," while also implementing "zero tolerance" policies to keep educational environments free from troubled youth.

While chapter 2 interrogated the folk categories that adoptive parents use to form their own representations of family, in this chapter we see both a potent source of these categories and a site where they are socially reproduced. The exploration of parents' relationships with adoption agencies shows the ways in which adoption agencies' language and practice contribute to the ritual and technical institutionalization of the "normal family." Agencies also enact several disciplinary techniques such as parent-fitness tests and postplacement reporting procedures that prescribe state definitions of family throughout the process. In both these indirect and direct ways, adoption agency rituals constitute the definition of the good and real family. The role of the child as emotional asset is also reaffirmed through these practices. Ultimately, examining the inner workings of the types of adoption agencies that parents at the clinic worked with demonstrates some of the ways that state agents aid in the construction of family as a social category in the United States.

Chapter Four

Prisoners in Our Own Home

Postplacement Realities of the Family

In fall 1997, Bev and Harry Meschler arrived home with Horacio, Rayna, and June, and the family briefly enjoyed what the parents described as an "idyllic" family life. According to Bev, however, only three months after legally adopting the children "the honeymoon was over." The children were sneaking around at night, and the younger of the two girls, June, had snuck into the pantry and eaten an entire five-pound bag of sugar. All the children were disturbed by physical attention, sometimes stiffening at Bev and Harry's touch. In addition to these behaviors, the children seemed to have attention problems, sometimes looking "glazed over" and sometimes being hyperactive. According to Bev, it made it difficult to do things with the children: "It was like there was no *there* there. We couldn't go out and have a good time. We didn't hang together as a family. They were either not interested or they freaked out."

Bev and Harry tried to deal with the problem on their own for about three months. However, after the terrible discovery that Horacio was secretly sexually abusing the two girls and that June was sexually abusing her older sister, Harry and Bev sought professional help. Within another three months, all three children were diagnosed with reactive attachment disorder. Horacio was placed in a group home for young sexual offenders, and

June began living in a series of group homes for girls. Rayna, the middle child, stayed in the Meschlers' home.

Like the Meschlers, other parents I interviewed at the clinic found that, despite their expectations that children adopted from institutions or foster care would easily make the transition to the nuclear family—and despite adoption agencies' encouragement that such transitions, no matter what the children's early history, were possible—their children did not easily adapt to the role of emotional asset. Almost immediately after adoption, such seemingly simple issues as hygiene, diet, and care of private property became the breeding grounds for serious struggle between parents and their adopted children. In some cases, children presented larger problems by behaving in ways that parents perceived as emotionally inappropriate within a family setting. In the most challenging scenarios, children exhibited violent behaviors, and adoptive parents and nonadopted siblings did not feel safe in their own homes. The expectations and assumptions that adopting parents made about the children who they would adopt and the ways in which the children would eventually become members of their family were more than just dashed expectations. As Angela Walker, a parent from Yuma, Arizona, said, "Our expectations turned out to be out-and-out fantasies."

In this chapter, I discuss several themes of the *postplacement* experiences of the parents I interviewed at the clinic. I first outline children's behaviors that challenged parents' expectations and alerted them to the need to seek help for their families. I then document the typical decision-making process parents underwent prior to turning to the Evergreen model of attachment therapy. Finally, I discuss the expectations that parents had for the therapy prior to coming to Evergreen. This information was gleaned from a further analysis of parents' intake discussions at the clinic as well as observations of parents' psychiatric consultations.

One of the objectives of this chapter is to demonstrate that parents' responses to children's postplacement behaviors vary. In particular, not all parents accepted a medical discourse to understand their child's behavior. The second objective of the chapter is to outline the large stakes for adoptive parents who *do* accept a medical discourse to explain their children's postplacement behaviors, and how these stakes shape the expectations they have for the Evergreen method of attachment therapy. As will be seen, parents fully expect attachment therapists to do what they could not do through their own altruism, and what adoption agencies could not do through their bureaucratic practices—therapists are expected to teach, or train, children to become emotional assets and to elicit children's genuine positive emotions toward adopting parents. In other words, adopting parents not only call on attachment therapists to cure their children, they depend on them for the preservation of their family.

Problematic Postplacement Behaviors of Children

Hygiene

In observing parents' psychiatric consultations, I found that the most emotional part of these discussions occurred when parents talked about their children's problematic postplacement behaviors. One of the first such behaviors that parents became aware of shortly after adopting was what they described as a lack of attention to hygiene. Parents complained of children's resistance to taking showers or baths, grooming their hair, or brushing their teeth, and of their desire to wear ratty clothing. Children took great pleasure in picking their noses, belching, and farting in public, despite repeated reprimands and punishments from parents. Of particular concern to parents, however, was the need to keep focused on the bathroom habits of children, even as old as twelve.[1] "We had to watch them 24–7 or we would be sorry," said Angela Walker, who adopted from social services in Arizona. Another parent stated that she became used to "having to use my nose when I first opened his door in the morning" to determine whether she might spend some time cleaning up urine or feces. Other parents stated they had to keep watch so that children did not urinate or defecate in their beds or in the bathtub, and some parents even did regular "poop sweeps" in seemingly unlikely places for bathroom activity such as closets, under children's beds, the side of the house, and the middle of the living room floor. According to some parents, such as Bev and Harry Meschler, this behavior seemed "unconscious," something that children did accidentally:

> HM: It was strange. It was almost like they wouldn't know they had to go to the bathroom.
> BM: Yeah, it would be like, "Do you have to go to the bathroom?" And they would say, "No" [imitating crossing her legs together to prevent urination].

[1] Literature on the phenomenon of children voluntarily or involuntarily holding in waste, or voiding in inappropriate places, which medical professionals call "enuresis" (in the case of voiding urine) and "encopresis" (in the case of voiding stool), demonstrate that enuresis and encopresis in children can be related to trauma experiences (Eidlitz-Markus, Shuper, and Amir 2000) including early childhood trauma such as physical and sexual abuse (Morrow, Yeager, and Lewis 1997; Reece 2005).

HM: So we'd say, "Well, come on, because it looks like you do," and we'd take them into the bathroom and sit them down, and they'd pee like a racehorse!
BM: And I was like, "Oh my Gosh." It was just very out there.

However, other parents, particularly those whose children regularly urinated or defecated in their pants or directly on the floor, or whose children habitually smeared feces and urine on their bedroom walls, considered the behavior to be purposeful. Said adoptive parent John Perkins:

Oh, it definitely felt like revenge for something…passive-aggressive. We did ask [our agency facilitator], 'Is this something related to the orphanage? The children weren't feral? No one mentioned potty training.' And she said, 'Of course [the kids were potty-trained].'…The strange thing is that it didn't bother them at all.

Becky and Pat Haskell-James, a same-sex couple who adopted two brothers from social services in Columbia, Maryland, had similar experiences:

Oh yes, we became very familiar with some very disgusting things…it wasn't just that Jonah pooped somewhere he shouldn't. He didn't tell us where he did it, and we'd clean up what we thought was all of it, but it would still smell and the whole house would smell.

Care of Belongings/Family Events

According to parents, in addition to displaying a lack of attention to hygiene, many children often took poor care of their belongings. While some children seemed to actually enjoy receiving new clothing and toys, as well as access to household goods, they often did not take care of them. One parent told me: "Oh! We found something wrong every day. Nothing was safe in the house." Parents readily listed and showed therapists photos of the damage that adoptees caused to personal property, including demolished beds, gouged mattresses, shredded books, beheaded dolls and action figures, broken windows, unpotted houseplants, irreparably stained carpets, and plugged drains and toilets. Some parents had replaced bedroom furniture so often that they refused to buy any more: children thus slept on plain mattresses with old linens. Attempts to teach children to care for their personal belongings, such as "positive reinforcement" techniques (gold-star systems) or chore schedules with built-in rewards, rarely elicited the kinds of results parents desired.

In addition to children's' shabby treatment of household goods, parents also were concerned about their children's lack of enjoyment and/or appreciation of parents' attempts to provide what they considered typical childhood experiences. As one parent put it, "A high as big as a family party or vacation was normally followed by a dramatic, dismal low." Such seemingly simple things as planning what to do for the holidays became a problem for many parents. Parents complained that their adopted children "could not handle" large family gatherings and receiving presents. Many children would act fine at parties but then "act out" at home in unpredictable and destructive ways. "The excitement seems to be too much for them," one parent told me. Another family, when discussing how their last Christmas holiday had gone sour with their adopted children, began arguing about the issue in front of staff members at the clinic. The mother explained she no longer wanted to participate in what she called the "family free-for-all." She was concerned that because the children in her husband's family were "spoiled rotten" and allowed to run around free of supervision, both of her children would not respond well. Thus when the holidays were over, the boys would act out, and she would spend the remainder of the holiday vacation disciplining them. Next year, she simply wanted to stay home with her husband and the children. She described it as her way of trying to take care of herself. However, this upset her husband, who said that to stay home with the boys would be depriving them all of a happy holiday with family.

Holiday parties and gifts were not the only things that parents reported children being unable to handle. Children also rejected family excursions to entertainment centers such as Chuck E. Cheese's or video arcades, and parents were especially disappointed when children did not have fun on their trips to amusement parks. This first became evident to me in an interview with Carl and Jane Maleski, a couple from Walnut Creek, California, who adopted two girls from Novosibirsk, Russia. Carl said that Disneyland was supposed to be "every kid's dream," but for them the dream quickly became "a nightmare." This became a common theme among many parents I observed:

> The first time we *really* knew something was wrong was when we went to visit my husband's parents in Florida. We took them to Disney World. We thought, "Disney World! How could a kid hate Disney World?" But they peed in the teacups, and they tantrumed while we waited in line. Every time we tried to pick them up they screamed like we were abusing them! Every day it got worse…we just stopped going. We went to the pool instead. They didn't like that much either. They wouldn't sleep in the hotel beds. We tucked them in, we turned

out the lights, we woke up the next morning—they were sleeping on the floor, next to the bed, under the bed, but not on the bed.

Illogical and/or Irrational Behavior

Parents also related what they thought to be another postplacement problem during our interviews: poor problem-solving skills, or what many parents called "illogical" or "irrational" behavior. Some of these behaviors turned out to be more confusing than harmful, such as the example of Madeline Voss, who temporarily fostered eleven-year-old Sarah:

> I had one little girl—Sarah—she had been with us for about a year and a half [for respite foster care]. She was in the process of reintegrating home. And her parents worked for American Airlines, so every weekend and then for holidays and in the summertime she would fly home. Well, I did my husband's laundry, and at that time he wore black socks to work. And he had tube socks for just regular stuff. So I washed up all of his laundry. I could remember folding his socks. I could remember putting them in the basket. Come Monday morning, it's time for him to go to work, and there's no black socks. And she's on her visit, right? We tear the house up trying to find these black socks. It didn't occur to me to look in her room. She'd been doing really well.
>
> Well, a little background on her life was that her mother had adopted her, and she was now eleven years old. Her mother had been married and divorced five times within that period of time. The daughter had always been with her, but the dads kept changing.
>
> So, she comes home and I just had this urge to ask her. I said, "Do you know where Dad's socks are?" "Oh yeah!" she says with a big grin on her face. She goes down in her room, gets the basket, brings it up and hands it to me. She was acting like a normal kid who had found a treasure, right? So I'm thinking, I should ask her why. So, I say, "Sarah, why did you take Dad's socks?" And man, she had this all planned. She says, "This is how I figured it. That if Dad didn't have his black socks, he couldn't go to work. If he couldn't go to work, he would have to be here when I got back and I wouldn't have to worry about him never coming home."

Other examples of illogical behavior, however, were not so benign. For example, Betty Korhonen's adopted son Jeffrey, a ten-year-old at the time, had dropped a quarter, which rolled behind the bathroom vanity in their basement. Instead of asking his parents for help or using the handle of the broom, which sat right beside the vanity, to retrieve the quarter, Jeffrey pulled the vanity out of the wall. Pipes burst and water leaked everywhere. Jeffrey's parents did not find out about the damage until hours later because he didn't tell them about the leaks, and when confronted, he nonchalantly shrugged and told them he needed to get his money. Betty was clearly confused and disturbed by her child's lack of ability to weigh the end against the means: "There was no thought to us and how much money it would cost us to fix the sink. Absolutely none. He wanted what he wanted, and that was basically it."

In another example, Melanie Jarvis, was at the supermarket with adopted son, Trevor, when he asked her if she would buy him an ice cream. Melanie said she couldn't because she didn't have enough money. That night Trevor went home and bashed his tooth out with a rock. When Melanie asked him why he did this, he told her it was because he thought if his tooth came out, he could put the tooth under his pillow and the Tooth Fairy would come and give him money that he could give to Melanie to buy him an ice cream. Again, this adoptive parent was concerned about the lengths to which her child would go to achieve a seemingly insignificant goal:

> The most disturbing part of it was that it had to hurt! And he did it even though it would hurt. In his mind, the ice cream was worth that. Can you imagine having that threshold for pain?

Resistance to Attachment and Indiscriminate Attachment

When discussing these problematic postplacement behaviors with the clinic's psychiatrist, parents' general tone was one of disbelief, sadness, and resignation. Parents also found these behaviors disappointing, inconvenient, and, in some cases, a cause for pity, embarrassment, or shame. However, many stated that they believed that these behaviors were reversible, and that there was still a chance they could minimize or eradicate them over time with discipline and love. Others mentioned that if, in fact, these were the only problematic behaviors their children displayed, they could live with it. However, it was rare that this was the case. Most parents interviewed at the clinic also witnessed far more disturbing behaviors in their children. The first of these—resistance to attachment—in which children push family and friends away—and indiscriminate attachment—in which children do not distinguish between adoptive parents or others as potential attachment figures—touched parents most deeply. It often brought them to tears as they described their children's inability to emotionally connect with them or anyone else on what seemed to them to be a genuine and appropriate emotional level. Parents often explained that their children displayed resistance to attachment or indiscriminate attachments in two areas. The first was at school with teachers and classmates. This is exemplified by Margaret and John Perkins, the couple from Parker, Colorado, who adopted two children from a Moscow orphanage. Said John:

> Sergei has what appears to be a superiority complex. He doesn't do things our way, preferring his own way even if it means screwing up and missing out. He doesn't seem to care. As long as we've known him, he has always had tremendous patience, and he thinks he can outlast anyone and everyone. He is stubborn as a mule. Sergei has friends at school, but we think he doesn't have many or any true friends. When his friends stop over, he'll go out to play. When they call him, he will never return their calls, and even when his Mom and I suggest ideas and tell him how to do them and what we will do to help make it happen, he just doesn't do it.
>
> He never invites friends to our home. He tends to gravitate to younger children, or occasionally an older boy in the neighborhood. He seems totally incapable of relating to us with honesty and true feelings. He appears to be trying to learn the rules and play the game to get what he wants emotionally.
>
> Bettina [their other adopted child] admits that at recess none of the kids want to play with her, and it's because she's been mean to them all. She will respond to authority, but she will not behave for empty threats and she pushes. Bettina has a hard time making true friends due to her desire—or maybe it's a need—to control the situation she's in.

Other parents commonly stated that their children could not keep friends because they "purposely set themselves apart from other kids."

This was the case with Myers, a twelve-year-old boy adopted from county services in Pennsylvania. According to his adoptive mother, Kathryn Weathers:

> Myers has problems getting along with his peers. He cannot handle losing a game or being embarrassed. If he sees he's going to lose he'll probably get angry and end the game with some excuse before that

can happen. He has been suspended from Sunday School, which is something that has never happened to anyone else I know—it's just not heard of in Pennsylvania Dutch country! He was removed from camp after the first week of a two-week session for starting something with another kid. He tends to pick at and tease other kids, then becomes terrified when they finally fight back. Last year in school, he had a student wait around the corner for him, then attempt to beat him up. Myers's response was to curl up in a fetal position and cry like a baby. He was moved by adults to another room, where I found him still in that position when I came to pick him up.

The second arena in which children had serious problems emotionally connecting was in the home, particularly with adoptive parents and even more specifically with adoptive mothers. Many parents revealed that their children rarely accepted physical affection, often stiffening at parents' touch or hug, and they rarely initiated physical contact with parents unless they wanted something. "It's hard to describe if you haven't experienced it. There's something…false about it, or fake. It's a *slimy* feeling," said Betty Korhonen, from Wisconsin, of Jeffrey:

> If I give him something he wants, then it's like, "I love you, Mom. I love you." But it's phony crap. It's like, he thinks about something later and thinks, "I better suck up because they're gonna be really pissed at me," so he's like, "I'm really sorry that I did that." And he can really play it genuine, I mean…but I don't think he is [genuine] though. If he were, he wouldn't keep doing bad things. He'll come back and say, "I'm sorry." Sometimes he'll even cry about it, but I don't know.

Other parents said the same thing. According to Bev and Harry Meschler, any sign of attachment their adopted children displayed seemed to have an ulterior motive. In this exchange between the Meschlers and one of their therapists, they described their daughter June's "empty" attachment patterns:

> Therapist: You're saying she is jealous? Vengeful?
> BM: Ugh. Horrible jealousy.
> HM: Pathological jealousy.
> Therapist: But there was a period where she did really well?
> HM: I would summarize it that there was a point in time when June allowed Bev to have input into her life. She allowed her to be there without being hostile and nasty. But I could not leave Rayna with

Bev and June during that time. June was horrible. It was the jealousy thing. June would say, "Oh when I'm out, you two are going to do such and such," sort of like, in her passive-aggressive way. And as soon as Rayna was gone [out of the house], June would be like [to Bev], "Hah, you're mine."

BM: And so, yeah, as part of that, there was a time when, for June, I was most definitely the chosen parent.

Therapist: And she even demonstrated some reciprocity?

BM: Some. Not much.

HM: But the reward was, she had Mom to herself.

Therapist: So ultimately, it wasn't a real attachment. It was actually splitting behavior [behavior designed to cause conflict between Bev and Rayna].

BM: Yes.

In addition to "false" attachments, children also displayed indiscriminate attachment. In other words, children do not identify their adoptive parents as their primary caretakers and even seem incapable of understanding that their relationship with adoptive parents is supposed to be permanent. Said Brandon Tucker of Ginny, a five-year-old girl he adopted from county services in Modesto, California:

Oh, she'll go up to anyone and start talking to them. I have no doubt that she'd go home with someone if they asked her, and I doubt that she'd even think twice about us. I don't think she'd miss us. It's like "insert parent here." It's like that cartoon, "Are you my Mommy? Are you my Mommy?"

Violent Intent/Realization

In addition to unrealized attachment or indiscriminate attachment, parents in some cases witnessed or experienced children's displays of what they perceived as "mean" or violent intent. According to several parents, their children seemed to take personal pleasure in others' discomfort or pain. For example, one parent said he thought his daughter received a lot of joy from observing his difficulty in getting time alone with his girlfriend and seemed happy when they had fights, and parents often complained that their children lied to other people and told them their adoptive parents were abusing them, starving them, or threatening to get rid of them. It then appeared to them that children took great pleasure in the confrontations that ensued. Even more disturbing for parents than these passive-aggressive behaviors were what parents commonly spoke of as "dagger looks" and incidents in which children had threatened, sometimes very graphically, to hurt them or others, or to set fire to the house. As one parent stated, "To be completely honest, I was afraid that if I turned my back at the wrong time, I'd get nailed." In other cases, children did engage in acts of violence against themselves or others, including hitting, kicking, scratching, and spitting. Children regularly physically attacked their family members—according to one parent, one of their adopted children often got so angry at his brother that he choked him so hard that he left hand marks on his neck. In another case, a mother described how, at age four, her son knocked over his eighty-year-old grandmother and injured her so severely that they had to take her to the emergency room. Parents were also targets. In fact, many parents—some boldly but most quite sheepishly—eventually showed therapists bruises, cuts, or scars that their adopted children had given them during a physical altercation.

Most disturbing to parents, however, were those cases where children acted out their violent feelings against adoptive parents or others in the household in what they understood to be cold and calculating ways. For example, Sylvia Garner, who adopted Gavin, a three-year-old boy from a county social services agency just outside Seattle, related a story about how Gavin, age ten, gave her a pillow for her birthday decorated with a heart design and some sentimental words. Initially touched by the rare gesture, she later discovered that the pillow contained a straight pin that "stuck straight out from the heart," sharp-side up. She believed it was purposeful and that if she had sat or laid her head on it, the pin would have hurt her.

In the most disturbing story I heard during a consultation, a respite foster care provider at the clinic related how Kiki, a three-year old who was adopted into a family in northern Colorado, committed an extreme act of violence. This is a statistically unique case, but it is offered here because it is indicative of the kind of intentions that parents sometimes described sensing or fearing:

> I have to begin by saying this. Kiki was the cutest thing. I cannot stress how cute this little girl was. When I met her she was four or five years old and she looked just like a teeny Snow White. She had black hair and these bright, bright blue eyes. The cutest little thing you ever saw. You just wanted to hug her every time you saw her. . . . She was adopted into a home that had four dogs, two Rottweilers and two cocker spaniels. Kiki had been having problems basically from the second she was placed in the home, and the parents had gotten right on it.

They took her to therapy and everything. They put her on Ritalin. But it didn't do anything for her.

Well, over the course of a few months, one cocker spaniel died and then the other one died. You know, the parents were devastated, and they didn't know what the heck happened. Were the neighbors using something poisonous in the garden on their lawn? They went all over town asking, and nobody seemed to be using anything bad.

It really was a mystery to them until they found one of the Rottweilers [dead]. The other one was kicked off of a deck and down the stairs, and they had to put it to sleep. These were full-grown Rottweilers. This is terrible enough? But later they realized it was Kiki that did it. She fed the first two dogs her Ritalin. Put the Ritalin in their dog bowls every day and it poisoned them and killed them.

I don't know why she did what she did to the other dogs, but the scary thing is that there was no remorse there. Four years old and this is how much rage this little girl had in her. You wouldn't think a little girl could do this. But I met this little girl when her parents brought her in for treatment. She didn't have any trouble telling everybody, with this little, little lisp, that she had a "kiwwing pwobwem."

As we see from these examples, according to parents, children do not always prove to be emotional assets but, rather, emotional liabilities in families. As one parent described her experience, "We thought we were building our family, but really it felt like less of a family than when we started." Children's postplacement behaviors often contradicted both the *doxa* and the institutionalized representation of the private nuclear family that parents and adoption professionals had constructed preadoption. Particularly, children undermined the offering of the various elements of the "good home" discussed in chapter 2. They refused to exhibit the aesthetics and behaviors associated with the private nuclear family. They also rejected the rituals and practices associated with this vision. Perhaps most disturbing to parents, children not only undermined their practical and symbolic work that was expected to oblige adoptees to love, children also responded in ways that put themselves and others at risk.

Traditional Therapies: When Discipline Fails

Adoptive parents like Kiki's, whose children actualize violence, claimed that they sought psychiatric or legal help immediately. However, those parents who did not experience behaviors that were life-threatening spent much more time trying to reduce or eradicate negative behaviors themselves—an average of three years—before seeking attachment therapy. As mentioned earlier in this chapter, parents often believed these behaviors were reversible with time, energy, and love. Before seeking therapy, parents first tried several different strategies on their own to reverse this behavior. One strategy was the reorganization of space, including:

- Creating line-of-sight supervision
- "Making the House Smaller" by making certain rooms off limits to children
- Making the playroom a common room for most activities
- Eating dinner only in the kitchen
- Only allowing adults to take children to school
- Installing motion detectors
- Not letting the kids be alone together (for those whose children were sexually acting out)
- Playing "musical bedrooms"—changing who shared with whom: originally, certain siblings were together, because one child seemed to be the victim, but then it turned out that another child was the victim, and they separated the children.

Another strategy was the reorganization of time, including:

- Putting time limitations on shower use
- Allowing more time for making and eating meals
- Instituting split shifts/tag-team parenting, in which one parent takes a night job in order to be at home during the day while the other takes a day job to be at home at night
- Not going out as much
- Creating a "revolving schedule" for out-of-town therapy and for the family
- Creating a schedule of "rotating babysitters" that includes extended family members and friends

However, children rarely responded to typical disciplinary techniques based on methods of positive or negative reinforcement. Said John Perkins:

We rather naively assumed we could just tell them what we expected and then help them keep their behavior within limits acceptable to us by using positive reinforcement of their good actions. But I suspect we actually changed to an attitude of negative consequences—time-outs and such—for inappropriate behavior sometime during the first twenty-four hours we were actually with the kids! By the time we had spent a month with them, we had degraded to using punishments and spankings to help control inappropriate behavior. But we determined that these kids had been through so much in their short lives that a spanking was not useful as a punishment. We continue to reward good behavior with money to teach them the value of money, words of appreciation, hugs and kisses, or the opportunity to do something they really enjoy. But bad behavior is still a problem for us to deal with. Time-outs and spankings are meaningless to our kids. Revoking a privilege is only marginally effective. Most of the time, in addition to revoking a privilege, we have them do exercises. Since both kids are hyperactive, this has worked somewhat as a deterrent and saps some of their excess energy. The down side is that we are raising two hyperactive kids with behavior problems that are getting very strong!

Other parents echoed this experience. One such was Angela Walker:

I cannot tell you how frustrating it was. No amount of punishment worked. One time, I gave both boys [her adopted sons, James and Mark] notice to be home from school on time. I told them, if they are not home on time, I had to be somewhere, so I would just leave. When they did get home and if no one was there, they were to sit on the patio and wait there until I returned. Well, James was on time, but Mark wasn't. I made sure that James and I were gone by the time Mark came home. When we came back, he was sitting on the patio crying his eyes out. I thought, "Eureka, he won't do that again!" I was wrong. He did do that again, over and over. He just doesn't seem to learn from his consequences.

Parents added that children always seemed to try to get out of punishments or having to deal with punishments by expressing what many called "a victim mentality," or the tendency to blame everyone else for their own actions or decisions. Angela Walker said:

I was called into school because Mark got into a fight. When I got there, he was sitting in the outer office. I shot him a look of consternation as I walked past him into the principal's office. He didn't seem worried, which made me madder yet. The principal and I discussed his consequences and Mark was brought in. When we told him that he would lose recess privileges for two days, he responded in this neutral voice, "Alright."

We also warned him that it was his third fight and if he got into another, he would miss recess for one whole week and be grounded at home as well. When the principal asked him to tell me what happened, he attempted to blame it on the other boys. He [said], "He grabbed me from behind and was holding me. He was hurting me!" He [cried], with real tears, "so I bit him." I ask the principal to bring in the other boy to verify this. She [did] and upon questioning, we [discovered] that the boy was restraining Mark. This older boy was restraining him while another boy went to find an adult, because Mark hit another child, knocking him to the ground. Still, you know, here's Mark contending that he was the one who [was] wronged. It was always like this.

When parents' initial attempts at dealing with the problem themselves did not work, the most common initial strategy was to seek out traditional forms of therapy for their children, such as play therapy and, depending on children's ages, talk therapy. Therapists often diagnosed the children with attention-deficit hyperactivity disorder (ADHD), posttraumatic stress disorder (PTSD), oppositional defiant disorder (ODD), and/or obsessive-compulsive disorder (OCD) and started the children on medication, most commonly Ritalin for hyperactivity, or antidepressants for sluggish or apathetic behavior. Some parents allowed doctors to place children on multiple medications when one alone did not work. This was so common that parents had a name for it: the "kiddie cocktail."

According to parents who sought treatment at Evergeen, they gradually unhappily realized that traditional therapies such as play or talk therapy did not work. Play therapy often elicited emotional responses, particularly from younger children, that confused therapists and did not fit their textbook guidelines for how to work with preverbal children. Play therapists then often referred parents to developmental psychologists and told parents their children were probably suffering from a form of mild mental retardation or other developmental problem. Once directed to the developmental psychologists, however, testing would often show that children did not appear to have any clear physical neurological problems and that many were actually of above-average intelligence. Frustrated, parents then discontinued their relationships with developmental therapists as well.

For those children who are eventually brought to Evergreen, talk therapy, like play therapy, also was ineffectual. According to many parents, talk therapists were easily "conned" into believing that the children were healthier than they were. As one parent succinctly put it, "Olivia was skilled enough at lying to convince or fool the common adult and most professional facilitators." Other parents claimed that after only a few sessions of talk therapy, their children became very good at "therapy talk" or "regurgitating what [he] thinks we [parents] want to hear." Said Justine Perry, a single mother from Oregon who adopted Martin, now twelve:

> I went to [Martin's] fall conference at school this year, and he literally lied to his humanities teacher three separate times during the conference. And he was extremely believable. Had I not known the truth, even I would have not known that he was lying, so you can imagine what he did to that poor therapist when I wasn't around.

In some cases, children were so convincing in their stories that therapists discontinued the therapy, asserting that there was nothing psychologically wrong with the children. Most often, however, parents discontinued talk therapy themselves when they realized that children were rarely offering therapists honest material to work with. As one parent put it, "When you realize that your kid is smarter than the therapist, it's time to stop the therapy."

Just as traditional therapy failed to work, so often did medications. In some cases, Ritalin and antidepressants only seemed to make children worse. In others, the medication would reduce or eliminate certain behaviors, which were replaced with others that were equally unpleasant. For example, children who were hyperactive before would become overly tired or hard to wake up in the mornings, and whatever activities they once had an affinity for now were no longer enjoyable. On the other hand, children who were sluggish before would have rages or tantrums. This was unacceptable to some parents, many of whom already felt guilty for medicating children, and they discontinued them. Others, admitting they were unwilling to give up the possibility that the medications might eventually offer them respite from their children's behaviors, continued to experiment with medication types and dosages.

The Depressive Parent: When Traditional Therapies Fail

When initial attempts to discipline children and subsequent attempts to get help from medical professionals fail, many of the parents I interviewed say they became deeply depressed. Some blamed themselves for their children's behavior. According to Carol Schenk:

> I was the mom that read all about skin contact, Ashley Montague's *Touching,* and was a champion of the Snugli [infant carrier]. I seldom used an infant seat. And then I couldn't figure out why my son was doing so poorly. We adopted three babies, all at the same time, and although two were doing well, Kevin was hurting us all. I didn't know my philosophy any more. He pulled the rug out from under me.

Parents also became depressed because their children had a negative impact on their social relationships with others. For example, Carol Schenk continued:

> After we adopted Kevin, in my marriage it seemed like I was always waiting for the "someday" when [my husband and I] could relax and have time to talk, be together, and just enjoy each other. This was way beyond what was involved in normal parenting of a large family. I described it as being held hostage by Kevin. I was a prisoner in my own home. The other young children missed out on my time and being able to participate in camping or other activities other families usually participate in. They saw me at wit's end with no energy left. My personal well-being was like a joke to me.

Others became depressed because they were just plain exhausted. Said Angela Walker, the mother who adopted two boys in Arizona:

> I'm tired and cranky. I've started taking antidepressants, Prevacid for my stomach, and Allegra for hives. More recently, I suffer from insomnia, rarely able to sleep until past midnight. And I've gained weight, as I tend to self-medicate with food. I know that I shouldn't take this out on myself, but it's hard not to.

That's My Kid!: Discovering Reactive Attachment Disorder and Deciding on Attachment Therapy

How did parents find out about the Evergreen model and then come to the decision to have their children undergo attachment therapy? Parents generally took one of two routes. In a minority of cases, traditional therapists, adoption agencies, or social service agencies referred families to attachment therapists, as was the case with Kim Schelling, who adopted nine-year-old Amelia from county services in Illinois:

> My caseworker did a ton of reading. She was open and matter-of-fact about everything. I knew what I was getting into with Amelia because I did spend a lot of time with her before deciding to adopt. And I know that my caseworker wanted this to succeed so badly. Amelia is good at heart. My caseworker told me that whatever it took we should try, and she told me about attachment therapy and that I should get on the Internet and see if there was a therapist near me. She even said that she'd try to get the county to pay for it.

In general, however, the case of the Schellings was not typical, because of the controversial nature of the Evergreen model of attachment therapy. According to Selena Marquez, a case manager at the Denver Department of Human Services:

> Although we encourage parents to obtain medical help during post-placement, there's not a lot of social workers that put stock in attachment therapy. You know, I personally feel it helps. I work with people, though, who think it's an invasion of children's privacy—it's therapy voodoo and retraumatizing. There are not many referrals from our office. I think I'm the only one who does it, and I can guarantee that there are even less throughout Colorado.

The second route to attachment therapy was through the parents' own discoveries in Internet searches, online support groups, or online chat rooms. There is a common story that most of these parents share. For many it took a long time to admit that they needed help beyond the usual avenues of traditional therapy and social service or adoption agency information. Getting online and entering child-development chat rooms to speak with other parents about their children made some feel as if they were admitting their failure as parents, but their desperation pushed them forward. When introduced to attachment theory and the reactive attachment disorder diagnosis, however, these parents began to feel differently about the prospect of attachment therapy. Said one parent, "It was a new world opening up. It was a new way to think about what we were going through."

On discovering the RAD diagnosis, a minority familiarized themselves with simple treatments and attempted to use them on their own for a while before traveling to Evergreen. More common, however, were parents who said they were so relieved and elated by their discovery of the RAD diagnosis and treatment that they searched out the means to get professional attachment therapy for their children right away. Said one parent of one RAD website:

> They show the checklist like, here are twenty things that your kid does if he's got RAD. And when I read it, I was like, "That's my kid!" You know, light bulbs everywhere.

Said another:

> You get so excited because after a while you feel like you're crazy, especially because RAD kids can turn people against you. People think you're the one with the problem and the kids are just fine and you're mean and evil because you discipline them so much and you're so hard on them. It almost always comes back to you. But when I read what these guys [RAD therapists] were saying, I thought, "Damn, somebody knows! Somebody else knows! So, OK, let's go. What do we have to do to make this happen?" This door finally opened.

It is important to discuss here that the excitement that parents report feeling at their discovery of RAD runs counter to the controversy that actually surrounds RAD's emergence as a recognized emotional disorder. Although it is the most common diagnosis associated with children who are brought to Evergreen for attachment therapy, the RAD diagnosis, like many forms of illness diagnosis (see Young 1995), is a culturally complex one. On the one hand, the disorder has been listed in the Diagnostic and Statistical Manual of Mental Disorders (DSM) since 1980, and mental health professionals have been able to come to some consensus on its diagnostic criteria (Chaffin et al. 2006; Hanson and Spratt 2000; Newman and Mares 2007). The most current diagnostic manual as of 2009, the DSM-IV-TR (American Psychiatric Association 2000), defines the essential feature of reactive attachment disorder of infancy or early childhood as, "markedly disturbed and developmentally inappropriate social relatedness that occurs in most contexts that begins before age five and is associated with grossly pathogenic care" (127). Additional diagnostic features of RAD are described as follows:

> There are two types of presentations. In the Inhibited Type, the child persistently fails to initiate and to respond to most social interactions in a developmentally appropriate way. The child shows a pattern of

excessively inhibited, hypervigilant, or highly ambivalent responses (e.g., frozen watchfulness, resistance to comfort, or a mixture of approach and avoidance) (Criterion A1). In the Disinhibited Type, there is a pattern of diffuse attachments. The child exhibits indiscriminate sociability or a lack of selectivity in the choice of attachment figures (Criterion A2). The disturbance is not accounted for solely by developmental delay (e.g., as in Mental Retardation) and does not meet criteria for Pervasive Development Disorder [disorders on the Autism spectrum] (Criterion B). By definition, the condition is associated with grossly pathological care that may take the form of persistent disregard of the child's basic emotional needs for comfort, stimulation, and affection (Criterion C1); persistent disregard of the child's basic physical needs (Criterion C2); or repeated changes of primary caregiver that prevent formation of stable attachments (e.g., frequent changes in foster care) (Criterion C3). The pathological care is presumed to be responsible for the disturbed social relatedness (Criterion D). (127–28)

In addition, over the past thirty years, a consensus has been building among pediatric psychologists that behaviors associated with RAD stem from a break in infant attachment to a primary caregiver (Zeanah and Smyke 2008). Both developmental and clinical researchers have clearly demonstrated that ambivalent and avoidant attachment classifications, such as those outlined by the Strange Situation Procedure (SSP) (Ainsworth et al. 1978) are some of the best indicators that a child will be diagnosed with RAD. Developmental researchers have established connections between insecure and/or disorganized attachments and increased risk for various types of disorders across the lifespan, including anxiety and personality disorders, as well as substance abuse and delinquency (see Allen, Hauser, and Borman-Spurrell 1996; Carlson 1998; DeKlyen 1996; Lyons-Ruth 1996; Rosenstein and Horowitz 1996; Warren et al. 1997). Clinical researchers (Goldfarb 1945; Main and George 1979; Wolkind 1974) have also documented that children raised in institutions, children who have been mistreated, and children who have been raised in extremely deprived care-giving environments are at particular risk for negative SSP-associated attachment styles as early as infancy. Descriptive studies of children kept for prolonged periods in orphanages have been especially helpful for documenting this observable phenomenon (see Ryan and Groza 2004; Zeanah, Smyke, and Dumitrescu 2002; Zeanah et al. 2005).

On the other hand, despite these general agreements, there is no consensus as to *why* early breaks in attachment to a primary caregiver as well as other forms of early childhood deprivation result in behaviors associated with RAD. There has been much neurological research in the last twenty years conducted on the relationship between neurobiology and the making of social relationships—particularly the process of attachment—that may shed light on the source of RAD in this regard. For example, one important theme in this literature is the demonstration of the neural correlates of maternal love. Studies use magnetic resonance imaging (MRI) to investigate a mother's brain response specific·to her child by having her view photo stimuli of her child's smiling or neutral face versus photos of other children's faces (Bartels and Zeki 2004; Leibenluft et al. 2004; Nitschke et al. 2004). Others have attempted to demonstrate the neural correlates of maternal behaviors by investigating the mother's response to infant cries or laughing. Some studies have also been carried out using the voice stimuli of young infants who were not the mother's own infants (Lorberbaum et al. 2002; Seifritz et al. 2003). Finally, some studies attempt to pinpoint a relationship between maternal love and social behavior in conditions close to actual interactions between a mother and her own one-to-two-year-old infant—the period understood to be the most important with regard to attachment (Noriuchi, Kikuchi, and Senoo 2007). For example, researchers took MRIs of mothers' brains while mothers viewed video clips of their own infants exhibiting a variety of attachment behaviors. This study found a strong and specific brain response in mothers to their own infants' distress.

A second theme in the scientific literature that attempts to better understand the causes of RAD are those studies that trace what has been called "the neurobiology of trust" (Zak, Kurzban, and Matzner 2004, 1). A particularly fruitful avenue in this regard is an investigation into the role that the two brain hormones oxytocin and vasopressin play in motivating animals (Carter and Keverne 2002) to engage in social relationships with one another. Animal research most often demonstrates that young animals naturally seek proximity to their mothers (Fisher 2004; Newberry and Swanson 2008; Shair 2007). Animal research also shows that oxytocin levels are largely a function of genetic inheritance and early maternal/infant bonding (Choleris et al. 2003; Winslow and Insel 2002). Animal research may provide insight into the role that the hormone oxytocin plays in the physiological process of trust in humans—a key component in interpersonal attachments (Bartz and Hollander 2006; Carter 2005; Carter and Keverne 2002; Keverne and Curley 2004; Lakatos et al. 2003; Zak 2008; Zak, Kurzban, and Matzner 2004, 2005). This research shows there is a strong hormonal basis for trust/ love among mother-child pairs as well as individuals more generally and that individuals with low levels of oxytocin cannot form bonds of trust.

This neurological research has risen in tandem with a third avenue for understanding the origins of RAD—the specific study of formerly institutionalized children's neurobiology. Such studies are also informed by earlier extensive studies on other genetic and prenatal influences such as antisocial behavior, hyperactivity, alcoholism, and drug abuse (Cadoret and Gath 1980; Cadoret, O'Gorman, and Heywood 1985; Cadoret, Troughton, and O'Gorman 1986; Cadoret 1990) and are marked by a focus on understanding the confluence of biological and environmental factors that may give rise to behaviors associated with RAD and other child psychopathologies (Rutter 2002, 2005). For example, in a 2007 behavioral genetics analysis of twins (Minnis et al.), a strong genetic influence to attachment disorder behavior was found, particularly with regard to males. This genetic influence, when coupled with abusive parenting situations, was found to correlate with the demonstration of RAD-like behaviors in children. However, others have demonstrated a link between environment and neural dysfunction; for example, Fries et al. (2005) have demonstrated two major differences in the brain-derived neuropeptides oxytocin and vasopressin between family-reared versus orphanage-reared children. The study of Romanian orphans, in particular, provides additional insight into the neural implications of early childhood deprivation. Such neural implications include children's poor executive functioning (Cermak and Groza 1998), decreased brain glucose metabolism (Chugani et al. 2001), limited brain connectivity (Eluvathingal et al. 2006), and dulled sensory processing (Groza, Ryan, and Thomas 2008).

In addition to the debates that surround the origins or causes of RAD, it should also be noted that there is much controversy over its use as a diagnosis. Problems in diagnosing RAD include how much to weigh a child's social behavior versus his or her ability to attach to others (James 1994; Zeanah 1996); uncertainty about the prevalence of RAD and its influence on children versus other pathologies, such as bipolar disorder (Alston 1996, 1999); lack of empirical evidence to support or explain the existence of multiple types of behaviors associated with RAD during childhood (i.e., "inhibited" versus "disinhibited" forms of RAD) (Minde 1999; O'Connor and Zeanah 2003); and lack of understanding about how RAD presents itself across the lifespan (Zilberstein 2006). As mentioned in the introduction to this book, there is also a lack of universally accepted diagnostic protocol associated with the diagnosis and treatment of RAD (Newman and Mares 2007; Zilberstein 2006). The Randolph Attachment Disorder Questionnaire (RADQ) is commonly administered by attachment therapists who follow the Evergreen model, but the tool is scientifically unsubstantiated (see Cappelletty, Brown, and Shumate 2005). It is also common practice for attachment therapists who practice the Evergreen model to create informal and un-standardized Internet "symptom checklists" on their websites that are designed to help parents determine whether their children have RAD. In fact, many of the children's postplacement behaviors that are discussed in this chapter are those that parents found on checklists of symptoms associated with RAD and which they explicitly said influenced their understanding of their children's behaviors. According to many of the parents, those who originally did not know how to describe their children's behaviors to others quickly learned how to talk about it from such checklists, "pick[ing] up the doctor's lingo." However, Prior and Glaser (2006, 186) have described these checklists as unreliable and "loose, if not wildly inconclusive."

Finally, despite some emerging agreement on what causes RAD, there is no consensus regarding the most appropriate and effective treatment, if any, for behaviors associated with RAD (Minnis and Keck 2003). Summarizing this debate, Vivien Prior and Danya Glaser (2006) have characterized it as an argument between those who encourage evidence-based interventions and those who support interventions with no evidence base. As discussed in the introduction to this book, evidence-based interventions vary, but they are most easily understood as those that either attempt to enhance caregiver sensitivity to infants and children, or, in the event that this first type of intervention does not work, to change caregivers to ones who can be more sensitive to a child's needs (Becker-Weidman and Hughes 2008; Chaffin et al. 2006). Interventions that currently have no evidence base include the Evergreen model of attachment therapy (Chaffin et al. 2006; Prior and Glaser 2006).

From RAD Kid to My Child: Parents' Expectations of Attachment Therapy

The initial excitement adoptive parents feel on discovering attachment therapy drives some very specific expectations for attachment therapy (the philosophy and methodology of which are described in detail in chapter 5). Parents' expectations are of three sorts: (1) the "quick fix," or the expectation that children will immediately respond to attachment therapists' new medication recommendations and intensive therapies; (2) "the eventual response," or the expectation of a positive response, but one that will take a lifetime of work on the part of the child; and (3) "the last ditch effort," in which parents' characterize therapy at Evergreen as a last attempt to help the child before they search for a permanent residence for the child to live in outside the adoptive family home.

No matter what their differing expectations about the effectiveness of attachment therapy, however, almost all parents who decided on attachment therapy had some basic presumptions about it. First, parents—recognizing they were at their wit's end—often entertained an "all or nothing" approach, claiming that attachment therapists would either cure their child or the child would have to live somewhere else, such as a group home or a boarding school. For example, said Nelson Ortiz of his five-year-old adopted daughter Annie:

> I don't know if another family will love her as much as we do. I don't know if there's another place for her. If she can't get better here, then where is she going to get better? Maybe at [the clinic], but then again, if she doesn't want to get better or can't, then I guess we'll have to make a decision. She can't live in our house. Things can't stay the way they are.

Second, parents also believed that postplacement problems lay with the child, and that, if possible, it was up to him or her to "get better." Many parents stated that they believed they had done all they could do to help their children and they were tired of working so hard. According to one adoptive mother, who, after bringing her daughter to the clinic for treatment, later went on to become a staff member at another attachment therapy clinic in Evergreen:

> There's a point you get to where you look in the mirror and you think, "I've aged about a hundred years. I look awful. I feel awful. I put in everything I have and it's never enough. You've just got to say, "Look kid, the deal is this. You've had a crappy life and crappy birth parents, but you've got an opportunity here. It's up to you to change your life. I'm not going to put more effort into your life than you do. Therapy's an opportunity. Take it, and you're on your way to having a family. Don't take it and you just end up with more crap in your life."

Third, parents had an important and complementary presumption about attachment therapy: that their role in therapy would be mostly marginal. In their minds, therapists would direct therapy and children would take direction. Said Sylvia Garner, adoptive mother of ten-year-old Gavin:

> It's their specialty to do the therapy; they're the experts. I mean, we'll do whatever they say, but you know, if we knew what we were doing,

we probably wouldn't be taking him [their adopted son] in to see them [attachment therapists] in the first place. I think we'll be doing a lot of watching, a lot of watching and learning.

Many parents also felt justified in their understanding that their role in therapy *should* be marginal. Just as parents believed during the adoption process that their primary duty was to provide love to children and that this love would serve as a curative agent, so now did they understand their primary role as supportive, or as one mother put it, "We'll just be the hand holders."

Angela Walker said:

My best hopes were that we had a truly good child with a modest problem that could be overcome with therapy, love, support, and positive reinforcement, and that with a loving family, we could overcome anything. I truly believed that.

Margaret Perkins, the mother of Sergei and Bettina from Moscow, said:

We were still in the mind frame of "love conquers all." *That* was our job. That's what parents do, offer unconditional love....These people [attachment therapists] get paid to be the bad guys. A lot of parents we've met whose kids had attachment therapy think that way. And it's hard to stop this way of thinking because it goes against every instinct you have. A child hurts, you want to hug them and "make the boo-boo go away." We didn't adopt to provide a *therapeutic* home, that wasn't the plan.

The last presumption that parents held about attachment therapy was that a "positive" or "successful" response to therapy would mean that the child would (1) learn to feel genuine love for the adopting parent(s); (2) learn to express that love and other genuine emotions appropriately; and (3) return to live with parents in their home. In other words, to varying degrees, parents expected or hoped that attachment therapists would teach their adopted children to perform as emotional assets in the home. Parents hoped that therapists would possess the specific skills necessary to rescue and preserve parents' *original* vision and understanding of family roles, composition, and culture by helping children learn to invest in the family as the adopting parents did. Parents rarely expressed an awareness of, or willingness to entertain, alternative visions of family life. Only by performing as emotional assets would children find their "full measure of joy," "long-term happiness," and/or "personal peace"; and only by experiencing this would children be happy, safe, healthy, "normal," and law-abiding.

It's Not Progress Like Other People Imagine: Helping Adoptees Adjust without Therapy

It is important to note that not all parents I interviewed thought that attachment therapy was the ultimate answer for their children. I spoke with four families who had adopted children whose postplacement behaviors proved challenging, but who decided not to medicate their children or treat them using the Evergreen model of attachment therapy. I include a lengthy, but powerful, excerpt from an interview with one of these parents, Melissa Barney. She and her husband Dan adopted Carrie, now six years old, from an orphanage in Tula, Russia, when Carrie was two. I learned of Melissa Barney through a newsletter published by a statewide support group for adoptive parents located in northern Colorado. The Barneys, like many in the organization, were working together to figure out ways to help their children adjust to family life in the United States. Many were doing so without resorting to medication or therapy. I met with Melissa Barney in her home in Littleton, Colorado, in April 2000. She discussed the strategies she used to help Carrie adjust to their home:

MB: We called it Mommy Time.
RS: How did you figure out to do this?
MB: I don't know. I had to go on my own instincts. I read a few books on children and adoption, but there wasn't anything that helped....
I felt like the problem with Carrie was that she didn't have anybody to love her for so long that it was weird for her to have somebody be nice to her and want to give her things and hug her.
RS: Do you think that your love made her do weird things?
MB: Oh yeah, when she came to us, she hated us. I would try to hug her and she'd stiffen up and get this funny expression on her face. Like it physically hurt her. She'd scream and wriggle away from me.
RS: So what did you do during Mommy Time?
MB: I just held her. I put her in my lap and told her that we were going to sit together. Every night. She hated it at first. She fought me like a little wild animal. She bit me! She scratched me on the face! And she screamed too. I would hold her in my arms and she would just growl

and scream. It didn't sound human. It was like the *Exorcist*! God, it was awful.

RS: How long did you do this?

MB: You mean how long did I hold her or how long did I do this every night?

RS: Both.

MB: I held her for an hour or so each night. And I guess it took about six months before we really started to make any sort of progress where she just let me hold her on my lap.

RS: That must have been exhausting! What did you do when you held her? You just held her?

MB: It *was* exhausting. Looking back, I don't really know how I did it. No, I talked to her, to tell her that I loved her and that I wasn't going to give her away. And this might sound weird, but we spent a lot of time looking at each other. Just looking at each other! I stared at her and she stared at me. It was disturbing at first because she didn't really seem to see me. She looked at me, but there wasn't any kind of recognition. Her eyes were glazed over sort of. That changed though.

RS: Did you worry that you would get in trouble? That people would think you were abusing her?

MB: Oh God, yeah. I thought that someone was going to hear her screaming and doing the Linda Blair thing—because she was loud!— and call the cops on us…and then I read that there was the woman in Greeley…

RS: Renee Polreis?

MB: Yes! That poor woman! She just lost it! I don't think that that boy killed himself. But everyone blamed her for killing him, and I can see how it happened…I know! Carrie was absolutely out of her mind sometimes, throwing temper tantrums, and she made me so angry. She didn't pee where she was supposed to. She went to the bathroom in her bed, on the rug in her room, in the living room. We didn't know what to do. She would get up in the middle of the night and take food. She wandered around, and it was hard to sleep because I didn't know what she was getting into. I was trapped with her, and really, it's not PC, but I really hated her for a long time.

RS: So you've heard of reactive attachment disorder?

MB: Yes. When I read about the Polreis case.

RS: Oh, right. Have you read up on it?

MB: Yeah, I have. I do. I use the internet, and sometimes I look at chat rooms. It's helpful to me because it's good to know—well, not *good* to know—that there are other people who adopted kids and are having trouble.

RS: Does Carrie have RAD, do you think?

MB: I am really not ready to say that Carrie has a *disorder* of some kind. She acts strange and she does have serious emotional problems that make her not like other people's kids, so maybe she does, but it seems like it makes sense that she acts like she does. I have to remind myself constantly that she grew up in an institution. She came here when she was two, and I saw where she lived for two years. [Her hometown] was a very depressing place.

I see a lot of articles about [how] putting your kids on depressants helps. But then I see later that putting your [RAD] kid on antidepressants helps. Which is it? How do you know the right one? I don't think medication is the thing she needs. I don't think if we stick her on Ritalin it will help. But I don't know.

RS: What about therapy?

MB: We tried it. Yeah. When she got older. Around four or so.

RS: Did it work?

MB: Well, the problem with that was that Carrie acted very different when she was in therapy or when we were out in public. She acted very friendly and was very sugar and spice when we went to friends' houses or to the supermarket. People really didn't believe that she was capable of doing the things we told them she was doing. It was so frustrating! People told us how sweet she was and how smart, but we knew what was really going on. And it was another reason we just couldn't stand our lives at that point. The therapists she went to—we took her to two...

RS: What kind of therapists were they?

MB: We did play therapy and just regular therapy.

RS: You mean like talk therapy? At four [years of age]?

MB: Yeah, it was like talk therapy. But mostly play therapy because she was really too young to go where the therapist wanted to go with her. But the therapists we took her to didn't think there was anything wrong with Carrie! She played and seemed fine to them. We told them what she did at home, and they said she was just having trouble adjusting and would be better once we had her home for longer. So after a few sessions, we didn't go back.

RS: So you did the work with Carrie on your own.

MB: Yes.

RS: And she's making progress you think?

MB: I think so. It's easier to live with her now.

RS: What did you do that helped her?

MB: The Mommy Time thing was a big one. I really can't tell you how much that helped. She went from fighting me to actually sometimes leaning against me without me having to hold her in my lap. We don't do Mommy Time as much now, but sometimes she'll ask for it. The first time she did that, I think, was when she was three and a half.

RS: How did you feel when that happened?

MB: Oh, I was really happy. I really felt like I had done something right. The fears I had that I was screwing her up even more finally started to go away.

RS: What else has helped?

MB: We spend time together, and she is homeschooled now. I think this has been important. She is behind her grade level a couple of grades, but that's OK with us because things are just easier for everyone when she is home with us...and we hope to catch her up. But we take her to swimming lessons. She plays soccer in the summer. She likes that a lot. She does well with other kids when there is a sport involved.

RS: Does she love you now, do you think?

MB: I think in her own way she does. I don't think that she wants to be anywhere else, but that maybe she is resigned to being here. It's tricky. It's hard to tell. There are times when she seems like a regular kid. The other day I made a joke about her hair being like a rat's nest, and she started to laugh, and when I asked her what was so funny, she said, "Oh, Mom, there are no rats living on my head!" It was the first time she ever just *laughed* at something I said and didn't make a big deal about it. Normally, she would just argue with me about brushing her hair. So I guess she's getting a sense of humor about herself. I think that's progress, but it's not progress like other people imagine. It's probably progress that other people take for granted.

RS: Do you love her?

MB: Of course. I watch her grow up, and I feel proud to be a part of it. I feel like I am her mother. But I don't really trust her. It's hard to live that way.

RS: Are you angry at her?

MB: Angry?

RS: For not being the child you wanted?

MB: Oh....That's a hard question to answer because it's not something that I want to admit, but...yes, I am angry, yes. Not really at her. Well, I'm angry when she acts like I'm a bad person or a stupid person for

wanting to help her. I get frustrated with her that she doesn't understand that we adopted her to take her out of her bad situation and
that we love her. I still get angry at the adoption agency for not telling
us what happens to kids in institutions. I get angry at God because I
think that we were only trying to do this good thing, and look what
happened to us. We ended up with a child who might never love us.
It's so tragic when you think about it.

RS: It is. Do you think that Carrie will get better?

MB: Yeah, I do. I think she's in the best place she can be to get better,
being at our home. I don't want to put her in a group home or anything. She doesn't need to be there.

RS: What do you want for Carrie when she gets older?

MB: I want her to be able to accept help and give help to people.
I want so much more for her, but that's all I can focus on right now.
If she can do those two things, then Dan and I think that it will be
the foundation for her just so she can cope with regular day-to-day
relationships. I think that what's probably going to happen, though,
is that she will just do the best she can with what we give her. We keep
our expectations low and our hopes high, if that makes any sense at
all. I don't know if she'll ever be the kind of person who will want to
have normal family relationships or have a boyfriend or a husband.
I don't know. We hope.

RAD as Black Box and Signal Symptom

We have seen that while family may be described and prescribed in the
ways outlined in chapters 2 and 3, children do not always take part in the
integration of the family, postplacement, in the ways parents had hoped.
Adoptees challenge the aesthetics, rituals, and roles that parents generally associate with the nuclear family. By rejecting parental love, children
who are eventually brought to Evergreen do not express the full range of
emotions commonly associated with family in the United States. They also
challenge the behaviors associated with these feelings, particularly ones re-
lating to discipline and parental control. They thus disallow themselves to
be labeled or treated as "emotional assets." By operating outside the role
of emotional asset, children destabilize basic modern constructions of the
child that deem them helpless, dependent, and useless. In addition, they not
only disrupt family relations, but indirectly frustrate the hegemonic *logic*
of the nuclear family. Love as a curative agent, and other forms of practical

and symbolic parenting work, does not turn the children toward the family, so parents must find a way to institutionalize this family feeling. They thus often turn to medical professionals.

The data presented here demonstrate that parents who eventually bring their children to Evergreen typically learn about attachment therapies and the reactive attachment disorder diagnosis in tandem. Parents of children adopted from U.S. foster care systems learn of the disorder and the therapies through caseworkers and the Internet. Parents who adopt children from abroad are more likely to learn from the Internet or through word of mouth. In both cases, when parents first learn about RAD, they are elated to discover that they are not alone and that there may be a reason for their children's behaviors that have nothing to do with their own parenting practices. Most parents were not initially aware of the RAD diagnosis' controversial aspects, and after educating themselves further about it, they didn't care if it was or not. Perhaps the best way to describe parents' initial relationship to the RAD diagnosis is their understanding of it as a "black box" (Latour 1987, 2), that is, a mechanism that is so complex in terms of its history or inner workings that one does not care how it actually works but only how much input they need to provide to achieve a desired result (in this case, child love).

The tendency for parents to view RAD as a "black box" is best illuminated by examining how RAD works as what medical anthropologist Howard Stein called "a signal symptom." In an article titled, "Alcoholism as Metaphor in American Culture" (1985), Stein provided a functional analysis of alcoholism as a culturally stylized and negotiated syndrome that socially integrates addicted individuals through conflict rather than cultural consistency. Stein also asked what new understandings of alcoholism might emerge if we understand alcoholism as a type of "signal symptom," a kind of tacit agreement between diagnosed individuals and others about the kind of unusual state that is present and how it is to be treated. Stein argued that alcoholism operates as a cultural mask, both revealing what can be tolerated and concealing what cannot. A signal symptom, then,

> denotes a specific type of symptom choice, one that embodies the deviant's inner state in a social form that serves the same function both for the identified deviant and for society, namely, to displace and project elsewhere the *location* of the shared conflict....Through a signal symptom, deviant and society focus and distract themselves. (201)

While I do not argue that children, and particularly formerly institutionalized children, are in a position to negotiate or resist being pathologized,

Stein's point that illness diagnosis operates as a culturally sanctioned way to safely shift attention from problematic realities for those who interact with a diagnosed individual is well taken. The RAD diagnosis can be argued to be a tacit arbiter of several forms of cognitive dissonance, the simultaneous holding of incompatible beliefs or attitudes (Festinger 1957), particularly with regard to the expectation that formerly institutionalized children can establish adoptive families. One the one hand, as we saw in chapters 2 and 3, adoptive parents in this data set both produce, and are subject to, social representations of adoptees and their emotional capabilities that are bound up in their belief that formerly institutionalized children can and will ultimately operate as functional family members. On the other, parents' discovery of the RAD diagnosis provides an attractive opportunity for them to reframe and define children's negative behaviors as pathology, which legitimates their own parenting practices and initial expectations for the family and at the same time locates the primary source of the problem as within the children. There are thus large advantages for adoptive parents in accepting a medical discourse.

Armed with a medical diagnosis that adequately explains the children's postplacement behaviors, parents turn to attachment therapies with specific expectations. Prior to coming to Evergreen, parents expect attachment therapists to do what they could not do through their own altruism—teach or train their children to become emotional assets with genuine positive emotions toward their adopting parents. They also expect their own roles in the Evergreen method to be marginal and that the therapy will help children to confirm the parents' vision of family life. In other words, adopting parents not only expect attachment therapists to cure their children, they depend on them for the preservation of the family.

In the next two chapters, which discuss child therapy sessions and therapeutic parent-training programs at the clinic in Evergreen, I introduce the people, philosophies, and therapeutic methods associated with the Evergreen model of attachment therapy. As we will see, attachment therapists attempt to condition children to perform as emotional assets through specific methods that address what they believe are children's drives to control adoptive parents. They also train parents in their methods. Whereas the RAD diagnosis *legitimizes* parents' initial expectations and hopes for children, family, and domesticity, transforming them into legitimated knowledge about the family in ways that neither they nor adoption agencies could, the specific methods that attachment therapists in Evergreen use reinvigorate parents' folk wisdom about children, family, and domesticity, providing confirmation, community, and hope to parents. Through the Evergreen model, parents who have temporarily lost faith in their original expectations for postplacement outcomes recapture the ability to project their family into the future.

Chapter Five

Good-bye to Birth Parents, Hello to Forever Family

Confrontation Therapy in the Clinic

The centerpiece of the Evergreen model of attachment therapy is what is commonly referred to as confrontation therapy, a main component of which is holding therapy. As explained in the introduction, during holding therapy, therapists conduct psychoanalysis while clients lay cradled, like an infant, across therapists' laps. According to therapists at Evergreen, this position allows them to force eye contact with children; it also provides the proximity necessary to physically provoke children to emote. During my nine months of fieldwork at the clinic, I observed holding therapy about three hours a day, five days a week. Fifteen families allowed me full access to their treatment over the course of this time. One of these was the Korhonen family.

The Korhonens were a large family, headed by Betty, a part-time librarian, and her husband Marvin, a self-employed appliance repairman. Betty and Marvin had adopted four children many years earlier through their county services agency, and they had come to Evergreen to see if therapists could help their fifteen-year-old son, Luke, who had recently been diagnosed with RAD. Their other son, ten-year-old Jeffrey, also displayed behaviors associated with RAD, and he accompanied Betty, Marvin, and Luke to the clinic. Assuming that all went well, the Korhonens hoped that after Luke received treatment, they would return soon to see Jeffrey through treatment as well. Their other children, seventeen-year-old Deidre and seven-year-old Zack stayed behind with relatives in their hometown. According to Betty and Marvin, neither Deidre nor Zack displayed behavioral problems.

The Korhonen family came from a rural county in Wisconsin and learned of attachment therapy through Luke's caseworker at the group home for boys where he was currently residing. The Korhonens had placed Luke in the group home about ten months before the family arrived in Evergreen for treatment. According to both Betty and Marvin, Luke's violent behavior in their home over the ten years he lived there escalated to the point where he set fires to buildings on their farm and instigated fist fights with Marvin, who was six foot five. Betty and Marvin and their other adopted children no longer felt safe with Luke in their home.

I liked both Betty and Marvin Korhonen right away. Betty was in her mid-forties, with curly brown hair that was graying at the temples. When I first met her, she was dressed in a denim shirt and cotton leggings and wore Keds. She was a boisterous woman who gesticulated freely and had a good sense of humor. During her family's sessions, she did most of the talking, sometimes answering for both her son and her spouse. Marvin was a tall, fit man who was balding on top. He had an infectious smile and a shy way about him. According to Betty, her worst fears about Luke were that even with all they had done for him, he would not succeed in therapy and would either end up killing himself or someone else. "Our best hopes," she said, "are that we'll have a son who is capable of loving us as much as we love him, that we can live a happy healthy life."

Luke's turbulent life began even before he was born. His birth mother, Jackie, was a chronic drug user who was taking medication for a mental disorder when she was pregnant with him. This possibly caused Luke to be born prematurely and with a cleft palate/submucal harelip (later surgically corrected) and partial hearing loss. His birth father was serving time in jail during most of Luke's gestation, and he never sought to make contact with Luke after he was born. It was documented that Luke's mother also abused drugs and alcohol after he was born. She neglected his physical and emotional needs while he was an infant. Social service records suggested patterns of physical and emotional abuse of Luke during his first six months, with many drug users and many sexual partners of his birth mother coming and going through the house. One of his mother's boyfriends stayed for a week at Luke's birth mother's home before he realized that she had an infant. According to the man's testimony, taken by county services, Luke's mother had hidden the baby in various places during the man's stay. One day, he heard a strange gurgling noise coming from behind the living room couch. He moved the couch to find something wrapped in a blanket and wriggling against the wall. After the discovery, he called Luke's mother into the living room and asked her what it was. She picked Luke up and drew back his blanket to reveal Luke's face, complete with harelip. The boyfriend testified that he expressed severe dismay at Luke's appearance, so Luke's mother placed him back behind the couch, and they left Luke's older sister to care for him while they went to a bar.

Shortly after this incident, Luke's birth mother asked a neighbor to take care of Luke and his older sisters for an evening. When Luke's mother failed to come back for the children two days later, the neighbor alerted social services. His sisters were placed in foster care, and Luke was placed in the hospital for behaviors and effects associated with failure to thrive (FTT). FTT is a term used to diagnose infants who do not take in, or who are unable to use, the calories necessary to gain weight and develop as medical professionals expect. He was hospitalized for FTT two more times before he was six months old. At the age of six months, Luke was placed in a series of three temporary foster homes, which lasted until he turned two. During this time, Luke's birth mother was asked by her Department of Human Services to undergo drug and alcohol abuse counseling and rehabilitation if she wanted to be reunited with Luke. However, she failed to complete the counseling and was arrested for drug trafficking and child abuse of her latest infant. While Luke was moving from foster home to foster home, his mother had given birth to another boy, Jeffrey—fathered by the boyfriend who had found Luke behind the couch—and the Korhonens also eventually adopted this boy as well. County services then placed Luke with his maternal grandmother, Virginia. This proved to be a bad match as she did not have the money or energy to look after Luke's special needs. After two or three weeks with Virginia, Luke was moved to another foster home for one month. It was then that the Korhonens learned about Luke, then four years old, moved him into their home as a foster child, had his harelip surgically treated, and adopted him into their family. On learning that Luke had three other biological siblings in foster care, they moved them into their home as well, eventually adopting two of them, Deirdre and Jeffrey. (The oldest, Andrea, had been convicted of fraud, and at the time of Luke's treatment was in jail.) Later, the Korhonens adopted a fourth child, Zack, from a different family.

According to Betty Korhonen, when Luke arrived at her home at age four, he "tried to be good and he wanted to be good," but he could not control his temper and had violent fits several times a day:

> We tape-recorded him once after we sent him to his room after one of the fits. And when we played back the tape we could hear he was saying to himself, "Why can't I just behave? Why can't I just behave?"

But Luke's behavior became steadily worse while he was living with the Korhonens. According to Betty and Marvin's comments on his intake packet, he began to lie, steal, act anxious and tense, bully other children and display cruelty to animals, fight, provoke, argue, brag, show off, demand a large amount of attention and get jealous very easily, obsess about things, talk too much and loudly, and show open hostility toward the rest of the Korhonens to the point of threatening them with violence and occasionally acting out physically toward them. In 1998, according to Betty, the family suffered the last straw when Luke set fire to their barn. According to Marvin:

> The worst thing about that was that when we caught him, he didn't show any remorse at all. He laughed. He didn't care at all that he could have killed the animals or someone in the family.

In October 1998, Betty and Marvin committed Luke to a temporary adolescent treatment center near their home. Then, in December 1998, they placed him in a group home for boys. Luke had not lived in their home since. Betty and Marvin thought that attachment therapy was Luke's last chance to remain in their family, and they were praying that it would work.

In this chapter, I outline the typical practices and goals of the Evergreen model of attachment therapy (see table 2), using the Korhonens' treatment experience as a case study.[1] I followed Luke Korhonen through nine of ten sessions that made up his two-week intensive at the clinic. Whereas parents are drawn to the RAD *diagnosis* because it legitimates the family through a "resignaling" of anxiety about its formation and provides an opportunity for parents to once again project their families into the future, parents are attracted to the *Evergreen therapy model* because it provides an actual blueprint for practice—one that promises to uniquely discipline children's bodies and minds in ways that will result in the restoration of the family as an internalized collective. Foundational to this restoration is the production of family feeling, which includes practices, rituals, and symbols that assist children in their demonstration of love for adoptive parents. The ultimate goal for therapists, then, is to produce child love in the clinic.

---

[1] The steps associated with the Evergreen model of attachment therapy have also been summarized elsewhere. For example, see Levy and Orlans (1998) and Myeroff, Mertlich, and Gross (1999).

Table 2. **Therapeutic methods and goals of the Evergreen two-week intensive**

Therapeutic goal	Clinical method
Setting up rapport	Introductions with family
	Sentence completion
Setting up the rules	Contracting
Demonstrating verbal reciprocity	Demonstrating eye contact
	Demonstrating holding therapy
	Fast and snappy; Mom and Dad's way; Right the first time
Throwing the child off-balance	Shoes off/Jacket off command
	Changing rules in therapy
	Changing therapeutic tone
	Third-party conversation
	One-liners
Reinforcing therapist control	Holding therapy
	Kicking exercises
	Jumping jacks
	Prescribing the symptom
	"Smart kid acting dumb"
	Making the child wait
Eliciting emotional response from child to trauma	Introducing the "cycle of need"
	Triggering body memories through touch
	Recreating early childhood history; role plays early childhood
Weakening attachment to birth parents	Introducing the "cycle of need"
	Demonstrating infant needs
	Recreating early childhood history; role plays
Prescribing attachment between child and adoptive parents	Teaching the child to ask for help from birth parents during role plays
	Giving the child's personal belongings to parents for safekeeping
	Tug-of-war exercise
Resolution of emotional response from early childhood	Psychoanalysis/talk therapy
	Therapeutic team de-roling from role play; real name introductions
Set up long-term therapeutic treatment goals	Meeting with parents, therapists, clinic administrators
	Evaluation summaries
	Send-off (varies by therapist)

Week One of Intensive Therapy: Initiating and Maintaining Therapist Control

The first week of attachment therapy is intended to introduce parents to the treatment team; figure out the parents' goals, expectations, and fears; conduct a diagnostic on the child; and let the child know that the therapist is in control. It is the time when the therapist begins to teach the child compliance and reciprocity rules. During my tenure at the clinic, many therapists served as key facilitators for my project. One of these therapists—Helen Ellis—was a licensed social worker (LSW) and licensed family therapist (LFT) who had interned under another therapist at the clinic in the mid-1990s. She began working as a therapist at the clinic immediately after her internship ended in 1996. Helen was Luke's therapist. She was joined by Brendan Farmer, a licensed LFT, who was co-therapist for the intensive, as well as Sasha Scott, who was Luke's therapeutic foster mother for the two weeks. Helen was a white woman in her mid-forties. She was well groomed but always casually dressed for therapy sessions in jeans and sweaters. Throughout the therapy sessions I observed with her, Brendan, and Luke's family, Helen acted professionally, outlining her expectations for all, including herself, and carrying them out in a consistent manner. A unique component of Helen's approach to the Evergreen model that I did not witness in other therapists' practice was her conscious incorporation of humor into her work. Helen often poked fun at herself, the families, and the children involved in the therapy. According to Helen the goal of such humor was to help clients prepare for, and ease into, the experience of the intensive. It was also designed, she said, to reinforce parents' hopes that the therapy did not signal "a death sentence for families." As Helen explained to Luke's family before his therapy began: "Even if this all happens to make perfect clinical sense to you, and you find the techniques acceptable and even easy, it is ultimately gallows [morbid] humor that's going to get you through this. Trust me."

Session 1: Introducing the Cycle of Need

In the introduction to attachment therapy, therapists first explain what attachment therapists call the "cycle of need." According to therapists at the clinic, the cycle of need can be described as follows: When an infant is born, it makes its needs known by crying. If no one comes to meet those needs, the infant cries louder. If still no one comes to meet the infant's needs, then the infant becomes enraged and its cries will take on more urgent and desperate characteristics. If an infant is left to cry and rage long enough in this manner, it will eventually cease crying. In effect, the infant "shuts down" and stops asking for, and eventually expecting, help. If this series of events happens often enough, the infant will internalize the neglect/rejections of others and remain trapped with raging feelings even as it grows up. Attachment therapists that practice the Evergreen model believe RAD children are stuck in this rage. RAD children do not trust that their needs will be met, so they do not even bother asking for help any more. They rely on themselves to survive, and they see their adoptive family's attempts to help them and take care of them as threatening, for it undermines their own attempts at control. Attachment therapists at the clinic thus characterized the Evergreen model as a series of exercises designed to help children express and rid themselves of their bottled-up rage. These exercises would also help children learn how to let their adoptive parents be in control and to trust that they are safe when their parents are in control.

THE TREATMENT FAMILY   After explaining that the main goal of the clinical work is to repair the break in the child's cycle of need, attachment therapists then explain to families that another important component of the two-week intensive is the time the child spends at his treatment family's home, where he or she will live apart from the adoptive family. The child is also informed that at the treatment family home, he or she is allowed to do only three things on his own: breathe, think, and feel. For everything else—from getting a drink of water and eating to going to the bathroom to petting the family dog—the child needs to ask permission. The child is also only allowed to see his or her family when the therapeutic foster parents decide that the child has earned the privilege.

BUILDING THERAPIST-CHILD RAPPORT AND INITIATING THERAPIST CONTROL   After the overview of the therapy, therapists then focus on building rapport with children. Therapists typically bring children into the treatment room, dim the lights, and raise curtains to reveal a two-way mirror through which families can see the treatment. Therapists also videotape every session. Children do not know that they are being observed, and therapists do not offer this information. However, if children ask, therapists tell the children the truth and show them the observation room.

The first time I saw Luke Korhonen from behind the two-way mirror in the observation room, I was surprised by his appearance. Because his case history had been riddled with stories about poor health, I thought Luke would be a skinny, undeveloped, and anemic-looking teenager. But Luke, although slight and short for his age, was a healthy and strong-looking boy. He had stylishly cut brown hair and deep brown eyes with long lashes—a very good-looking teenager—and he was dressed hip-hop style with baggy jeans and sports jersey. He was also wearing a fashionable pair of expensive space-age sneakers. He wore a gold chain and a gold watch and had a beeper in his back pocket. He didn't look very nervous to me as he sat down to begin therapy. He appeared somewhat cocky, like he could handle whatever was about to happen. According to Helen, he was also displaying what many attachment therapists at the clinic called "the smirk," an expression that connotes that the child thinks he is going to be able to lie or trick his way through attachment therapy.

The therapist usually begins the attempt to build rapport with a child by using small talk—about their love for sports, for example, or the child's school. Throughout this small talk the therapist directs the child to look into her eyes when being talked to. This direction happens subtly at first, and then more insistently whenever the child fails or forgets to do so. The therapist will also have the child sign a contract agreeing to do his or her emotional work at the clinic. In particular, the child must answer two questions of importance to the therapist: "Are you ready to accept partial responsibility for the bad things that have happened to you?" and "Do you agree to do it my way while you're here?" The therapist believes that it is important for the child to agree to the terms of the clinic and to prove seriousness about the therapy. In addition, whenever a therapist directs the child to do something the therapist says, "Got it?" The child must respond "Got it." Not "OK," "Sure," or "Alright," but "Got it." The child is also expected to respond immediately to any therapist request quickly and without question.

SENTENCE COMPLETIONS AND ASSESSING THE CHILD'S NEED TO CONTROL   The next part of the first session is devoted to reviewing sentence completions. Sentence completions are sheets of paper with partial sentences on them that children are expected to have completed prior to their first clinical session. Sentences begin with phrases such as: "When I was young…"; "Most kids think I'm…"; and "When I grow up, I want to…" Sentence completions are given to the child by the treatment parents. They are designed to provide insight to the therapists into the way children see their lives and current life situations. In particular, it helps the primary therapist determine how much a child is "stuck" in the bad things that have happened to him or her. As one attachment therapist at the clinic stated:

> Sentence completions help me to see how honest a kid is willing to be, and which emotions are dictating his responses. Is he hostile? Too nervous to answer? Also, it's an opportunity for me to show that I am in charge by having a conversation with him. I can reinforce his eye contact and my "Got it" rule at this time. I can also see how he communicates and do some corrections.

For instance, according to Luke's therapist, during his first session, Luke had a tendency to maintain eye contact with her when she spoke with him, but when he responded, he lowered his eyes or closed them completely. Also, if he did not want to answer a question such as "Did you miss your parents while you were at the residential facility?" Luke would conduct what the therapist called a "stalling device," repeating her question as if it were the most important question in the world, but never really answering it, She said to me later:

Did you see him? I asked him the question about his parents, and he put on the theatrics…"Huh…Did I miss them? Hmm…Did. I. Miss. Them." He was buying time, diverting attention! So we corrected that behavior, which is really just a little controlling thing that he did, not really knowingly, but something he does with his parents when they try to talk to him about things he doesn't want to talk about, I can guarantee, and it probably makes them crazy.

Luke's therapist attempted to correct Luke's behaviors during his first session in many ways. The most prominent way was to address the behavior head-on and make a joke out of it, as we see during this exchange when Luke employed what the therapists considered to be a stalling device:

Therapist: Did you see that?
Co-therapist: Yup. Looks like we got ourselves a question repeater. And he's acting like that's the most important question in the world. But really, he just doesn't want to answer it.

At other times, Luke's therapist addressed Luke's behaviors more directly and with some feigned hostility. In response to the stalling device, she would look at Luke and say, "Is there some reason why you won't look at me when you're answering my question?" Another tactic she used to show she was in charge was by asking Luke a question, having him answer it successfully with eye contact and clear enunciation, but then picking out a word Luke used in the response to trigger an entirely tangential conversation with the co-therapist. This technique is called third-party conversation. For example, in response to a question from his therapist about things Luke was afraid of, Luke responded, "Big dogs." This brought the therapist to shift attention away from Luke and ask the co-therapist about his own big dog at home and how "Sparky" was doing lately. The therapists talked about the dog for a full thirty seconds in an extremely jovial tone, laughing about Sparky's tendency to dig holes in the garden and track mud through the house in winter. This tone contrasted sharply with the one the therapist had been using only seconds before with Luke, and this left Luke completely bewildered. The therapist then moved on to the next sentence completion item as if the conversation with the co-therapist had never happened. Acting as if the conversation had never happened was a tactic that was intended to let Luke know that he not was in control of the conversation.

Still another strategy that Luke's therapist used was to seem mostly indifferent to the negative early life experiences Luke had. For example, when they arrived at the sentence completion item that stated, "When I was young, I..." Luke answered it, "I was abused." Luke then began to animatedly speak in detail about his cleft palate and all the surgeries he had to correct it. He also talked about being left alone and how his birth mother used drugs. Later, the therapist told me that it was common for children with RAD to learn to talk about their exposure to neglect and abuse in ways that elicited sympathy from adults. She said, "RAD kids love to be the center of pity parties. They invite as many people as they can, and a lot of adults come." Luke's therapist believed that by engaging her and the co-therapist in narratives about his difficult childhood in such animated ways, he hoped they would dwell on these hardships and say that they felt sorry for him. However, instead, his therapist actively listened to his stories for only a few seconds, validating that he had been treated badly and that this was part of the reason why he was in treatment at the clinic but that it was now necessary to get past that part of his life and to live "in the now" so he would not become a criminal. She then moved on to the next question, without giving Luke time to respond to what she said.

KEEPING KIDS OFF BALANCE: ADDING RULES AND MAINTAINING EYE CONTACT   After sentence completions, therapists continue to try to confuse children and keep them off balance by adding other rules. One popular rule they put forward is that children may only answer questions affirmatively by saying, "Yes, sir" or "Yes, ma'am." They may not say, "Yeah," or "Yeah, sir or ma'am." At this point, therapists also begin to forgo the verbal directives for children to maintain eye contact and instead actually put the palms of their hands directly on children's heads to physically remind them of their duty to maintain eye contact whenever they forget. Therapists may also begin to move closer to children and ask them if they like to be touched. If children say no, therapists may hug them and indicate to them that they are glad that they have the chance to teach them that hugging is safe and fun.

INTRODUCING HOLDING THERAPY   One of the most important techniques of attachment therapy is holding therapy. Holding therapy is a term used in several different types of therapy. The holding therapy used at the clinic at the time of my research was based on the Welch Method Regulatory Bonding "holding time" (Welch 1989) which, according to the clinic director, replicated as closely as possible the holding of an infant by a mother. The clinic's therapy was meant to diverge from Welch's model in one important way, however, in that it was understood by therapists to be voluntary. Children were allowed to stop the therapy at any time by asking the therapist to do so. According to Helen, this type of holding therapy was markedly different than that intended to restrict children's movement to keep them from harming themselves or others.[2]

To begin holding therapy with Luke during his intensive, the therapist shifted to one side of the couch and told him that she was going to ask him to do something that he would find very weird. She reminded him that he had signed a contract that stated that he knew that the therapist was in charge and that he was safe. Did he remember that? He said that he did. The therapist then told Luke that he was going to sit in her lap.

Luke sat down in the therapist's lap right away with no questions asked, although he seemed confused. She laid him across her lap in a prone position, like a baby, with his head resting on the arm of the couch and his head tilted up to look at her. Her face was approximately one foot away from his. She placed Luke's right arm behind her back, between her back and the couch, and then placed the palm of her hand on his head to direct him to maintain eye contact with her. She then placed her other hand on his chest. The co-therapist moved his chair in and leaned forward toward Luke. He grabbed Luke's free hand and held it tight. Luke, all five foot six inches of him, looked like a big, vulnerable baby being held by a mother and gazed at by a father. "This," said the therapist, "is the way we do therapy around here."

At this point, Luke's facial expression and body language changed. Although he was tense and his arm behind the therapist's back was stiff and not resting on her at all, his body was limp across her lap and his face bore

---

[2] For a discussion of the similarities and differences between holding therapy as it is practiced in Evergreen and restraint models, see Shechory (2005). Martha Welch also compares holding therapy and "compression therapy" in her popular book, *Holding Time* (1989). For a discussion of the concerns regarding holding therapies, see Boris (2003). For studies on the rates of effectiveness of holding therapy as it is practiced in Evergreen and elsewhere, see Myeroff, Mertlich, and Gross (1999) and Shechory (2005).

an expression of fear mixed with sadness. Several people in the observation room commented on how heartbreaking it was to see him looking so confused. The therapist began to explain to Luke why *she* thought he had entered treatment. She said that bad things had happened to him and so he felt he needed to be in control all the time, but here at the clinic, he wasn't in control. She was. She added that he was safe in the treatment room even when he wasn't in control. She also added that when he was in his treatment home with his therapeutic foster parents, that he wasn't in control there either, but that he was safe there too. She repeated to him what she said to us: He could do three things for himself—breathe, think, and feel—and for everything else, he had to ask for permission. She then told him that he wouldn't be allowed to see his mom and dad except at therapy sessions and when his therapeutic foster parents said it was OK. She also stated that she was willing to work hard to help Luke get better, but that she wasn't going to work any harder than he was. The same thing went for the therapeutic foster parents, and, most important, the same thing went for his parents. She said, "You've treated them badly for long enough. They're not going to do this anymore. Do you understand that?" Luke looked at her and responded, "Yes, ma'am." Finally, the therapist asked him if he understood that it was his choice whether he wanted to be a part of the Korhonen family or not, and that at any time while he was at the clinic he was free to say, "I give up. I don't want to be a part of my family. I'm going to go live in a residential home." If he said that, she would stop therapy, refund his parents their money, and then his parents would send him off to a residential home, a military school, or wherever they thought best. "They will still be your real and forever parents," she said, "and they will always love you wherever you live, but that's your choice. Do you understand?" Luke responded, "Yes, ma'am."

Throughout this conversation, the co-therapist also piped in with certain questions and comments. He asked Luke if he'd ever been in trouble with the law, to which Luke replied no. The co-therapist told him if he kept on with his bad behavior, it wasn't a question of whether he would end up a criminal, but when. The primary therapist then added that the Air Force (which is where Luke expressed he wanted to go when he turned eighteen) wouldn't accept a man with a criminal record. The co-therapist also asked Luke what he did when he got really scared or angry. For example, did he run away? Luke replied no. "That's good," said the co-therapist, "because there are mountain lions and bears up around your therapeutic home, and if you run away, I can't promise you that you won't be eaten alive." The co-therapist also contributed to the rules of therapy by making Luke practice answering him and the therapist in full sentences, such as, "I feel disappointed and mad at myself because I almost burnt down the barn."

SAYING GOOD-BYE TO PARENTS   After some more questions and answers in the holding therapy position, Luke's therapist told him to get off her lap and sit down. She told him that his parents were going to come in to say good-bye to him and that after this session he would officially be going to live with his therapeutic foster parents for two weeks. He would see the rest of his family very rarely. Luke would not be allowed to live with the rest of his family during the two weeks of therapy because Betty and Marvin would need "to practice being a family" with the treatment family while he was working hard in therapy. The therapist left him alone for a few moments and retrieved Betty and Marvin from the observation room. Until this time, they had been mostly quiet and observing, with Betty making occasional comments about the therapy, anticipating Luke's answers to certain questions out loud, expressing surprise when he climbed onto the therapist's lap, and making jokes about some of Luke's misadventures in the residential home. Marvin, however, cried from time to time, particularly when Luke got into the holding therapy position. He also commented on Luke's scared expression more than once.

When the therapist brought Betty and Marvin into the therapy room to say good-bye to Luke, she had them sit in chairs facing the couch. Marvin started to tear up immediately. The therapist put Luke back into the holding position and told him it was time to say good-bye to his mom and dad. At this point, Luke also began to cry a little. "Do you have anything you'd like to say to your parents before you go?" the therapist asked him. Through a few tears, Luke told Betty and Marvin that he'd miss them. The therapist then asked Luke who he trusted most in his family. Luke said his father. The therapist told Luke to give Marvin his wallet, gold chain, and beeper, and said that his dad would keep them for him while he was at the clinic. Luke, however, remained motionless.

"Don't you think you'll get your things back at the end of your time here?" she asked him. Luke hesitated, but then said yes. Luke gave Marvin his things. The therapist then asked Luke which parent he'd like to say good-bye to first. Luke chose Betty and started to cry again. He was still in the holding position. The therapist turned Luke's face to look at Betty. She said, "Tell your mom that this is hard." Luke looked at Betty and told her this, crying a little harder. Then the therapist told him to say good-bye. He did. "Now tell your dad good-bye." Luke did. Then Luke got up to give Betty a hug. They hugged, and Betty held Luke a long time. The therapist, watching the two of them, got up from the couch and corrected the way Luke was hugging his mother, placing his hands, which were clasped together around her back, into a position where his palms were actually lying flat on her back, touching her all the way around and not, as she called it, "hugging himself." Betty told Luke that she loved him and would miss him. Luke echoed this, very softly in her ear. Then he hugged Marvin and they exchanged I love yous. Betty and Marvin left the therapy room, returned to the observation room, and sat there while the co-therapists sat with Luke and processed his feelings. Then they told him to put his shoes back on and to wait until someone came to get him.

ASSESSING CHILDREN'S "GENUINE EMOTION"   The final part of the first session of the Evergreen therapy consists of a debriefing with parents. It is the therapists' attempt to elicit feedback as to whether parents think the child's emotional responses to the therapy were genuine. In the Korhonens' case, when the co-therapists entered the observation room, they pulled the curtain down in front of the two-way mirror and turned off the surveillance monitor so we could no longer see Luke. They wanted to focus on Betty and Marvin. Betty spoke and said that this was the first time she'd ever seen Luke cry real tears. She was amazed but still skeptical. Marvin said that he thought there was real progress made. He was surprised Luke had gotten up on the therapist's lap. The therapist commented that the tone of her voice and the way she took control made it impossible for him to not consider it as an option. "It never occurred to me that he *wouldn't* get on my lap," she said. Marvin also mentioned that this was one of the few times he'd ever seen Luke cry since the age of four, when they first adopted him. The only other time was when Luke tried to run away and Marvin brought him to county services to transfer him to an institution. Luke's tears ultimately kept Marvin from placing him there.

After the debriefing, the co-therapist prepared Luke's belongings so he could take him to the treatment family's house while the therapist went in to tell Luke that he would be leaving now. She also told him that if he got angry and wanted to express rage while he was there, he should not take it as a cue to try and run away, but rather, a cue to take it into the treatment room. This is because there were ways to express emotions that were appropriate and inappropriate: acting out in violent ways and not telling anyone what is wrong is inappropriate; however, communicating with words to adults what you are feeling is appropriate. She then told him that there were four feelings that he should communicate: mad, glad, sad, and scared. When she asked him to repeat these back to her, he couldn't. She then told him that there were three additional rules for behavior at his treatment family home: when the treatment parents asked him to do something, he was to (1) do it fast and snappy; (2) do it Mom and Dad's way; and (3) do it right the first time. Could Luke remember those? Again, when asked to repeat these rules back to the therapist, Luke could not remember them all. In the observation room, Betty commented to me that Luke always had trouble with memory work and math. Later, however, the therapist told me that what she had asked Luke to do was not a hard thing and that she was fairly sure it was just another bid on Luke's part for control.

Session 2: Exercise and Discipline

Therapy is generally designed to be tougher for children during session 2 than in session 1, in the sense that the therapist will purposefully use a more forceful tone and be more liable to challenge children verbally than on the first day. They also direct children to complete physical exercise if they do not obey an order. In Luke's case, by the second session, his therapist had become completely intolerant of any back talk, hesitation, or what she called "snark." Within the first ten minutes of the session, the therapist disciplined Luke for failing to ask her where he should put his coat. For this, she made him do five push-ups. During the rest of the session she also made him do five push-ups for pretending to forget her name. After he did the push-ups (complete with verbal counting of each one), he remembered Helen's name. "Miraculous!" she cried. "We're making progress already!"

After the therapist asserted that the rules of respect were the same in therapy as they were at his treatment family home, she sat on the couch and immediately told him to come up onto her lap and into a holding therapy position. Co-therapist Brendan, also present, held Luke's hand, which Luke did not seem pleased about, as his face registered immediate disgust. The therapist later explained to me that this response was not surprising as Luke probably felt that he had done very well at his treatment home, so he expected to get a more lenient therapy session today. In fact, she said, the opposite was true; the sessions would continue to get more difficult until Luke either gave up or "started to get real" or "genuine," that is, indicate that he wanted to be in the Korhonen family by working hard in therapy. Again, the phrase, "We aren't going to work any harder than you" was repeated to Luke throughout the session.

ELICITING CHILDREN'S RAGE AND HELPING THEM EXPRESS IT APPROPRI-ATELY   The therapist used harsh tones with Luke for the first thirty minutes of his session and then quickly turned them off. She took about twenty minutes and explained to Luke about the "cycle of need." She prefaced this by asking him if he thought that he currently had a bad life, to which he replied, "Yes, ma'am, I have a crappy life." She also asked him if he had bad feelings, and he replied yes. The therapist told him that she was going to tell him why that was. She explained that infants have needs, that infants call for help, that sometimes parents neglect the infants' calls for help and, when they do, this causes rage within the infant. She then explained that if this keeps happening, the infant, as it gets older, will learn to take care of itself as best it can, while holding on to the rage toward adults. She explained all this in a very soothing tone of voice. "Now, do you think this happened to you?" Luke said he did. Helen, being careful to use Luke's birth mother's first name instead of calling her his mother, asked him, "Did Jackie rock you and hold you like a mom should?" At this point, Luke began to cry tears, which the therapist wiped from his cheeks, and he replied, "No, ma'am." The therapist then began to relate Luke's early history to him, repeating things she knew from the case history provided to her by the Korhonens. She stated that Jackie did not want to get pregnant with him and that she treated him badly while he was still inside her. She spoke of Jackie's probable drug and alcohol addictions and explained to him that he was a "failure to thrive" baby. She also told him that he was neglected and never got any of the things he needed when he was a baby. She asked Luke if he thought that he, as a baby, deserved that. Luke said no and once again, he began to cry. The therapist told Luke that he probably thought he was a bad baby because he was neglected. Luke said yes. She turned the conversation to the bad feelings of hate and rage that this left Luke with, that he still had inside him today. She talked to him about some of the times that he misbehaved as a kid and as a teenager, and she asked him to think of the time when he was the maddest he ever was. Luke complied, stating that the maddest he'd even been was when he was at church with Marvin and his father punished him for something he didn't do. It wasn't fair.

At that point, Helen and Brendan changed their tones. Helen told Luke in a loud voice to look at the co-therapist and imagine that the co-therapist was "your dad's face." She told him to say, "I'm mad at you, Dad." Luke smiled a little and did it weakly. The therapist yelled at him, "There's nothing funny about this Luke, so I don't understand why you're smiling. Your dad just punished you for something you didn't do! Tell him you're mad at him!" Luke did it again—weakly.

The therapist sat back a bit, seeming to relent for a second. She asked Luke if that yelling helped him. Luke said, "A little." She asked him to score it on a scale of 1 to 10 on how much better it made him feel. He said "half," and the therapist asked, "Half of 10?" Luke said, "No, half of 1." The therapist then changed her tone again to nurturing and said, "I know why that might be true." Then she and the co-therapist told Luke to make a fist and squeeze it as tight as he could, to where his nails were digging into his palm. She asked him to hold it there for a good thirty seconds. She did it as well. After a second, she started to wince. "Doesn't that hurt *your* hand muscle?" she asked him. "Because it sure hurts me." Luke agreed that it hurt his hand. The therapist continued, "Well, that's because you've got your hand all tightened up, hard and tense. And you know…that's just like your heart." For the next few minutes, she explained to Luke that the way to unclench his heart, held all tight with hatred, was to learn to unflex it like a fist. She had him unflex his fist little by little until he had a relaxed open palm. "That," she said, "is what we want your wounded heart to look like."

With this, the therapist once again changed her tone. She shook her head and said that she didn't think that Luke was working very hard to get his rage out. She knew that Luke could get madder than this because his mom and dad told her so. She made Luke, who was still in the holding position, look her directly in her eyes and told him to start kicking his feet like he was swimming. Luke looked at her questioningly and then began to kick his feet weakly up and down on the couch. The therapists made a few remarks about how if he was actually swimming, he'd drown. The therapist told him to stop kicking and he did. When he stopped, she told him to put his ankles together and keep his legs straight. "It looks like you've got stupid feet, Luke," she said. "So keep your legs together and straight. Now Kick!…Fast!!"

With this, Luke kicked a little faster. The therapist looked him in the eyes and said, "Keep kicking." She leaned into his face while he kept kicking. "I'm going to tell you something. The way you're kicking now, the way you're behaving, is exactly the way that your birth mom behaved with you, OK? Weak. Not trying. Luke, you're not working! Do you think that's true?" Luke, who now began to kick harder, looked the therapist in her eyes and said, "Yes, ma'am." The therapist replied, "Yes, what? In a full sentence!" Luke said, "Yes! I'm acting like my birth mom." Then Luke started to cry again. The therapist kept him kicking another full thirty seconds, making him look at her. He was not allowed to look away. Then she began to yell loudly at him: "Do you hate kicking? Tell me!" Luke yelled, "Yes, ma'am! I hate kicking!" The therapist instructed him to say it again and again until he was screaming it.

She then said, "Do you hate me for making you kick?" Luke screamed at the top of his lungs, "Yes, I hate you! I hate you!" He cried harder. The therapist looked at him again, let her eyes travel down to his feet, which continued to kick more and more furiously and then said, "Good." She instructed him to stop kicking and look at Brendan. She directed Luke, "He has your dad's face."

At this point, the co-therapist began to recreate the scene in the church in which Marvin punished Luke, saying, "Come over here, Luke, because you are grounded. And I don't care what your excuse is, because you know what? I don't believe you anyway. I know that you did that bad thing because you've done so many horrible things before."

With this, Luke exploded with anger and screamed as loud as he could at the co-therapist how much he hated him. Then, with the therapist cueing him, he screamed this over and over, or repeated the things she told him to. She told him that she knew that he was capable of saying the worst possible things with curse words and everything, because his mom and dad had told her some of the things he'd said to them, and she told him that this was the place to use them, in therapy. Luke went on repeating more and more of her cues until finally he didn't seem to need them and screamed, "I fucking hate you! Get the hell away from me! I don't want you to be my father!"

Then Luke began to sob. He couldn't yell anymore.

The therapist let Luke cry for a moment or two and then made the point to Luke that even though he had lashed out, she and the co-therapist were still there. "Did your hatred kill us?" she asked him, and then answered her own question. "No, we're still here." She then processed the feelings he had with her. Luke was crying uncontrollably now, and when the therapist asked him why, he said he felt bad for the things he said. So the therapist had Luke practice saying he was sorry to the co-therapist. Then she asked Luke if he was ready to have his real dad come in so that he could apologize to him in person. Luke hesitated, said it would be hard, but finally said yes.

FOSTERING EMOTIONAL BONDS WITH ADOPTIVE PARENTS   Helen then went to the observation room to get Marvin, who was nervous about going into the treatment room to sit with Luke. Betty told him that he couldn't say the wrong thing and that he should just be himself. Marvin and Helen went to the treatment room, and Helen had Marvin hold Luke in a holding therapy position. The therapist put her palm on Luke's forehead so that he would maintain eye contact with Marvin while apologizing to him. In order to coax Luke, she once again brought up parts of Luke's family history with the Korhonens. She told him that she understood that he thought his hatred could kill Marvin, because Marvin had had a stress-related heart attack in 1998. With this, Marvin and Luke both began to cry. Luke apologized for saying the things he said. He also told Marvin that he missed and loved him. Marvin responded with encouragement, saying that he hoped Luke would keep working hard so that he could come home. The therapist was now using a nurturing tone, asking Luke if he thought his dad was a quitter. "Are you a quitter, Dad?" she asked Marvin. Marvin said no, that he would never quit, and that he didn't want Luke to give up on him. The therapist asked Luke if he was going to give up, and Luke said, "No, I won't give up, Dad." He then began sobbing uncontrollably once more and grabbed for Marvin and hugged him close, sobbing for a good three or four minutes. Luke and Marvin cried together during this time. The therapist and the co-therapist dimmed the lights in the treatment room and stepped out to let them be alone for a bit.

The therapist and the co-therapist joined us in the observation room and watched Luke with his father through the two-way mirror. She remarked that Luke's body was "soft" and leaning into Marvin and was in the fetal position. He seemed "regressed" to her, appearing genuine as a young child might be. She turned to Betty and asked her whether *she* thought that Luke was being genuine. Betty was crying and said that she'd never seen Luke sob like that. When the co-therapist asked Betty if she was crying tears of hope, Betty said yes.

When Marvin came back from holding Luke and saying good-bye to him for the day, he had a big smile on his face, and he and Betty cuddled a bit. The therapist asked Marvin how he thought Luke did on a scale of 1 to 10 and Marvin said, "Nine." He also said that he felt that Luke came a long way during the session but that he still felt he had a long way to go for the rest of his life. The therapist made the comment that if she went in to the treatment room and asked Luke how much he'd taken care of his feelings today, he would probably say a 9 too, and that he wouldn't be lying if he said that. But she actually thought that he had taken care of his feelings at a rate of 2. She said that Luke didn't realize how much was really deep down in his heart, but he would find out that more work needed to be done soon enough.

Session 3: Regression Work via Role Playing

In general, third sessions are softer in tone than those of the previous two days. For Luke's therapy, the third day of therapy was conducted by the therapist and Sasha, Luke's therapeutic foster mother. The first five minutes were spent repeating compliance exercises. However, this day, after Luke took off his coat and placed it on the chair of the therapist's choice, she added even more rules and had him take off only one shoe and put it somewhere. He had to leave the other one on. Luke complied and then responded quickly when the therapist told him to come into the holding position with her.

The therapist began the therapy by talking to Luke about his good progress, but she also told him that just because he'd been good so far, didn't mean that he would necessarily get to go home with the Korhonens. She reiterated the hard work mantra. Then she began to talk about Luke's birth mother, Jackie, and told him he should be ready to do some regression work, which was when a therapist tried to help children remember what it was like for them to be a baby. The therapist then changed places with Sasha, so that Sasha was doing the holding. Sasha purposefully used a "soft touch" in therapy, using a very quiet and soothing voice and asking questions rather than ordering or telling. This added to the quieter tone of the day.

The regression work with Luke was done with a brief role play, a dramatic account of Luke's early childhood experiences. In this role play, Helen portrayed Jackie, Luke's birth mother. While Sasha held Luke, the therapist told him to close his eyes and go back to when he was in Jackie's stomach. Relying on the words of Betty and Marvin and Luke's case history, she began to replay what Jackie might have been like as a pregnant woman who didn't want her baby. Then, she said, Luke was born and now he was a little baby. The therapist, recreating details specific to Luke's childhood and pretending to be Jackie, approached Luke and told him he was ugly and that his mouth was disgusting and the noises he made were gross and that she didn't want him. She put her face right next to his and told him about the drugs she took and how many boyfriends she had and how ashamed she was of having him and wished that no one knew he was hers. Luke looked at her with no emotion in his eyes. Subsequently, the therapist called the co-therapist into the treatment room by yelling loudly for him. The co-therapist came in and yelled at Luke, bossing him to express himself: "Your birth mother is in your face telling you how ugly you are!" he yelled, "Doesn't that piss you off?"

The therapist continued to role-play Jackie by walking in and out of the treatment room, telling him how worthless he was and then leaving. After some time, Luke began responding to her when she screamed in his face. He told her he was sad about what she was saying to him, and then he told her he was angry. Eventually, after the fourth time the therapist came in and told him how worthless he was, Luke began to argue with her about it. For example, when the therapist would say, "I'm pretty and you're not," Luke told her, "Not if you were turned inside out you wouldn't be pretty. You're ugly inside."

With this session, the therapists' stated goal was to regress Luke through his toddler stages, before his first surgery for his cleft palate. Although the role play was limited this day, the therapist thought it would be a good idea to have Betty go in and hold Luke. This would contrast the nasty behavior of Jackie with the loving behavior of Luke's adopted mother. The therapist told Betty to cue Luke to tell her what happened in the treatment room with Jackie just a moment before, but not to talk herself. Sasha and the co-therapist left Luke alone for a few minutes to collect himself. About two or three minutes later, Betty went in.

When Luke saw Betty, his face registered surprise, but not necessarily pleasure. According to Sasha, even if he was happy to see her, he probably wouldn't have shown it. Happiness would suggest that he was feeling secure. When Betty told Luke to get in her lap though, he did it right away. Betty asked him what happened in the room with Jackie. She did as Helen had suggested and didn't say much to Luke; she did say, however, that she felt that what Jackie had told him wasn't true and that she thought he was a beautiful baby. She also stroked the surgery scar on his face, all the while making him maintain eye contact with her. Co-therapist Brendan then went in to aid the process and wrap up the session. Later, he told me that children don't get to spend very much time with their parents in therapy. This is because the therapists want them to develop a genuine feeling of longing for the adoptive parents. They want the children not only to want their parents to "rescue" them from the therapy, but also because they truly want to be with them.

This said, when Brendan entered the session room and sat down next to Luke and Betty, he used a drill sergeant's tone. He sat next to them on the couch and got right in Luke's face to tell him that he was sure he was "gonna give up." When he did this, Luke went to Betty's chest for support in an attempt to get away from Brendan. During the last few minutes of Luke's therapy, the co-therapist asked Betty if there was anything she wanted to say to Luke. He asked her if she thought Luke was going to give up. Betty said that she had faith in Luke, and she made him look at her and told him to stay tough. Luke began to cry very hard and reached for Betty to hug her. The therapist, who was observing through the two-way mirror, commented that his arms were around Betty the entire way and his hands were gripping her back. She said she was surprised he initiated a real hug with Betty.

After Luke's session, the treatment team planned to head to a staff meeting. The co-therapist told Luke to sit tight in the treatment room for about an hour by himself and reflect on the day's session. About thirty minutes into the staff meeting, the co-therapist went to check on Luke. He found him in the room clutching a box of tissues, crying hard. When the therapist went to check on him again soon after, she moved him to a different room to help him compose himself. After she moved him to another room, however, he asked her for paper and a pen to do some homework in what she perceived as an "arrogant way." This, she told me, let her know that even though he is working hard, he also thought that he had the program beat. She also told him that he should think again.

Session 4: The Psychodrama

The typical fourth session is an intense psychodrama of the child's early life history. This psychodrama is similar to the introductory role play and is designed to pick up where the earlier regression work left off. But it is also designed to evoke on an even deeper level the pain and anger resulting from the child's negative early life experiences.

In Luke's fourth session, the psychodrama took about an hour and a half. His case history served as the material for the script of the psychodrama, and it was written out and tacked up on a bulletin board in the observation room so that all psychodrama "players" could figure out who was to perform in the treatment room and when. The co-therapist Brendan served as the "director," in that he put Luke in the holding position and did the holding therapy with him and helped him to process his feelings as he was led through the events of his life. Helen played Luke's birthmother Jackie. Clinic interns played Luke's grandmother and various foster parents, and I played the role of the foster mother in Luke's shortest foster home stay because it was the most minimal role available.

After the treatment team determined who would play what roles and in what order they were to be performed, the therapist excused herself. She said she "needed a beer," and was going outside to take a few swigs and a couple of drags off of a cigarette. Assuming this was a joke, Betty and Marvin laughed out loud. However, the therapist told them she was serious. When I asked her why she was going to go do this, she said that olfactory memories are very powerful reminders of early childhood memories. Often, when she smelled of beer and cigarettes, children regressed much more quickly and took the role play more seriously. Other attachment therapists at the clinic agreed. Said one:

> Beer and cigarettes are the smells of neglect. Many diagnosed with RAD are genuinely disturbed and scared by these smells. When they smell alcohol or cigarette smoke, they associate it with extreme abuse

and pain. So it's a useful clinical tool. It cuts through a lot of the bullshit and triggers genuine emotions in the kids.

The treatment team rewrote Luke's life history to include the following elements, which were incorporated sequentially into the psychodrama:

- Jackie's neglectful parenting
- Two visits to the hospital for the effects of failure to thrive (FTT)
- Surgery to correct his cleft palate
- Two stints in temporary foster homes
- Living with Jackie's mother, while Jackie served jail time for child abuse
- Placement in another foster home
- Placement with the Korhonens

To begin the psychodrama, Brendan wrapped Luke loosely in a blanket and put him in the holding position. He then told Luke to close his eyes and imagine himself as a fetus, a fetus that wasn't wanted, a fetus being fed drugs and alcohol while he was in the womb. Then he told Luke to think of himself as a little baby. Helen then entered the treatment room and portrayed Jackie as a flighty, addicted woman who was sickened by, and angry about, Luke's cleft palate, and who was a neglectful mother. During this session, it didn't take Luke long to respond to these attempts at regression. While the therapist was sitting there, pretending to smoke a cigarette and telling Luke how horrible he looked, the co-therapist was holding Luke and asking him how he felt about what was happening, asking him things like, "What do you need from Jackie right now?" He was also telling him what was happening, saying things like, "She's here, but she's not feeding you right. She's here, but she's ignoring you. How does that feel?"

The rest of Luke's psychodrama looked like a revolving door, with many "surgeons," "foster parents," Jackie and her boyfriends flitting in and out of the room. The room bustled with people yelling and physically moving Luke from place to place. Certain scenes from his life were replayed, such as when he was being treated for FTT and when he had his cleft palate surgery done. Luke was hastily moved from one "surgery table" to another (sets of chairs pushed together), was "operated on" (complete with a bandaging of his nose and lip), and swaddled loosely with a blanket to replicate the helplessness that Baby Luke might have felt then. Later, the therapist, simulating Jackie's return to Baby Luke, acted very sweet and responsible in front of the doctors, but then, when they left, she began to yell at Luke about how upset and angry she was.

Scenes from Luke's home life were also reenacted, with another therapist playing Jackie's boyfriends cursing and pushing the therapist/Jackie around. They also replayed the night when one of Jackie's boyfriends found Luke behind the couch and expressed disgust at his appearance. Then Luke was brought back to "the hospital," where another member of the treatment team commented on how thin and malnourished Baby Luke looked and wondered whether he would die.

Each time that Baby Luke was brought to the hospital without Jackie, only to have her return sometime later, Luke would appear to get more and more upset, particularly when Helen, acting as Jackie, would come in, tell him that she was going to take him home and then leave him all alone swaddled and helpless on the chairs in the room. Whenever they left, Luke would cry out for her and ask the co-therapist, "Why did she leave me? She left me!" Eventually, when it was not Jackie but "foster parents" who began passing through the treatment room, Luke, who seemed completely regressed by this point, would ask, "Are you my new Mom? How long can I stay with you?"

Various therapists who worked or interned at the clinic at the time of my research continued to reenact Luke's various foster care placements and the therapist/Jackie continued to make several brief appearances. This continued until Luke began to get angry whenever "Jackie" appeared. At first, when she left, he was sad and crying for her. However, after a while it became clear to him that he'd been moved around many times and that every time she came, she eventually left him. He soon began to cringe whenever Helen/Jackie would come into the room. Brendan, continuing his role as the director of the psychodrama, attempted to help Luke process her comings and goings with statements such as, "She's gone again" or "She's gone to drink and do drugs, what do you think of that?" These comments encouraged Luke to get angry at "Jackie." At one point, about an hour into the psychodrama, when the therapist/Jackie came back to the treatment room, she moved very close to Luke and asked him if he wanted her out of his life. Luke screamed, "Yes!" The therapist moved even closer to Luke and hugged him hard. The therapist told Luke that he could get rid of Jackie with his words if they were loud enough and angry enough. He then incited Luke to yell at Jackie as loud as he could to tell her to get away from him. Luke became so enraged that with the co-therapist's inciting, he eventually got up from his holding position, undid the blanket around him, and pushed Helen/Jackie out of the room, screaming, "Get lost! I don't want you around!" Then he sat down on the couch and sobbed and sobbed in the co-therapist's arms.

After a few minutes, once Luke had stopped sobbing, Brendan the co-therapist told him that the psychodrama was over, that he'd seen enough of what it was like for him when he was little and that it was time for him to be his fifteen-year-old self again. The co-therapist told him he was safe and that now it was time to take off his bandages and be older. He also took on a nurturing tone and told Luke that his life was much better now than it was when he was an infant. The co-therapist told Luke that he had a special opportunity to put his early life behind him, because Luke now had "real and forever" parents that wanted him for a son. He asked Luke if he wanted to see his parents. Luke replied, "Yes, sir." With this, the co-therapist called for Betty and Marvin, who came into the treatment room, sat with Luke between them and held him. They cried together.

Session 5: Inner Child Work

A large part of the fifth session of the Evergreen intensive is devoted to doing "inner child work." Inner child work is designed to help the child identify himself or herself as an individual in need of care. In Luke's case, this involved the presentation of a teddy bear that would represent Luke's inner child. The therapist told him that the bear was named "Baby Luke" and that it was Luke's job to take care of it as if it were himself as a little baby. Luke was charged with keeping Baby Luke safe and talking to him when he was "having a feeling."

When the therapist pulled the bear out and told Luke it was his, his eyes lit up and he said, "I have a bear at the group home (the residential treatment program in Wisconsin where Luke had been living for the last ten months)!" He took the bear and cuddled it and touched all its parts. He listened carefully when the therapist told him what he should do to keep the bear safe. Later on, I told the therapist I was interested in Luke's positive reaction to the bear. Helen said that she felt that his positive reaction was because he was "stuck." "He's really at seven or eight years old in his development," she said. She then recalled a conversation with Luke's therapeutic foster father in which he made the comment that when he sees Luke at home in his pajamas at night, he swears that Luke looks like a little kid. Both she and the therapeutic foster father thought that this was further evidence of the break in Luke's cycle of need.

During this fifth session, Luke wanted to know if and when he was ever going to go home with the Korhonens. Until this point, Betty, Marvin, and the treatment team had not told him how long he was going to be in treatment. For all Luke knew, he was going to be there until he turned eighteen. The therapist responded to his question by telling him, "You're on a need-to-know basis. You keep working. The adults will decide if and when you're ready to go home."

Week Two of Intensive Therapy: Rejecting Birth Parents, Embracing Adoptive Parents

Session 8: The Tug of War

Evergreen intensives typically continue to use holding therapy, regression, and inner child work in sessions 6 and 7 or until therapists determine that children appear ready to reject their birth parents and embrace their adoptive parents. Therapists may also use some time during these sessions to conduct holding therapy with the parents. In Luke's case, Helen and Brendan conducted both types of work during his sixth and seventh sessions. In addition, during the second week of Luke's intensive, Helen began to introduce a series of exercises designed to encourage Luke in his acceptance of the Korhonens as family. One such exercise is called the Tug of War. The goal of the Tug of War exercise is to help children both physically and symbolically choose adoptive parents over birth parents. Another point of the exercise is to encourage children to think about who it is that they would like to emulate—their birth parents or their adoptive parents. As attachment therapists described it to me: Do children want to continue to give superficial love, like their birth parents taught them? Or do they want to choose the "real love" that their adoptive parents offer and expect?

In Luke's case, the Tug of War exercise was conducted during his eighth session. The exercise was conducted as follows: The therapist told Luke to stand in the middle of the treatment room floor and look in the mirror. An intern at the clinic stood behind Luke with her hands on his shoulders. Betty and Marvin came in and stood on Luke's left side. Helen, role-playing Jackie, called co-therapist Brendan into the room to play one of Jackie's many boyfriends. She and Brendan both stood on Luke's right side. Then Betty and Marvin began pulling on Luke's left arm while at the same time the therapist and co-therapist started pulling on Luke's right arm. As they pulled, each couple whispered, talked, or shouted things in Luke's ears. For example, Betty and Marvin told Luke how much they loved him, how much they wanted him to work hard to come home, and how they were not going to give up on him. Jackie, however, was telling Luke that he was ugly but that she sort of loved him anyway. Not enough to change, but that "hey, I'll send you some cards every year. Don't you want my kind of love?" The co-therapist, playing Jackie's boyfriend, kept yelling at Jackie that she didn't want an ugly kid like Luke, and also, if she took him home, he'd leave her. To which "Jackie" replied, "Yeah, you're right." As minutes went by, both couples implored Luke to choose them. They also increased the volume of their pleas. In the meantime, the intern stood behind Luke, whispering things like, "You need to choose between these two loves. Do you want the kind of love that Jackie gives or the kind the Korhonens are offering? Choose, Luke."

In this session, it took Luke about three minutes to get upset enough to start pulling away from Jackie and her boyfriend, and to start edging toward Betty and Marvin. When this started happening, the intern said, "If you don't want Jackie's kind of love, then tell her that." Without any more prompting, Luke began yelling at the therapist and co-therapist, telling them he didn't want their kind of love. The intern then said to Luke that if he didn't want Jackie's kind of love, he could show her by pushing her out of the room. "Push her out, Luke! Push her out!" the intern implored. Luke needed no more prompting to wrench away from Betty and Marvin and to push "Jackie" and her boyfriend out. "Get out of here!" he yelled. "I don't want to be like you! Get away!"

Once he had pushed them out, he ran to Betty and Marvin and grabbed them in a hug and held them both tightly. The intern led them to the couch, sat them down, dimmed the lights, and left the room.

Session 9: Forgiving Birth Parents

The ninth session of the Evergreen intensive focuses on working through the child's anger at his or her birth mother with the goal of having the child forgive her. Without forgiveness, attachment therapists believe, children's negative emotions may be left open and unresolved after an intensive. Luke's ninth session was devoted to encouraging him to forgive his birth mother. For this session, Helen told Luke that she was going to role-play Jackie in a "healthy mode," a state in which she could listen and understand and care about the things he was saying. She conducted this session with Sasha and directed her to do the holding with Luke and lead him through what she called the "forgiveness cycle." Luke climbed into Sasha's lap, and Helen, playing Jackie, sat down next to him and began explaining to Luke why she acted like she did when she was young. She then asked for forgiveness.

Luke listened to what she said but gave Helen/Jackie a hard time about her apology. For example, he held her to typical clinic rules, saying things like, "I actually can't forgive you right now because you didn't say 'I' in your apology" or "I can't forgive you because you didn't look me in the eye." These were all things that the therapist had told him over the course of the two-week intensive that he should do when he apologizes to somebody. Luke was attempting to hold "Jackie" to the same kinds of rules that he was being subjected to. Ultimately, he never did forgive her in the session or at any other time during his intensive.

Emotional Management and the Production of Child Love

The data included in this chapter demonstrates that whereas the *RAD diagnosis* normalizes certain understandings of family, as well as children's roles in that family, the two-week intensive component of Evergreen attachment therapy is designed to specifically *discipline children's bodies and minds* in ways that will result in the restoration of the family as an internalized collective. The Evergreen model explicitly and unapologetically operates as a form of emotional management of children, and the techniques that therapists use at the clinic are uniformly designed to return children to what attachment therapists understand to be their natural state as emotional assets. Foundational to this restoration is the production of family feeling. In turn, the successful production of family feeling relies on the production of child love in the clinic.

As we see, therapists at the clinic seek to produce child love in at least three important ways: First, they seek to rid children of the notion that they are, as one therapist called it, "beyond family." In other words, therapists go to great lengths to demonstrate to children that they cannot, and no longer need to, take care of themselves. Children are now part of an adoptive (real) family, and one of the stipulations of being in a family is the need and privilege to let adults be in control and keep children safe. Therapists at Evergreen understand children diagnosed with RAD to be preoccupied with self-caretaking, so much so that they seek only to control others at all times. Therapists seek to challenge children's compulsion to control others by demonstrating that "the therapist is in control" through a series of practices such as holding therapy, confrontational communication, demanding immediate conformity to therapy rules, and providing consequences to children who do not comply. By applying, and demanding, therapist control at all times during the two-week intensive, therapists believe themselves to be providing children with the opportunity to practice relinquishing control with them in the present, so that they can relinquish their need for control over adoptive parents later.

A second way that therapists attempt to produce child love in the clinic is through the series of exercises designed to divest children of their interest in their birth parents. Therapists reconstruct children's early histories through regression work and role plays that illuminate birth parents' lacks vis-à-vis the *doxic* notion of the nuclear family. For example, therapists piece together fractured narratives about birth parents' biographies, including their relationship and sexual histories, their alcohol and drug use, their medical histories, and even their feelings about giving children up for adoption. These details are presented to children as evidence of their birth parents' inability to truly care for them, as well as to demonstrate children's innocence in their own early histories. Therapists demonstrate that birth parents made poor decisions and treated children poorly; thus, it is understandable that children have strong and intense feelings about their lot in life. Therapists represent birth parents as unrelenting and immutable in their abuse and neglect of their children. Children are assured that birth parents will, in fact, *never* be in a psychological position to be able to, or want to, parent them in the present or in the future. Children are challenged to accept this fact, to process it, and to recognize the abundant opportunities that their adoptive family provides to them.

A third way that therapists attempt to produce child love in the clinic is through a series of exercises designed to nurture children's interest and investment in the adoptive family, which is also held up as the ideal form of family. This is evidenced through such examples as role plays in which adoptive parents "rescue" children from their past, and Tug of War exercises in which therapists physically and verbally encourage children to choose adoptive parents over birth parents. In these exercises, therapists explicitly and consistently compare birth parents to adoptive parents, almost always ranking them below adoptive parents in desirable attributes. For example, birth parents (as role-played by therapists) are often unclean, addicted, loud, irresponsible, dangerous, and without remorse about abusing, neglecting, and/or abandoning children. One the other hand, therapists encourage adoptive parents in the therapy room to be unambivalently reliable, loving, soft-spoken, helpful, and safe. Therapists present two options to the children at the moment of their therapy—either hold on to the fantasy of being returned to their birth parents or accept the adoptive family. They strongly encourage children to choose the adoptive family over their birth family.

In analyzing some of the practices associated with the two-week intensive at Evergreen, it can be argued that at least one goal of the Evergreen model is to integrate children into families by creating an affinity between adoptive parents' and adoptees and to create a solidarity of interest between adoptive parents and children. The data included in this chapter also demonstrate, however, that illuminating an alignment of interests between children and adoptive parents is not thought to be enough to produce child love in the clinic. Children's bodies and minds must also be strongly disciplined through a series of rigorous behavioral modification exercises. Throughout the two-week intensive, children are exposed to repetitive rote exercises that force a"practicing" of compliance to adoptive parents. Just as role plays and Tug of War exercises prescribe for children the roles, behaviors, practices, narratives, and symbols associated with "real" family, so do these exercises discipline children to take on the role of emotional assets. Over the course of the two weeks, children are expected to start to become compliant, respectful, receptive, passive, and even grateful to parents on a day-to-day basis. Only by practicing this behavior can child love eventually come to be born.

However, the "genuineness" of this emerging child love is always in question. As seen in this chapter, therapists at Evergreen are the first to say that they are never really sure whether their child clients are truly responding to the therapy or not. They feel compelled to create and employ informal assessment tools to determine the "genuine emotion" of their clients. For example, therapists consistently touch base with parents to rate children's "genuine emotion" on a scale of 1 to 10. They have also devised a series of techniques that they assume to be effective indicators of genuine child love, such as working hard in therapy, compliant communication, and "proper" ways of showing affection to adoptive parents (i.e., the correct way to give a "real" hug). On the one hand, attachment therapists in Evergreen find it necessary to construct the simulacra of family in a therapeutic setting; however, one is never really sure whether the therapy is actually producing the family it intends.

If confrontation therapy as it is practiced in Evergreen is designed to condition children to accept their roles as emotional assets, then the second important piece of Evergreen attachment therapy—therapeutic-parenting training—is designed to discipline *parents* to accept their roles in the family: namely, as the provider of the therapeutic home, or refuge. The methods and goals of therapeutic parenting are outlined in the next chapter.

Chapter Six

Fast and Snappy, Mom and Dad's Way, and Right the First Time

Constructing the Therapeutic Home

Another important component of the two-week intensive at the clinic is the therapeutic parent-training program, in which parents are taught the skills that therapists believe necessary to emotionally condition children once they leave Evergreen. As one long-time staff member at the clinic stated:

> The secret of life with attachment disordered children is…there ain't no secret. There's no switch you turn on or off and they suddenly become the kid you always dreamed of. You have to change as much as they do. You really have to investigate why you committed to the child in the first place, what your goals are for your family, and if you're ready to do what *you* have to do to do your part in solving this problem. That means things are probably not going to be the way you think they should be.…It's still your family though.

Thus, in addition to emotionally conditioning children, a second goal of an Evergreen intensive is to teach parents how to control RAD kids at home. This is also known as the process of turning one's house into a "therapeutic home." Attachment therapists use many methods to teach parents to turn their houses into therapeutic homes. These include parent-skills training classes; adult holding therapy; couples-counseling sessions; invitations to treatment-family homes to witness firsthand the skills taught in the parent-training sessions; and the establishment of a long-term treatment plan for when they return home with their child. First, I outline in detail the processes by which clinic staff members train parents to turn their houses into therapeutic homes. Once again I use Luke Korhonen's two-week intensive to demonstrate the ways in which the therapeutic home is made at the clinic.

Parent-Skills Training Sessions

Parent-training sessions at the clinic typically take two forms. The first are specially scheduled parent-skills classes taught by a trained therapeutic foster mother and employee of the clinic, who, at the time of my research, had worked at the clinic for almost ten years. The primary changes that attachment therapists teach parents to make in their households to accommodate children diagnosed with RAD are:

Physical changes to the house
    Putting alarms/motion detectors on doors
    Creating sitting places for children
    Creating chore sites/project sites
    Creating separate eating spaces (e.g., having children sit at a breakfast bar while adults eat at the dining table)
    Creating safe places for pets and/or vulnerable members of the family

Scheduling changes
    Alone time for parents and respite time
    Debriefing time between parents
    Strategizing time between parents
    Built-in time for frustration with, and anger at, children

Expected changes in children's behavior
    Physical and verbal compliance
    Material goods must not be seen as entitlements
    Sitting/chores
    Writing time
    No interrupting

No arguing
Family time must be earned
Creative consequences for acting out

The second type of parent-skills training was conducted by the primary therapists, who taught parents any lessons they thought were applicable to the family's situation. In fact, it was common to spend twenty minutes before each intensive therapy session on what was called a "parents-skills primer." For example, every morning, when Betty and Marvin Korhonen arrived to observe Luke's therapy from behind the one-way mirror, they had a discussion with the therapist and the rest of the treatment team about how they were going to parent Luke and the rest of their children after leaving the clinic. These sessions usually had three components.

First, therapists stressed the relationship between good parenting skills, a parent's individual physical and mental health, and the metaphorical health of the parents' relationship. For instance, in the case of the Korhonens, the co-therapist talked to them about how it would be necessary for them to get their own marriage on solid ground before they could get their relationship solid with the kids. He also insisted there was no way the latter could happen without the former. "What is good for the parents is good for the kids," he told them. "So let's figure out what's good for you."

Second, therapists identified parents' current methods of parenting to address why they hadn't been effective and to then set specific new goals. In the Korhonens' case, the co-therapist suggested to Betty that she could, for example, change the way she dealt with Luke when he was being bossy. According to Brendan, there were two parts of her exchanges with Luke that she needed to be aware of. First was the content of the exchange, and second, was the structure. The content of an argument with RAD kids, he said, hardly ever actually matters to RAD kids, so it's useless to enter into fights with them. He cited an example of a fight that Betty and Luke had gotten into only a couple of days earlier about whether Betty should purchase milk at the grocery store. He told her:

Whether there are two gallons of milk at home in the refrigerator or one doesn't matter. The point is, that by arguing with you about the milk, or correcting you about whether or not there is milk in the fridge, Luke doesn't really care whether it's there or not. He cares that he's got your attention and he's got you locked into a power struggle, and by keeping you in it, he is automatically winning.

The structure of the exchange is also important. According to attachment therapists, parents have the power to change the structure at any time. For example, in the Korhonens' case, the co-therapist's advice to Betty was for her to figure out what attachment therapists call a good "one-liner" to use to extract herself from the conversation, such as "I love you too much to argue with you."

During this part of the session, the therapist and the co-therapist also focused on some of Betty and Marvin's marriage issues and how they might relate to parenting Luke and the rest of the kids. They told Marvin that from what they'd observed during the last two days or so, he needed to have more confidence in controlling his children. Marvin said that he usually doesn't tell his kids to do anything because he thinks that they "just won't do it." The therapists then told Betty that she was the dominant parent. She replied that she wished Marvin would help her parent more, but, on the other hand, that she didn't think that he'd do it right. The therapist and the co-therapist told Marvin that he needed to be more forceful and "mean it."

With Betty, they tried a more indirect approach, so as not to raise her defenses. The therapist began to tell a story about "her friend John," who was a dominant parent and who made it difficult for his wife to contribute to parenting because he didn't give her space to learn and fail on her own. To this, Betty replied that it would be difficult for her to let Marvin parent because she knows "what works." "Yet," she said, "I'm frustrated by the way my kids are turning out."

Third, therapists answered questions parents had about the treatment program at the clinic. They also addressed parents' concerns about what might happen to their families once treatment was over. During the ninth session with the Korhonens, for example, the treatment team dealt with two issues of great importance to the Korhonens: how they could educate others about their new parenting skills, and how the therapists at the clinic could help them get their county services to pay for any future treatment for Luke, since they were currently relying on family members and charitable donations to pay for the therapy. Days earlier, the Korhonens had asked the therapist if she would write a general letter that they could give to people that described the new parenting techniques that they were learning as part of the program, so that, as Betty put it, "people won't think we're nuts." The therapist said there was a general letter that the attachment therapists at the clinic used to help "outsiders" understand the behaviors associated with RAD kids. During this session, she produced and read aloud the letter she had written for the Korhonens, and this put them at ease. In response to the Korhonens' second concern—paying for Luke's therapy—the therapist promised that the clinic director would speak to their caseworker and any other agents necessary to advocate for the Korhonens. Other members of the treatment team also suggested that the Korhonens speak with the judge who originally awarded them some of the payment for Luke's treatment.

Adult Holding Therapy

In addition to parent-skills training sessions, attachment therapists expect parents to also undergo holding therapy, and they sometimes even devote entire sessions to parents. According to attachment therapists, conducting therapy with adults, as well as children, is valuable. This belief is based on their interpretation of Murray Bowen's family-systems theory (1978), which interprets the family ecologically, in that the capabilities of the family is thought to be greater than the arithmetic sum of its parts (Glick, Berman and Clarkin 2000). Said one therapist at the clinic:

> If one part of the [family] organism fails, the whole organism fails. If one part falls out of balance, the other people quickly rearrange to make up for the lack of balance and to get equilibrium again. In this organism, it is important for the mother and father to be a strong unit, the core of the family. Without this core, the family cannot function.

This therapist also stated that since RAD kids are experts at figuring out "how to push parents' buttons," and are adept at figuring out how to divide parents by preying on their fears and sensitivities, parents need to deal first with their own issues.

Attachment therapists also consider holding therapy with parents important because it helps parents reprioritize themselves and their own needs:

> The idea of the self-sacrificing mom who puts aside her own happiness for her child doesn't really wash in these situations, because RAD kids will take advantage of that instinct.

As mentioned in chapter 5, a portion of session 6 in the Korhonens' case focused on holding therapy for Betty and Marvin. Prior to their holding therapy, the therapist had introduced and worked through something called a "life script" with them. Life scripts, as they are understood at the clinic,[1] are a series of questions that adult clients are expected to answer to help the therapist understand, in a general way, what happened to them during their childhoods. It also helps the therapist direct adults' holding therapy. During session 6, the therapist stood in the observation room with a marking pen and wrote Betty and Marvin's answers on a whiteboard as they read aloud their answers to their life-script questions. When Betty read hers, several issues surrounding what she interpreted as her father's physical and emotional abuse emerged. Marvin read his answers, stating that everything in his childhood had been fine. The co-therapist said that he thought this was interesting since he had already heard Marvin mention many times that his childhood was lonely because other kids thought he was stupid and that he had felt alone in that stupidity.

After the therapists discussed Betty and Marvin's answers, Betty accompanied the therapist and co-therapist into the treatment room for her holding therapy. She engaged in this therapy for about two hours. During that time, Luke's co-therapist, Brendan, who did the actual holding, and Luke's therapist, Helen, who sat by Betty with the intention of helping her process her feelings, dealt with Betty's father's abusive attitudes regarding Betty's weight as a child. Betty revealed how her father used to weigh her and her sister every morning before church on Sundays, and if Betty had not lost weight from the previous Sunday, he would yell at her or spank her. Helen and Brendan then talked to her about her low self-esteem in relationship to these experiences. As they had done with Luke, they told her to imagine Brendan was someone she was angry with—in this case, her father—and incited her to release her rage at him. Betty did this, crying and yelling at Brendan.

However, Marvin's holding therapy did not go as smoothly. Although he had told Brendan that he was open to the therapy because he "wanted to see if something was wrong," he did not meet Helen and the Brendan's therapeutic expectations that he would "open himself up emotionally" during the holding. With another therapist's help, they tried for about three hours to tap into some sort of memory that would help him to express sadness, fear, or rage. This did not happen, however. When they asked him why he was not tapping into his "true" feelings, Marvin told them that even though

---

[1] Whereas therapists who use transactional analysis (see Berne 1973; Steiner 1994) have popularized the term "life script" to describe an unconscious story that a child makes up at an early age and that governs the way his or her life is lived out, attachment therapists at the clinic use the term to describe a client's literal *written* description of their own childhoods, ones that therapists use to direct the client's holding therapy.

his childhood could have been better, and even though he was now scared about the "screwed-up" nature of his current family, he felt that every person was responsible for their own self and that there wasn't anything he could do about other people. He kept saying that everything was "OK by me," even when Brendan, in what he explicitly stated was intended to be a therapeutically based strategy, called Betty a "beached whale."

Although the day's session did not go as well as the therapist and cotherapist had hoped, they later told me that the work they "had done with the Korhonens was important for the family. They thought, for instance, that Betty had learned that the abuse she endured at the hands of her father when she was young, as well as how she reacted to it, was being replayed every day in her interactions with Luke, who was also verbally abusive and often caused Betty to want to withdraw or crack jokes to hide her own pain and hurt. By bringing this to Betty's attention, and then working her toward resolution of her anger toward her father, the therapist thought that Betty might find it easier to do some things that seemed "unnatural" to her, such as shrugging off Luke's abuse or taking control even when she was feeling scared or low. She might even get to the point where she could let Marvin take control of some of the parenting.

Couples Counseling: Reflective Listening

In addition to parent-skills training classes and holding therapy with parents, parents might also undergo couples-counseling sessions with certified therapists on staff at the clinic that are designed to give parents time to assess the impact of parenting children diagnosed with RAD on their relationship. Indeed, Betty and Marvin underwent couples therapy with Luke's co-therapist Brendan during the first weekend of Luke's two-week intensive. Their session, which Brendan felt was necessary to conduct in addition to the ten sessions usually scheduled for clients was held in the hotel room in which they were staying during Luke's two-week intensive. During this session, Betty was upset. Before the session even began, she related a story about something that had taken place that morning that had been unexpected and horrifying for her and Marvin. Throughout Luke's therapy, she said, his ten-year-old brother Jeffrey, who was staying with them in Evergreen, had been becoming increasingly jealous of the attention being paid to Luke, and he was acting out more and more. He had also told Betty and Marvin the day before that he thought that they didn't really love him and that, because of this, he was going to run away. "All I need is some money," he told them. Marvin, inspired by the therapist's suggestions that he stand up to his children more often, pulled out all the money he had in his wallet and told him that he could have it. Jeffrey looked sheepishly at him and then told Marvin that soon he would indeed run away, but not from Colorado. He needed to go home first and get more clothes.

Betty and Marvin reported feeling proud of themselves when they went to bed the night before. They felt that they had successfully used some of the new skills they were learning at the clinic. In the morning, however, Jeffrey continued to talk about his feelings that Betty and Marvin didn't love him, and he began to outline his plans to run away again. According to Betty, Jeffrey was also bossy, interrupting her and Marvin when they were trying to talk to each other. Betty, utilizing some of the clinic's methods, disciplined Jeffrey by assigning him several push-ups, which he completed. But eventually he became so exasperating to Betty that she sat him in a chair facing the wall and told him to sit there until she told him to get up. She then went to go to the bathroom. When she came out, she found that Jeffrey was out of his seat and in the kitchen. At this point, Betty turned her back on him, but she told Marvin to watch him. Marvin watched as Jeffrey went to a drawer where the knives were kept, put his hand in, and calmly told Marvin he was going to kill them.

Betty said that Marvin felt panicked, but that he remembered what he'd been told to do during the parent-skills class just the day before. He went to the phone and told Jeffrey that if he touched a knife, he would call 911. It was Jeffrey's choice, he said calmly, but he said it like he meant it. Jeffrey and he stared at each other for some moments until Jeffrey backed down. He closed the drawer, and Marvin told him to get back to the chair where he was supposed to be sitting. Betty related to Brendan that she'd never been so scared in her life. Even though she wasn't scared of Jeffrey, she was scared of his rage.

The Korhonens' couples session came just hours after the incident with Jeffrey. It consisted primarily of them completing what the co-therapist called "reflective listening" exercises. Earlier in the week, the co-therapist had pointed out to Betty and Marvin that they seemed to have communication problems. This translated into problematic parenting because Betty operated as too dominant and Marvin as too passive. The point of their reflective listening exercise was to teach them how to communicate with each other better so that they could provide a united front when dealing with their kids.

The couples session was conducted as follows: The co-therapist asked Betty and Marvin to sit in chairs facing each other, knees touching. The exercise dictated that one of them say something and then stop. Then the other was supposed to reflect out loud what they heard from their partner by saying, "What I heard you say was…" Then, the first person would say whether the second person understood all or some of it. The second person was then allowed to respond to what the first person said or to change the subject altogether. The point of this exercise was to introduce a rhythm to a couple's conversation that would clarify the content and what the co-therapist called the "metamessage" produced by the body language of the speaker. This session lasted about an hour and a half. In this short time, the co-therapist elicited several themes that he believed would help the Korhonens relate to each other. For example, Betty revealed that her self-esteem was low because her father always abused her because she was overweight. Marvin, on the other hand, revealed that he could hardly read, had always been called stupid by his teachers, and had serious anxieties about learning. When the co-therapist asked them how they thought these issues might affect the way that they tried to team parent children like Luke and Jeffrey, they discussed the possibility that Betty might have personal stock in "rescuing" all the kids as a way to feel better about herself. Marvin might also let her control everything because he thought he was too stupid to contribute, and Betty did little to counter that perception. The co-therapist then had them continue this conversation with a renewed attempt at reflective listening. He closed the session by warning Betty and Marvin that during the last week of the two-week intensive, they were going to be expected to work on their own childhood issues as hard as Jeffrey and Luke were expected to work.

Visiting the Treatment-Family Home

In addition to parent-skills training, adult holding therapy, and couples counseling, attachment therapists often direct parents to take a field trip to the treatment-family home so that they can see parent skills in action. The assumption is that parents will then attempt to copy them. For example, the same day that Betty and Marvin had their couples session, they were invited to visit with Luke at his treatment-family home. Luke's treatment-family home was a large five-bedroom stucco house tucked away in the woods, about ten miles from the clinic. It had a large open living room with a cathedral ceiling and two sets of stairs at opposite ends of the living room. One led up to a loft that was used as a TV room and playroom, and the other led up to a bedroom that was used by another child being treated at the clinic. There were also three other bedrooms clustered off the living room, which were used for other children as they rotated through their two-week intensives, short-term therapy, and long-term therapy. The house looked lived in, with magazines scattered on the coffee table and letters and files on the dining room table. The kitchen was slightly messy, and the back-yard looked like it was in the middle of being landscaped. In the words of the therapeutic foster parents, it was "a place where a lot of little children can do some chores."

At the time of the Korhonens' visit to the house, the therapeutic-treat-ment family was hosting four other children who were being treated at the clinic. When Betty, Marvin, and I walked into the house, Luke and another boy, about ten years old, were practicing the clinic's therapeutic method of "sitting," which requires children to sit quietly where a parent places them until they are called to do something else. In the context of the therapeutic home, sitting can take place anywhere at anytime that parents deem nec-essary. There may be several reasons for telling a child to sit. These range from giving a child time to cool down after he or she has expressed feelings in a way that the parent deems inappropriate, to reminding the child that spending time with family members is a privilege, to wanting to remind the child that the parent is in control in the home. A younger boy was sitting in a chair, facing the wall, and Luke was sitting Indian-style on the landing of one of the staircases. Both boys were silent, and when the Korhonens walked by them, they did not turn around, but instead remained staring at the walls. This particular therapeutic-treatment family had also been watching Jeffrey while Betty and Marvin were having their couples session, but he was no-where to be seen. The therapeutic-treatment mother greeted us from above in the loft with a cheery hello. She came down and offered the Korhonens some iced tea and talked about her family's plans to improve the backyard.

As the Korhonens spoke to the therapeutic-treatment mother about her backyard, the children remained stock still, until a third boy, a teenager who looked to be about Luke's age, came down from the loft and asked for help moving an inflatable chair into his room upstairs. The treatment father told Luke to stand up. Luke said, "Yes, dad, sir" and let the boy pass by. Then he sat down again. As the treatment mom then showed the Korhonens around the house, the treatment dad went into one of the bedrooms and returned with Jeffrey. The treatment mom explained that Jeffrey had been bossy with her and so she had told him that since he was no fun to be around, then she guessed the only person he could be around was himself. She then put him in the bedroom with a book. While in there, Jeffrey had fallen asleep. The treatment dad rousted him with a shrill whistle and then had him come out into the living room. When the treatment dad told Jeffrey to say hello to his parents, Jeffrey did it, but in a robot voice. The treatment dad then made Jeffrey do twenty-five jumping jacks for what he called his "snotty reply." He told Jeffrey he had to do them with a straight back and to clap after each one while saying, "One, Dad, sir..." and so on. After Jeffrey went through his twenty-five jumping jacks, the treatment dad asked Jeffrey, "Why wouldn't I have liked those?" Jeffrey said he had no idea. The treatment dad then told him he would need to do another twenty-five. Jeffrey did twenty-five more, and the treatment dad asked him again, "Now, why wouldn't I have liked those?" Jeffrey shrugged. The treatment dad had him do another twenty-five. This occurred four more times. The treatment dad was trying to get at the fact that Jeffrey had missed clapping between some of the jumping jacks or had slouched while doing them. When Betty asked the treatment mom what was going on, she said that even though it didn't seem like it, Jeffrey knew exactly what he was doing by not doing his jumping jacks correctly. She said that controlling things meant *that* much to RAD kids. Eventually, though, Jeffrey got them right.

The next step in the process of visiting the therapeutic-treatment family's home was learning how to teach children to conduct appropriate introductions. The other teenager who was staying with the family had finished moving his chair upstairs to his bedroom, and the therapeutic dad called him into the room. Then Betty and Marvin were introduced to him. When the teenager was introduced he put his hand out for them to shake and was very cordial. He then stated his name and age.

A last step in the visit to the treatment-family house is for parents to observe a typical family event, paying particular attention to the ways in which the treatment parents discipline children's speech and actions. In this case, later in the evening, the Korhonens joined the treatment family for dinner. Luke and the other teenager in the home were instructed to make most of the dinner under the treatment mom's supervision. They were also ordered to set the table and pour the water for everyone. After dinner, they also cleared the table, and Jeffrey and another younger boy were told to wash the dishes. While the children completed these tasks, the parents sat at the dinner table and talked. When the children were done with dinner chores, they were instructed to sit at their own end of the table. They had to say "Excuse me..." before they said anything, and they were not allowed to interrupt. If they did, they had to do push-ups. Jeffrey was particularly boisterous, being bossy to the other children, talking back and interrupting the adults during their conversation. The treatment family dad instructed him to do push-ups every ten minutes or so.

After dinner, the treatment dad told one of the boys to get up and tell his life story to us. Then he instructed Luke to do the same. Similar to the life stories written by parents before holding therapy, the children's life histories were narratives that explained why they were in the program. Luke was nervous during his presentation, and Jeffrey was in the kitchen making noise to interrupt him. As a result, Betty and Marvin's attention was more focused on Jeffrey's noise in the kitchen than on Luke's narrative, and they ended up interrupting Luke to yell at Jeffrey. The co-therapist told Luke to keep going with his story until he was finished, and then he told Betty and Marvin not to reward Jeffrey's bad behavior with so much attention.

Setting Up a Long-Term Treatment Plan

The final tool that attachment therapists use to teach new parenting skills is the long-term treatment plan, which parents will use as a guideline for parenting during what therapists call "reintegration." Reintegration is the process of helping a child to rejoin the family and live with them under one roof. If attachment therapists determine that a child is ready to return home after the two-week intensive, then plans for reintegration are always discussed and cemented during the tenth and final session. As the intake packet handed out to parents prior to the acceptance of a child to the clinic states:

> Your child has made some changes. You have made some changes. A well-thought out treatment plan makes this process effective. The process of reintegration may include several extended visits and trials. It should include some contingency plans. Placing parents (the clinic's term for client families) can anticipate some testing behavior. Regular phone contact between placing parents and therapeutic parents can help provide opportunities for support and for parenting strategies. A visit to the placing family by our therapeutic foster parent can provide the opportunity for additional training and support. Our therapeutic parent might also work with a respite provider, a support group, school systems, etc. to enhance the support network you have available to you. The option to send your child back to [the clinic] for a period of respite can help you to maintain gains.
>
> It is important to request help before things get too far out-of-control. "A stitch in time saves nine" is good advice when it comes to addressing your child's behaviors. Do not hesitate to ask for help.

Your hometown therapist is part of this process. On-going therapy by a trained attachment therapist will help all of you to maintain the gains you have made and continue to progress. Your therapist should help you to develop parenting strategies that work for your child, and should help to empower you in your role as parents. Insist on this.

In the case of the Korhonens, Luke's therapist introduced the discussion of the family's treatment plan during the last session just before going in to tell Luke that he would be returning home with his family in a day or two. Earlier in the week, the treatment team had spoken with the Korhonens about whether Luke should return home to try living with them again. The therapist indicated that she thought he should. Betty and Marvin agreed, and said they felt that they could take the skills they learned at the clinic and apply them at home, not just with Luke and Jeffrey, but with the whole family. Betty then made the joke that this was actually a moot point, though, because they couldn't afford to keep Luke in long-term treatment at the clinic anyway and that it was a good thing that he had made so much progress. She was happy, however, that he would not be returning to the group home again and was excited to try to work with him in their home. Marvin agreed.

The particular long-term treatment plan that Luke's therapist designed for the Korhonens was tailored to help them deal with both Luke's and Jeffrey's behaviors. It outlined each of their medication schedules and dosage amounts, schooling options, and a list of things that the Korhonens and the clinic staff needed to work on together to ensure that the Korhonens' county services would either subsidize or pay for Luke's (and now Jeffrey's) attachment therapy in Wisconsin. The other half of the treatment plan outlined the specific parenting skills that the therapist and co-therapist thought would be most effective for the Korhonens when parenting Luke and Jeffrey at home. In Luke's case, the Korhonens were told:

1. When using one-liners, be empathetic without rescuing.
2. Remember the concept of "the expandable box," meaning that Betty and Marvin had control over how big or small Luke's choices in life were going to be.
3. Reinforce verbal/physical compliance, such as eye contact and "Got it."
4. Reinforce that Luke is always on a "need-to-know basis."
5. Help Luke confront his feelings and help him express them in words.
6. Stand by your decisions and "Let your yes be yes and your no be no."

The therapist and co-therapist thought that when Betty and Marvin parented Jeffrey, however, they had to use some different tactics. With Jeffrey, the therapist said, the important thing was to keep him and the whole family safe. She recounted the situation where Jeffrey threatened Betty and Marvin with the knife. Betty and Marvin said they felt they handled it well, but they wanted to know what to do if it happened again. The therapist and the co-therapist told them there are several things they needed to do to prepare for a child like Jeffrey who acts out: First, there must not be any locked doors in the house and there needs to be an alarm on Jeffrey's bedroom door. Second, she said, if you say you're going to call 911, consider it a promise, not a threat, and be prepared to carry it through, no matter what. Third, hide the knives. Fourth, pick their battles, and only use the parenting skills they have learned at the clinic about 50 percent of the time that they experience some conflict with Jeffrey, because without the therapy to back up the feelings that the new parenting skills will induce in Jeffrey, it could be dangerous. Fifth, get in touch with the local police and ask them what they'd like the Korhonens to do in a situation when Jeffrey rages. Also, a preemptive call would prepare the police and make them take the Korhonens' situation more seriously in the future. Finally, letting the police know ahead of time that Betty and Marvin would like to have a "paper trail" of Jeffrey's behavior makes it more likely the police will be less lenient with him. Sixth, don't say to Jeffrey, "I'll love you wherever you live," because he's anxious about being thrown away. In response to Jeffrey's acting out, just use one-liners like "Good work on giving up on being a part of the family this morning." Finally, tell Jeffrey that suggestions one through five are going to happen so that Jeffrey can't complain of "being tricked." She told them to practice these skills until Jeffrey could attend the clinic for his own two-week intensive.

Saying Good-bye to the Korhonens

After the treatment plan was agreed on, Luke's therapist stood up and said it was time to tell Luke that she and the Korhonens had decided that he had worked hard enough in therapy to go home with the Korhonens the next day. When she told him, he looked surprised and did not do anything except smile. She also told him, however, that just because he got to go home, it didn't mean that she wouldn't be seeing him again. "There are plenty of kids who work hard in therapy and then go home and blow it," she said. "There's always room at your therapeutic-treatment family's house for you." But then she gave him a hug and wished him good luck.

Saying good-bye to Luke was very sad for everyone, including Luke, who cried. But he was also beaming and looked truly excited to go home. The treatment team gave Luke hugs and told him not to forget what he learned at the clinic. The Korhonens would stay one more night and then begin their long drive home to Wisconsin.

CHAPTER SEVEN

LOVING EACH OTHER FROM A DISTANCE
Life after Attachment Therapy Failure

The Korhonens were a family for which Evergreen therapy was successful in helping them to meet their goal of preserving the family as a physical body. Luke Korhonen understood the goals and objectives of attachment therapy; Betty and Marvin accepted many of the attachment therapists' philosophies and methods; and Luke was reintegrated into the home after only two weeks of intensive therapy. However, even in the case of the Korhonens, which Luke's therapist later admitted to me turned out better than most, family members did not accept attachment therapists' methodology, philosophy, and goals absolutely. Three weeks after Luke completed his two-week intensive, Betty reported to me on his status via e-mail:

Luke is doing okay. I do see him being dragged into some old things from the past with the other kids, and I let him know right away so he can correct himself. He really tries, but sometimes he gets lazy as far as sharing his feelings with us, and we have to ask him to share. He does share them when we ask though.

I had to laugh last week when we met with [Luke's hometown therapist]. He asked the kids if they thought there was anything that should be different at home. Luke said, "Yeah, dad needs to start spending more time alone with mom." [The therapist] laughed, and looked at Marvin and said, "Busted." Then he made him schedule time with me alone, and told us that if we didn't do that we would always be too busy.

We still haven't met with County Services yet [regarding payment for continued attachment therapy for Luke], but that is about what we figured would happen. Oh well—just another hurdle to jump—it's not like we aren't used to jumping them.

Thus, Luke did not make a "complete" recovery in the way that Betty and Marvin had originally hoped or expected, because he did not entirely cease his negative behaviors, nor did he completely reject his birth mother and accept the Korhonens as his new parents. Later, Betty and Marvin also reported misgivings about transforming their home into what Betty referred to as "the Stepford Family," a reference to the popular 1970s film *The Stepford Wives* in which a group of affluent men develop the technology necessary to turn their spouses into robotic household servants. According to Betty, however, Luke did accept the attachment therapists' tenet that having a family is a privilege and one that he had to work hard to earn. Luke thus changed his behaviors and began to show Betty and Marvin that he appreciated the opportunity to have a family, and that he had an investment in the family that more closely matched Betty and Marvin's. Simultaneously, Betty and Marvin began to realize their original hopes for Luke's progress and their expectations for his behaviors were unrealistic, given his history of abuse, neglect, and experiences in foster care. They learned to consider alternative family roles and practices and, as Betty put it, "to live each day as it comes." The needs of each of the individual members of the family began to inform the possible futures for the Korhonens.

While the case of the Korhonens is exemplary for the goals and methods of the Evergreen model of attachment therapy, and may be held up as an ideal outcome of the therapy, my observations at the clinic between 1999 and 2000 demonstrate that Evergreen therapy actually aids families in their quest for reunification about as often as it fails. Between 1995 and 1999, for example, the clinic where I conducted my fieldwork completed 129 two-week intensives for as many children. Of this number of children, 68 (52.7 percent) reintegrated, that is, returned home with their parents after the intensive, but 61 (47.3 percent) did not. Of the 61 children who did not reintegrate, 48 remained in "long-term care" in a therapeutic-family home at the clinic, and 13 were admitted to a group home, military school, or boarding school, where, according to attachment therapists, they would no longer be challenged emotionally. Attachment therapists call outcomes such as these, "loving each other from a distance," a term that denotes family obligations between members even though they do not live together in one household. The objective is to preserve some semblance of family.

In this chapter, I explore the phenomenon of "loving each other from a distance," through typical scenarios in which many children ultimately come to live at the clinic or are admitted to other institutions after undergoing attachment therapy. I highlight two cases of "loving each other from a distance." The first case is that of twelve-year-old June Meschler, sibling to Horacio and Rayna, whose family was introduced in chapter 2, and who, after a two-week intensive at the clinic, was admitted to long-term (but not permanent) care at the clinic to "practice being in a family." The second case is that of fourteen-year-old Jamie Haskell-James, who, after undergoing attachment therapy, was enrolled in military school instead of returning home to his family. In examining these two cases, we see that Evergreen therapy does not always succeed in helping adoptive parents achieve their vision of the home as an emotional refuge where children can be trained to perform as emotional assets; however, the phenomenon of "loving [family] members from a distance" does continue to preserve what Bourdieu has called "the family spirit" (1998, 64).

Practicing Family: The Case of Long-Term Treatment Kids

According to attachment therapists, "long-term treatment" is an optional residential program at the clinic designed to help those children whom therapists agree need more than a two-week intensive to effectively learn the skills that they believe are necessary to live in a family setting. During long-term treatment, the adoptive parents return to their hometown while the child lives in a therapeutic-family home, usually within ten miles of the clinic. Long-term treatment is often temporary, and typically ranges from one month to one year or longer. In a small number of cases, long-term treatment may last until the child emancipates from the clinic at the age of eighteen. According to therapists in Evergreen, the goal of long-term treatment is to change patterns of behavior, teach reciprocity, enhance the ability to trust/attach, and teach the child to make good choices to help them return to their adoptive parents' home as quickly as possible.

In long-term treatment, the child receives therapy as frequently as therapists determine is needed, but at least weekly. Quarterly psychiatric reviews as well as quarterly treatment planning are required during this time.

Therapeutic families report on progress weekly to clinic administrators. A monthly progress report is also sent to placing families or agencies. Regular contact between placing families and therapeutic families and clinic staff is intended to facilitate a team approach. Adoptive families are encouraged to continue to work on individual or family issues at home during this time. In addition, according to attachment therapists, this is a good time to begin to develop community resources that will be helpful when the child returns home. Therapists encourage families to locate a support group and trained respite care and to form working relationships with a local therapist, schools, physicians, extended family, and anyone who can provide time and energy to the ongoing progress of the child and family. Attachment therapists believe that a well-informed and coordinated support team helps make parenting children diagnosed with RAD easier and helps children maintain whatever gains they have made in the program.

A most vivid example of a case of a child who is placed in long-term care is that of June Meschler. As mentioned earlier, Bev and Harry Meschler adopted June and her two older siblings, Horacio and Rayna, when she was six years old. Originally full of high hopes for their new family, the Meschlers were devastated to learn later that the children, ages nine, ten and fourteen, were regularly having sex together. When Harry and Bev discovered the sexual behaviors between the three siblings, they began to seek help from their county services and psychologists. Through therapy sessions with the children they first learned that Horacio was the primary instigator of the sexual activity, and they moved him out of their home to a residential facility for sexual offenders in the state. However, even with Horacio removed from their home, June and Rayna continued to have sex with each other. More sessions with psychologists pointed to June as being the primary motivator for the most recent behaviors. June had also been witnessed sexually molesting girls in her first-grade class. Soon after this, the Meschlers admitted June to a group home about three hours from their house, where she resided until just before her two-week intensive at the clinic. Rayna was the only one of the three siblings who still lived at home with the Meschlers. However, Rayna did undergo attachment therapy in Ohio about a month after the Meschlers admitted June to the group home.

By the time the Meschlers arrived for June's treatment at the clinic, they had also discovered that June's birth parents and extended family, including grandfather and grandmother, physically and sexually abused June and her siblings as toddlers to the point that Bev and Harry believed that the children were actually used for prostitution and pornography in the Denver area. Both June and Rayna recalled white lights being shined in their faces and groups of people watching them as they had sex with various family members. They also remembered being "paraded" naked before people with cameras.

As is typical with the Evergreen method (and as described in chapter 5), when June arrived at the clinic, her primary therapist attempted to establish rapport, reciprocity, and control rules with her. He also explained the "cycle of need" to her and began holding therapy. For most of the rest of June's intensive, her therapist concentrated specifically on her history of sexual abuse, first eliciting from her a list of children she had sexually molested, and then creating a series of role plays and a psychodrama outlining what he thought were the key events that led to what he referred to as her "constant need for power through sex." During these sessions, the therapist used what he called "body triggers" through "nonthreatening touch" to encourage June's emotional responses. For example, according to June, when she was younger and Horacio abused her, she recalled he would often convince her to have sex with him by threatening her with very hard kicks to her shins if she refused. During therapy, then, the therapist tapped her shin firmly while he talked to her about Horacio abusing her, in an attempt to trigger her to remember those times when Horacio did kick her. According to the therapist, this technique worked to regress June more quickly when he was trying to get her to "have a feeling" about the abuse. Another trigger that June's therapist discovered and utilized therapeutically during the session was the placement of his hand over her mouth to remind her of the feeling she said she had when she was performing oral sex. The therapist also occasionally placed June's arms over her head to trigger memories of restraining her the way Horacio did. Sometimes he held June tightly in his arms to simulate June feeling suffocated. Whenever the therapist used these triggers, June struggled against him, sometimes to the point of becoming hysterical. When this happened, the therapist continued using the trigger, but continued to talk to her, saying, "Stay with it" or "Take a breath, you know where you are. Am I really going to hurt you?" June would then calm down, regroup, and continue on with the therapy.

Although June's therapist thought she was responding well to certain elements of the therapy, in that she was accepting attachment therapists' philosophy that she needed to work through her anger at her birth family for mistreating her and that she believed that her new family was something she had to "earn" and was complying with them in treatment, her treatment family reported that she was not doing well in their home. According to her treatment parents, June did not follow directions, often made bad choices, and acted out. The therapist discussed this with the Meschlers and then with June during her second week of therapy. He recounted what he described as June's less-than-desirable behavior and told her that this kind of behavior was just the kind that would keep her in the program long term: "It seems that you understand what we're telling you here in therapy, but you don't know how to act at home." Because what they considered to be negative behavior came in the wake of a discussion he'd had with June about the probability that her parents would be leaving her in long-term treatment in a few days, he also raised the possibility that her bad behavior was related to her anger with them for bringing her there and then thinking about going home. She eventually stated that she was sad and angry that her parents were leaving.

Later in the week, June continued to state that she was angry with the Meschlers. Although she had known that her admittance to long-term treatment at the clinic was possible after her two-week intensive, and perhaps even probable, she expressed that she was scared that they would forget about her when they left. She also worried that they would enjoy their life without her, so much so that they would decide that they did not want her back or that they would decide that she was too much trouble and disown her. June continued to express these feelings, perhaps most poignantly when she addressed a group at her treatment family's home one night, in which she recounted the history of her early life, why she had to come to the clinic, and what she thought she needed to work on to leave. She began to cry halfway through her story, and when her therapeutic father asked her why, she said it was because she was "scared" and that "there are people here that I don't know, and I don't want them to think I'm disgusting. Who will love me if I'm this disgusting?"

Before June even began her two-week intensive at the clinic, Bev and Harry had assumed they would leave her in long-term treatment there, but they had not discussed this with her. Their reasoning was that they thought the clinic would be the best place for June because they truly believed that she did not love them or want to be a part of their family. By the end of June's two-week intensive, however, Bev, Harry, and June's treatment team agreed that June seemed to feel genuine love for the Meschlers and wanted to do the work to be in their family. The Meschlers also agreed that they were willing to continue to change their expectations for their adoptive family, to practice the new parenting skills, and to keep both girls at home if that's what it took to help June and Rayna. However, they thought that even if the therapy made clinical sense to June, there was a big difference between her understanding her therapeutic goals and actually meeting them. They felt torn, and even though they dreaded telling June that they saw value in leaving her at the clinic for a while, they decided to have the conversation and treat her as an equal in the discussion.

As it turned out, June responded differently than they thought she would. In response to the therapist's comments about her being angry at the Meschlers for thinking about leaving her at the clinic, June stated that she had thought about the possibility and decided to "see it as good." Later, many months after she was placed in long-term treatment, she had this to say to me:

> I'm not going to lie. I hate it here. I don't like having everyone control me. I don't like the food. I can see their point [though] about being here for a while as probably a good thing. If I'm going to be in a family, I have to practice being in a family.

After speaking with June, the Meschlers decided to register her for three to six months of long-term treatment. They left the following day, and June made progress with the treatment. Inspired, a few months later, the Meschlers enrolled June's sister Rayna for intensive attachment therapy at the clinic, and eventually Rayna switched places with June. In late 2000, the Meschlers admitted Rayna to long-term treatment at the clinic for six months while June returned to live with them in their home. Two years after June's two-week intensive, the Meschlers continued to alternate living at home with each of the two girls, and even though Bev reported that the girls competed for their attention whenever the family was together during visits and drop offs at the clinic and reverted to old negative behaviors on a daily basis, June and Rayna decreased their sexual activities and were, Bev believed, learning to express genuine emotions appropriately. According to an interview I conducted with Bev after June's initial treatment:

> The "loving them from a distance" thing felt like a cop-out at the time....We struggled. We'd already been doing it while June was at the group home; and to keep doing it, while we felt it would keep us sane and while we knew it was the right thing for us, felt like the wrong thing in our souls for her. But now we're glad we did it....We're not your typical family, but it's working.

When Living in a Family Is Too Hard: The Case of Institutionalization

While attachment therapists frame some cases of "loving each other from a distance" as the result of a child's need to practice being in a family, they believe that other cases result from a child's *choice* to undergo permanent institutionalization of some sort, rather than return home to live with adoptive family or to enter long-term treatment at the clinic. The most striking example of this phenomenon that I witnessed was the case of fourteen-year-old Jamie Haskell-James. I met Jamie's family in November 1999, about six weeks after I arrived in Evergreen. When I met them, Jamie had already completed a rocky two-week intensive at the clinic in September and had temporarily stayed in long-term treatment with one of the clinic's therapeutic families at the request of his parents. According to his therapist, his intensive had been an especially difficult one because Jamie had become physically violent during one of his sessions, and his primary therapist and therapeutic foster care had responded by temporarily restraining him on the floor until he calmed down. Jamie was discharged to his home in Maryland just before I arrived in October, but, according to his mothers, Becky and Pat (a same-sex couple), his progress there had been slow. According to them, Jamie had "behaved better" in the home immediately after treatment in that he was more compliant and seemed "more genuine" to them. They reported that since being home, however, he had resorted to what they considered his usual behavior: obsessing over things, acting withdrawn and depressed, bottling up his feelings and then exploding in physical and verbal ways, and directing this hostility toward his thirteen-year-old brother Jonah.

When I met Jamie and his family, Jamie's two-week intensive had been completed and the therapists at the clinic had begun treating his brother Jonah in a separate two-week intensive. Becky and Pat had decided to bring Jamie to Jonah's therapy, however, with the hopes that Jamie could somehow participate and aid in his brother's progress. They also thought it would be helpful to bring Jamie in for what they called "a tune-up." They had also flown in Jamie's female hometown therapist, in case it turned out that Jamie needed some extra help.

Although people often commented on how much Jamie and Jonah looked alike, in reality, the two boys could not have been more different. Jonah was a tall lanky boy, with long arms and rail-thin legs. He had a mop of blond hair that fell into his eyes, which were wide set and rarely focused. Neurological testing had determined that he had developmental problems and his early childhood history suggested that he had been affected by his mother's use of drugs during pregnancy. His behavior also suggested this. He had little control over his facial expressions at times, widening his eyes at strange moments and biting his lip over and over again. He would often look in the two-way mirror of the treatment room and make faces to amuse himself. He also told himself elaborate stories when no one else was in the room. His hygiene was very poor. He always smelled a bit sour or of urine, and he suffered from bad breath because he disliked brushing his teeth.

While Jonah's primary therapist at the clinic said that he thought that Jonah clearly had neurological issues, he also stated that he believed there were some behavioral issues that were entirely treatable. Said his therapist, "You'll notice that he smirks all the time. It's like he's saying "fuck you" to everyone. And it lets me know that his actions, even if they don't seem it, are very calculating in some respects. So that's something we need to work on." The therapist also commented on Jonah's lack of attention to hygiene, interpreting it as a calculated attempt to make himself the kind of client that no therapist would want to do holding therapy with. In fact, the therapist spent a part of every session with Jonah telling him that coming in "with dragon breath" as a form of passive aggression would not deter the therapist from working with him. He would come back again and again to work with Jonah no matter how dirty he became.

Jamie, on the other hand, was fit, with well-groomed hair and stylish clothes. He was a bit shorter than Jonah and had bright blue eyes. Compared to Jonah, Jamie looked wiser and very aware of everything that was going on around him. He was silent most of the time, and spent a lot of time observing others. When Jamie did speak, he was very charming and articulate.

I had already observed Jonah for four intensive sessions when I finally met Jamie. These sessions had been devoted to introducing Jonah to the cycle of need, holding therapy, and assessing his need for control in the home. According to Jonah's therapist, these sessions revealed that Jonah's need for control in the home correlated with his need to compete with Jamie for Becky and Pat's attention. The therapist also said he thought the two boys shared a "trauma bond" (see Carnes 1997), that is, Jonah looked up to Jamie and sought to bond with him even though Jamie was verbally and physically hostile towards him. The therapist thus thought it would be a good idea for Jonah and Jamie to undergo some therapy together.

Usually Jonah spoke in a little-boy voice or mumbled, and he appeared very vulnerable in his sessions with the therapist. However, when the therapist told Jonah that his older brother Jamie would be joining him in therapy that day, a change occurred in Jonah that was completely unanticipated. As soon as he heard that Jamie was joining him, he sat up straight, his eyes focused, and he began asking questions about how long he would be allowed to be with Jamie and what they would do. When Jamie entered the treatment room, Jonah became even more animated, talking incessantly about such things as Pokémon, video games, and toys. He literally threw a barrage of words at Jamie. Jamie attempted to take part in the conversation, but could not, because Jonah kept talking over him. Eventually, Jamie appeared to be trying to defend himself against the force of Jonah's words. Every once in a while he would roll his eyes and sink further down in the couch, as if trying to get away from his brother. At other times, he would take a deep breath and try to reenter the conversation, just to make an effort. After about twenty minutes of observing this, the therapist entered the treatment room and told Jamie it was time to go. Jamie eagerly left the room. The therapist then told the treatment team that he would be showing the tape to the boys the next day to use as a visual aid for his discussion about competition and trauma bonds.

The next day, the therapist brought Jonah and Jamie into the treatment room and sat them down next to each other. A TV and video recorder were put in the room, and the boys watched a video of their interaction the day before. The clinic therapist and Jamie's hometown therapist watched the tape with them. A quick discussion ensued about how they behaved together. During the course of this conversation, however, Jamie began to talk back to the therapist. The therapist began asking about Jamie's feelings of hostility toward his brother. Jamie became increasingly more verbally hostile toward the therapist, increasing the volume of his voice and telling the therapist to "shut up." The therapist, in response, told Jonah to leave and sit in another part of the treatment center and wait, which Jonah did. At this time, Jamie's treatment father arrived at the session, joining the primary therapist. Jamie climbed up into the therapist's lap in the holding therapy position, and the therapist began to explore why Jamie was, as he put, in such a "foul mood."

During the holding, the therapist questioned Jamie's motivation to be in a family with Pat and Becky. He said that Jamie's mothers had reported that he was having "killing feelings," to which Jamie responded with silence. Jamie also closed his eyes and refused to look at the therapist anymore. Jamie's therapeutic father moved in closer to the two of them and held Jamie's hand. The therapist repeatedly told Jamie to open his eyes and look at him, but Jamie refused. The therapist then proceeded to open Jamie's eyes with his fingers and hold his eyelids back, all the while questioning him and talking to him about his "killing feelings": "Who do you want to kill, Jamie? Your moms? Your brother?" Jamie would not answer. All that were visible were the whites of his eyes. Then, suddenly Jamie went into a rage, jerking his body to get up. He flailed his arms, striking the therapist. The therapist and the therapeutic father then restrained him on the floor. There they remained for about an hour, restraining Jamie and attempting to talk him through his feelings of rage.

A good portion of the time that he was being restrained, Jamie remained silent. His therapeutic father lay sprawled across his chest with Jamie's arms pinned over his head, while the therapist lay across his legs. The hometown therapist was looking on from a nearby chair. The therapist repeatedly tried to talk to Jamie about his feelings of anger—he asked him such questions as, "Are you angry at your birth parents? Your moms? Your brother?" When Jamie finally answered, it was only to tell the therapist that it was he and his therapeutic foster father that he wanted to kill for restraining him on the floor. Jamie yelled obscenities and screamed dirty words. In the observation room, the hometown therapist commented that she felt like she was witnessing an exorcism. After a few more minutes, Jamie complained that his elbow hurt, and he began calling for Pat and Becky. Pat and Becky, who were watching the session from the observation room and who were crying, both said to their hometown therapist that they were not going to go in to the treatment room to rescue him. They said that they had witnessed this exact same scenario a couple of months earlier when Jamie had undergone his first two-week intensive. They also commented that it had taken a lot longer during that intensive for him to get to the point where he was expressing rage, but that they felt he was calling to them for the wrong reason—not necessarily because he genuinely wanted them, as parents, to rescue him, but because he did not want to be restrained. So they refrained from going in.

The therapist and the therapeutic father continued to restrain Jamie, with the stated intention of trying to evoke Jamie's emotions. After a few more minutes, the therapist then began presenting Jamie with options. He told him that it was important that Jamie comply and be honest about his killing feelings. He then told Jamie that he believed that Jamie's refusal to be honest about these feelings indicated that Jamie had no real interest or desire to manage his emotions in the ways that he needed to in order to be in a family. The therapist then explained to Jamie that this was his last chance to prove that he wanted the family he currently had, and that if Jamie decided not to be in the family, then that was fine, but he needed to tell Pat and Becky that this was his decision.

What happened next was, as Jamie's hometown therapist would later say, was "something out of a horror movie." The therapist told Jamie that they were about to release him and that this was his last chance to prove he wanted to be in a family. When Jamie heard these words, he winced as if someone had stabbed him in the chest, and then he emitted a wolflike primal scream. His face then turned as expressionless as stone, and he no longer talked, yelled, or communicated. He lay on the floor, face up, and stared into space. Pat commented that it looked as if Jamie had been cracked open and that there appeared to be nothing inside. After a few minutes of observing Jamie this way, the therapist told Jamie that what he really felt about him was that if Jamie did not learn to face his true feelings, he was going to end up killing somebody and going to jail. Jamie then began to cry and said that he didn't want to go to jail. The therapist called Pat and Becky in.

While Pat and Becky went in to hear what the therapist had to say, Jonah's therapeutic foster mother went to check on Jonah in another room. There she found him curled up on the floor in the corner of the room. He was crying and petrified. She asked him what he was scared of, and he told her he could hear through the walls of the therapy room and that he didn't want Jamie to kill him and his family. Jonah's therapeutic foster mother hugged him and told him that he and his moms were safe. Jonah then revealed to her that Jamie was regularly sexually abusing him at home and that he was scared that Jamie would kill him if he told. The therapeutic foster mother asked him if he would like to go in and tell Becky and Pat about it. Jonah said no. However, Jonah's therapeutic foster mother later sat with Jonah as he disclosed this information to Becky and Pat, and Jonah's therapist eventually began processing this new information with Jonah during his intensive.

Back in the treatment room, the therapist explained the options for Jamie to Pat and Becky. He said that he thought that Jamie was too dangerous to stay with them in their hotel, and that he needed to be placed in a facility until the weekend, when Becky, Pat, Jonah, and Jamie would leave Evergreen and then begin looking immediately for an appropriate place for Jamie to live outside the home. They agreed. But Becky and Pat also told Jamie that while he would be going back to Maryland with them over the weekend, he might not be living at home anymore. They felt that he was just too dangerous. Becky then went to be with Jonah while Pat told Jamie how she felt about his inability or lack of desire to be with them. She told him that she wished he could do it, but that since he couldn't, he had to go live somewhere else, and she and Becky would "love him from a distance." Becky then came in with Jonah, who listened to the rest of what Pat had to say. He looked worried about Jamie, but didn't seem to understand that Pat and Becky were, in essence, saying good-bye to his brother. Eventually, both parents came back into the observation room, Jonah was sent to sit with his therapeutic foster mother and Jamie was left to sit briefly in the treatment room. Becky and

Pat cried for some time, and Becky said that she felt horrible, but that even this morning, when she was with Jamie and Pat in their rented cabin, when she had needed to leave the cabin to get something from their car while Pat was in the shower and Jamie was in the living room, she stopped herself on the way out the door, because she did not trust Jamie not to kill Pat while she was gone. She said that she couldn't live like that.

At the end of the session, the therapist processed with Jamie the fact that he wouldn't be living with Pat and Becky when they got back to Maryland. Jamie lay stiffly in the therapist's arms and hardly said anything, including when the therapist told him that this was probably going to be the best thing for him, not being pressured to be emotionally honest or deal with his feelings. The therapist said that "sometimes, kids are just like that, and the best thing for them is no family." Eventually, the therapist left Jamie in the therapy room and headed to the observation room, where he cried for several minutes with Becky and Pat. The three then went to explain to Jonah what was happening with Jamie.

For hours after the session, the treatment team attempted to make sense of what had happened. There was much crying and hugging and people comforting one another. Later, the treatment team and Jamie's hometown therapist, who seemed to be having the most severe reaction to Jamie's therapy, went to lunch. As she said, "You just can't believe that a kid would choose what he's chosen. You just wouldn't believe it if you hadn't seen it."

Within a day, Becky, Pat, and the hometown therapist had a discussion with Jamie about the way he'd like to live his life. Jamie told them that he realized he couldn't "make it" emotionally in a family. He also told them that he wanted to live near them, but not with them. Ultimately, Pat and Becky found a military academy about ten miles from the house where Jamie could live full time and get an education, but still come home occasionally for weekends and holidays. According to Pat and Becky, Jamie would eventually be very happy with this outcome, as would they. Months later, Jamie was continuing to do well in school and planning on entering the military. According to Pat:

The military, I'm sad to say, is the perfect place for him. I'm one of those peaceniks, and it's hard for me to think that one of my kids is going to be all gung-ho about fighting and war and killing people, but, you know, he still can't connect emotionally…so I guess he should be somewhere where that's an asset, where it works for him. Although as he gets older I think he feels like he needs to control less…and so far, he hasn't hurt anyone. I feel like we did the right thing, and frankly

I feel like he chose the right thing for himself that day at Evergreen. It got a lot easier for us after Evergreen because we let our fantasies go once and for all and we forgave ourselves—and the boys—for not being the All-American family. We gave ourselves a break.

As this chapter has shown, the same methods that appeared to work for the Korhonens in helping Luke to live with his adoptive family can fail to work for other families. Instead, those children who are not reunited with their adoptive families may be "loved from a distance." This includes being (re)institutionalized in long-term care at the clinic or elsewhere, such as in group homes, military schools, or boarding schools. Implicit in this framework is the assumption that the exiling of the child from the adoptive family is a result of either the child's need for more practice in being in a family or the child's conscious *choice* to live outside of families, where there will not be an expectation to form attachments to others. In both instances, the responsibility for the shortcomings of the therapy is placed on the child. In the case of June Meschler, for example, June was found not to "be working hard enough" to take full advantage of the therapy, and this led to her placement in long-term treatment at the clinic. In the case of Jamie Haskell-James, living in a family was determined to be too hard for him, and so his adoptive parents enrolled him in military school. In both cases, making the child accountable for the failure of the therapy served to refocus attention from the less-than-desirable outcome and reframe it as a productive one.

In chapters 5 and 6, I argued that, despite its controversial nature, the Evergreen method of attachment therapy persists as a popular treatment because it both explicitly promises to produce child love in the clinic and to provide parents with the means and information to discipline children into families. This allows parents to continue to project their vision of their family into the future, despite children's difficult behaviors. In this chapter I argue that a second reason for the therapy's popularity lies in the fact that attachment therapists' framing of therapy failure as "loving each other from a distance" provides a unique opportunity for parents at the clinic to transform family from a physical to a metaphorical collective without diminishing it as a social category.

As we have seen, when children do not respond well to the Evergreen model of attachment therapy, parents feel at their wit's end. For most, the Evergreen model was considered a last chance for success. When the Evergreen model fails, their typical next step is to make arrangements to remove the child from the home. While removing the child from the home solves immediate problems perceived by parents, such as increasing their and other family members' safety and/or reducing their own frustration/fatigue levels, this decision presents a new problem: parents' original vision of the home as emotional refuge is challenged, if not eradicated altogether. However, by offering parents at the clinic the option of "loving children from a distance," attachment therapists offer parents the opportunity to continue to count children as family members. The Evergreen model of attachment therapy thus allows adoptive parents to preserve the family in spirit, if not in actual body.

CHAPTER EIGHT

OUT OF EVERGREEN

Theorizing the Social Reproduction of Attachment

As we have seen, the road to Evergreen, Colorado, is a long and difficult one for children and parents. Parents who adopt formerly institutionalized children and who later enter them into attachment therapy at the clinic in Evergreen typically rely on folk wisdom about family in framing their expectations of the postadoption experience. For the parents discussed here, the family is initially viewed as a sanctioned site—"the good home"—in which disinterested emotional reciprocity will take place. While the decision to adopt formerly institutionalized children is bound up in altruistic discourse, it sets in motion a series of difficult and important tasks for adopted children. While there is ample evidence to suggest that biological parents and adoptive parents share the same ideas about family, and that biological children perform the same work in their families as adopted children (Englund 1983; Diener, Heim, and Mangelsdorf 1995; Delmore-Ko et al. 2000; Welsh et al. 2008), one difference is that formerly institutionalized children who end up at Evergreen become involved in an altruistic discourse that increases parents' investment in the actualization of the family. A second difference is that the process of adoption itself serves as a trial by fire for parents. Agencies subject parents to rigorous disciplinary practices such as parent-fitness assessments, home visits, and postplacement reporting.

Many adoption agency practices work to cement these commonsense ideas about family and children that potential parents bring with them into the adoption process. In this way, adoptive parents' projections of themselves as altruistic providers, their home as an emotional refuge, and their children as emotional assets are legitimated and normalized during the adoption process. This is not necessarily the intent of the adoption organizations or the adoption agents; they are beholden to the state to strive for bureaucratic permanence and professional efficacy, which is achieved largely by placing as many children with acceptable parents as possible. But giving specific form to the idea of the family is an interesting unintended consequence of those acts. The state acts on the agencies in ways that reify certain conceptions of family; agencies then export those same concepts to the level of the individual home, where they continue to "live" through the practices and symbols of the "good home." They assure parents that, despite their adopted child's early mistreatment, the transformative effect of the good home, including material goods and love, will repair the wounds and change the child's behavior. Agencies imply this indirectly through representations of the idealized family, or, in the case of adoptions through domestic county services, through the narrative reinforcement of adoptive parents as "rescuers."

Rather than act as emotional assets, however, the formerly institutionalized children that parents adopt prove most often, postplacement, to be emotional liabilities. Their behaviors both challenge and undermine parents' *doxic* representations of family. Some parents, hopeful that it is the children, and not their expectations, that is the problem—and one that may be fixed—turn to a biomedical discourse to explain and alter children's behavior. Reactive attachment disorder, the centerpiece of this biomedical discourse, serves as both a "black box" and a "signal symptom" for parents, one that reorients the problem away from parents' original expectations for the family to the child's body, mind, and past. While RAD is a pessimistic diagnosis in that a child's current behavioral issues may be emanating from a developmental chapter that, in most cases, has long since been firmly closed, the Evergreen model's reinterpretation of the diagnosis accomplishes an important task at the level of the preservation of the family in the present and, more importantly, the future.

For example, the RAD diagnosis situates children's problems in their own biological development. While this "resignaling" is initially encouraging for parents, in that it places the burden of the family's problems on the child, that the problem is fixed in biology can make the disorder seem immutable and insurmountable. *Attachment therapy,* however, and particularly the Evergreen model with its primary focus on repairing broken children by revisiting earlier developmental stages in a therapeutic setting, gives the RAD diagnosis the potential to preserve the family as a field. The Evergreen model promotes a perspective about the plasticity of attachment, and frames broken attachment as relatively immediately reparable. Parents are (or become) aware that children have died in therapies inspired by, if not actually performed within, the clinic. And yet they are drawn there, oftentimes after other more conventional treatments fail.

It is not enough, however, to say that "desperation" drives parents to Evergreen—desperation does not account for adoptive parents choosing *this* unconventional therapy, rather than some other. Parents are drawn to the Evergreen model of treatment because it is guaranteed to "save" a number of categories that are important to them, only one of which is the child. Whether the Evergreen model ultimately returns children to the adoptive home or not, attachment therapists reframe therapy outcomes in ways such that the model saves the idea of family.

This said, when I first learned of the Evergreen model of attachment therapy, it seemed radical, in the sense that its practices and philosophies run counter to those of mainstream pediatric psychology. However, seen in the light of preserving the *doxa* of the family, the model can actually be argued to be quite conservative. It conserves the idea of the family that preexisted the adoption, complete with the transformative power of love, routine, and the material trappings of a good home. Parents are attracted to the Evergreen model because it invigorates and legitimizes the same ideas about families, children, and domesticity that they themselves socially reproduced, and then had reinforced for them by the adoption process. To return to the thinking of Pierre Bourdieu, they are simultaneously forging and fixing the category of family itself.

Once families arrive in Evergreen, they find that the use of confrontation therapy and therapeutic-parenting training reframes attachment as a negotiable social contract, one that is positively responsive to a disciplinary process. Treatments that fail at the attachment disorder clinic reveal the limits to our understanding about attachment. They also reveal what we may not want to admit: that developmental deficits resulting from maternal loss or deprivation is a lifetime-long grievable situation for adoptees and is not resolvable with a quick fix. However, if children do not respond to the therapy at Evergreen, attachment is reframed as a matter of the child's conscious decision to live apart from family. Using this new framing, parents are able to own the successes in this therapy and disown the failures. Even if they are not able to salvage the physical family unit, they are still able to keep family as a category with which to structure their social reality. While therapy may not achieve physical proximity to the family for the adopted child, it still allows parents to use the category of family to organize and achieve their social order.

Lessons Learned in Evergreen

Just as there are many roads leading to Evergreen, so are there many that lead out. Families carry what they learn in the town's clinics back to the cities and towns where they live, practicing the methods in their own homes and sharing the central practices of the Evergreen model with hometown therapists, doctors, and other parents. Children who are not reunited with adoptive families also continue their difficult work in the group homes, boarding schools, and military schools to which they are assigned. Therapists who work in Evergreen may leave the clinic but continue its practice elsewhere. Parents form new "Evergreen" support groups via the Internet. It is safe to say that the Evergreen model is not only practiced within the town's boundaries but in a nationwide therapy network with Evergreen at its center.

The Evergreen model of attachment therapy is also exported around the world. Foster Cline and Jim Fay, cofounders of the Love and Logic Institute, an organization located in Golden, Colorado, that is dedicated to teaching the "Love and Logic" philosophy on which much attachment therapy in Evergreen is based, continues to sell thousands of books and videos each year, as well as putting on seminars in several countries on topics ranging from managing toddler behavior to disciplining adolescents. International conferences extolling the virtues of the Evergreen method now take place in Great Britain and Japan. And therapists from these countries regularly visit Evergreen for training seminars in their techniques. Today, Evergreen is not just a town in Colorado—as one parent at the clinic told me, there is a new way to "*think* like Evergreen." Indeed, "Evergreen"—and all its symbols and practices and all that it connotes about children, the family, and domesticity—has become a state of mind.

Theoretical Issues

While the main goal of this ethnography has been to present a snapshot of one process by which the social category of family is constituted, institutionalized, internalized, and negotiated in the United States, there are other, equally important theoretical issues that ethnographic research at the clinic raises, ones that have to do with the ways in which children in particular are bound up in the making of family.

The Need to Examine How the Medical Model Is Used for Social Ends

Michel Foucault (1976 [1954]) and Christopher Lasch (1977) have written extensively on the use of the illness diagnosis to discipline individuals into accepting their roles in the Western nuclear family. However, it is worthwhile to reconsider the specific ways that children in particular are disciplined to this end (Katz 2001, 2005). Based on the data presented here, it especially seems productive to further explore the possible relationship between the ways in which medical professionals try to reproduce attachment and the attempt to mold children into "family material." Such an avenue would be informed by an analysis of what anthropologist Monica Casper has called the "culturing" of social objects. According to Casper, "'culturing' usually refers to growing a virus or other organic material in a laboratory. But it also captures the intensive activities and meanings around a particular social object at certain historical moments" (Casper 1998, 17). The data presented here demonstrate that adoptive families, adoption agencies, and attachment therapists are indeed "culturing" attachment through their activities, representations, and language, slowly changing its meanings and signifiers. It is interesting to think about what this phenomenon may mean not only for children diagnosed and treated for RAD, but also for children more generally. In other words, in what ways is the remaking of attachment influencing a variety of objectifications, personhoods, and subjectivities of children?

The Need to Hear from the Children Themselves

A second set of related theoretical issues that this research raises is the extent to which so-called RAD kids can, or should, speak about their own experiences of adoption and therapy (Stryker in press). While this book did not address RAD Kids' representations of family, the analyses here were informed by the words of twenty-one formerly institutionalized adoptees, between the ages of three and eighteen, who were interviewed with parents' permission during the course of this work. Scholars of childhood have long debated the value of, and problems with, presenting children as protagonists in their own stories (Bluebond-Langner 1980; Bluebond-Langner and Korbin 2007; Boocock and Scott 2005; Cocks 2006; Goodman 1970;

James and Prout 1997 [1990]). Scholars both within and outside anthropology have called such work "thinking from children's lives" (Mayall 2002, 4) or "thinking beyond Piaget" (Jenks 1996, 29; Van Ausdale and Feagin 2002, 7); these scholars have also raised many questions about the paradoxes of child-centered analysis. These questions are compounded further when conducting ethnography that centers on the narratives of children diagnosed with RAD. A popular, if unfortunate, joke among attachment therapists goes something like this:

Q: How can you tell if a RAD kid is lying?
A: Is his mouth open?

The point of the joke, of course, is that RAD kids are not capable of telling the truth. While this joke, on the one hand, is a form of "gallows humor" common to attachment therapists in Evergreen—indeed, it is a reworking of a gag that is more commonly told about politicians or lawyers to convey distrust of people in those notoriously disingenuous professions—it also contains within it an unsettling grain of truth, since one of the typical behaviors of RAD kids is pathological lying. Therapists may tell this joke to discharge the anxiety they feel about having to evaluate the genuineness of a RAD kid's response to therapy; the joke remains with me, however, because I have the same uneasy questions about how to regard the ethnographic material I gathered from the children. One feels acutely aware that one cannot always take their narratives literally, but one is also certain that it is important to figure out how to regard them in order to better understand the ways in which the children themselves make meaning of attachment therapy. A serious ethnographic treatment of the words and actions of RAD kids, then, is a subject that merits a book of its own, and is an important direction for future research.

In the end, determining the truth value of the statements made by the children discussed here was not central to my current goals, which focus on the social construction of attachment, attachment disorders, and attachment therapies, set within the broader social construction of the family— all of which are created in conversations that for the most part exclude the children themselves. Adoptive parents, adoption agency workers, and therapists, do most of the talking here. Children such as Luke, Jeffrey, June, Jonah, and Jamie are the object of this discourse rather than its initiator. From my interviews I do believe in the genuine pain that these children experience, before, during, and after the process of adoption, and it was my reaction to the difficulties that the children faced both before and after adoption that pushed me to try to understand the social forces shaping their lives. My hope is that children such as these will be the beneficiaries of my work and that, in the future, they will be subjects in, as well as objects of, the discourse on family and attachment.

The Need for More Empirical Research

A final set of issues raised in this book surround the question of how a more empirical understanding of children's experiences of family can be used not only to influence social scientific research on children but, also, to inform and reform both adoption practice and pediatric psychology more generally in the United States. As we have seen here, the consequences can be dire for formerly institutionalized children who come to be diagnosed with RAD if one ignores the reasons why parents are turning to controversial therapies such as the Evergreen method to preserve the family. It is also important to remember that for every formerly institutionalized child that has been adopted in the United States and who may ultimately be brought for therapy at Evergreen, there remain thousands of children in orphanages in countries from which the United States currently adopts, as well as within U.S. foster care systems. It is well documented that institutionalized children in both these settings face tremendous difficulties being raised in these cultures of care. These difficulties include higher rates of psychological and behavioral problems (Dementieva 2000; Hussey and Guo 2005), increased rates of juvenile violence (Jonson-Reid and Barth 2000), and increased rates of sexual and physical abuse (Jonson-Reid et al. 2007). In addition, when children raised in child welfare systems in the United States and around the world emancipate, they face higher rates of substance abuse (Smith and Thornberry 1995; Wall and Kohl 2007), incarceration (Jonson-Reid and Barth 2000), teen pregnancy (Southerland, Casanueva, and Ringeisen 2009), psychiatric disorder (McMillen et al. 2005), and homelessness and unemployment (Collins 2001; Courtney and Heuring 2005), as well as lower levels of education (McMillen et al. 2003) than children who have not been institutionalized (Iglehart and Becerra 2002; Shang 2002). Even children who eventually are reunified with their birth parents after spending time within institutions have much difficulty readjusting to family life (Bellamy 2008).

There is thus not only a pressing need for theoretical work that explores the boundaries of "child-centered" research; there is also a desperate need for *practical* work that is based on more empirical and phenomenological understandings of formerly institutionalized adoptees' experiences. While such a call is not new (see Finn 2009; Johnson and Fein 1991; Karr-Morse and Wiley 1997), little progress has been made in this regard. As Lynn Nybell (2001) has written, troubling children such as formerly institutionalized adoptees are still treated as "a problematic byproduct of an endangered world....Like toxic waste, [they] present a problem of containment—as they are conceived as threatening, unpredictable, and without a destination" (227). In particular, an empirical understanding of children and the workings of attachment is a glaring lacuna in the literature on formerly institutionalized adoptees (Ghennie and Wellenstein 2009; Mennen and O'Keefe 2005). The data presented here allude to the traumatizing and polarizing effects of maternal loss and institutionalization for adoptees. There is a great need for ways to reach birth parents of young children so as to decrease instances of breaks in attachment and to provide more attention to young children in institutional settings who have already suffered breaks in attachment. There is also room for greater opportunities for disclosure on the part of adoption facilitators about children's early history so that those who adopt children who have suffered breaks in attachment understand what they are taking on when they commit to become parents of such children, with space for more honest discussions about the potentially long-term challenges. And finally, there needs to be a way to promote more realistic expectations for families and children. In other words, not only is it our task to investigate our tendency to attempt to change children who are perceived to threaten our systems. The new task before us is to "swim upstream" to focus our attention on those systems that result in harm to children.

DEMOGRAPHICS OF CHILDREN TREATED
AT THE CLINIC BETWEEN 1995 AND 1999

Table A1. Gender

Gender of children (n = 129)	Number of children	Percentage (%) treated at the clinic (1995–99)
Male	84	65.1
Female	45	34.9

Table A2. Age

Age of children (n = 129)	Number of children	Percentage (%) treated at the clinic (1995–99)
0–3	0	0.0
4	1	0.78
5	5	3.9
6	10	7.8
7	10	7.8
8	11	8.5
9	18	14.0
10	19	14.7
11	7	5.4
12	19	14.7
13	12	9.3
14	11	8.5
15	1	0.78
16	2	1.6
17	2	1.6
18+	1	0.78

Table A3. Ethnicity

Parent-reported ethnicity of children (n = 129)	Number of children	Percentage (%) treated at the clinic (1995–99)
Caucasian	90	69.7
Hispanic	9	7.0
Biracial	9	7.0
African American	5	3.9
Russian	5	3.9
Romanian	5	3.9
East Asian	3	2.3
Chilean	1	0.78
East Indian	1	0.78
American Indian	1	0.78

Table A4. Home state

Home state of children (n = 129)	Number of children	Percentage (%) treated at the clinic (1995–99)
California	21	16.3
Colorado	16	12.4
Virginia	13	10.0
Minnesota	10	7.8
Florida	8	6.2
Pennsylvania	6	4.7
Missouri	5	3.9
Nebraska	5	3.9
Illinois	4	3.1
Canada	4	3.1
Kansas	4	3.1
Washington	4	3.1
Texas	3	2.3
Wyoming	3	2.3
Alaska	3	2.3
Alabama	2	1.6
Arkansas	2	1.6
Arizona	2	1.6
Connecticut	2	1.6
Ohio	2	1.6
North Carolina	2	1.6
Iowa	1	0.78
Louisiana	1	0.78
Maryland	1	0.78
New York	1	0.78
North Dakota	1	0.78
Oregon	1	0.78
South Dakota	1	0.78
Tennessee	1	0.78

References

Ainsworth, M. D. D., M. C. Blehar, E. Waters, and S. Wall. 1978. *Patterns of Attachment*. Hillsdale, NJ: Erlbaum.

Allen, Joseph P., Stuart T. Hauser, and Emily Borman-Spurrell. 1996. "Attachment Theory as a Framework for Understanding Sequelae of Severe Adolescent Psychopathology: An 11-year Follow-up Study." *Journal of Consulting and Clinical Psychology* 64(2): 254–63.

Alston, John F. 1996. "New Findings in Diagnosis: Correlation between Bipolar Disorder and Reactive Attachment Disorder." *Attachments* 1996:49–52.

———. 1999. "Correlation between Childhood Bipolar Disorder and Reactive Attachment Disorder, Disinhibited Type." In *Handbook of Attachment Interventions*, ed. Nancy Thomas, 193–243. San Diego, CA: Academic Press.

American Psychiatric Association. 2000. *Diagnostic and Statistical Manual of Mental Disorders*. 4th ed., text rev. Washington, DC: American Psychiatric Association.

Anderson, Michael. 1971. *Sociology of the Family: Selected Readings*. Harmondsworth, UK: Penguin Books.

Anderson, Michael, Frank Becchofer, and Jonathan Gershuny. 1994. *Social and Political Economy of the Household*. New York: Oxford University Press.

Aries, Phillipe. 1960. *Centuries of Childhood*, trans. Robert Baldick. London: Jonathan Cape.

Aronson, Naomi. 1980. "Working Up an Appetite." In *A Woman's Conflict: The Special Relationship between Women and Food*, ed. J. R. Kaplan, 203–29. Englewood Cliffs, NJ: Prentice-Hall.

Association for Treatment and Training in the Attachment of Children (ATTACh). 2005. "Registration List." Lake Villa, IL: ATTACh.

———. 2008. "Registration List." Lake Villa, IL: ATTACh.

Auge, Karen. 2000. "Alternative Therapies Not New in Evergreen." http://web.archive.org/web/20010309205804/ http://www.denverpost.com/news/news0617d.htm (accessed June 30, 2009).

Bakermans-Kranenburg, M. J., M. H. van Ijzendoorn, and F. Juffer. 2003. "Less Is More: Meta-analysis of Sensitivity and Attachment Interventions in Early Childhood." *Psychological Bulletin* 129(2):195–215.

Bartels, A., and S. Zeki 2004. "The Neural Correlates of Maternal and Romantic Love." *Neuroimage* 21(3): 1155–66.

Barth, R. P., D. Brooks, and S. Iyer. 1995. *Adoptions in California: Current Demographic Profiles and Projections through the End of the Century, Executive Summary*. Berkeley, CA: Child Welfare Research Center, School of Social Welfare, University of California, Berkeley.

Barth, Richard P., and Julie M. Miller. 2000. "Building Effective Post-Adoption Services: What Is the Empirical Foundation?" *Family Relations* 49(4): 447–55.

Barth, R. P., D. A. Gibbs, and K. Siebenaler. 2001. *Assessing the Field of Post-Adoption Service: Family Needs, Program Models, and Evaluation Issues.* Contract No. 100-99-0006. Washington, DC: U.S. Department of Health and Human Services.

Bartz, Jennifer A., and Eric Hollander. 2006. "The Neuroscience of Affiliation: Forging Links between Basic and Clinical Research on Neuropeptides and Social Behavior." *Hormones and Behavior* 50(4):518–28.

Becker-Weidman, Arthur, and Daniel Hughes. 2008. "Dyadic Developmental Psychotherapy: An Evidence-based Treatment for Children with Complex Trauma and Disorders of Attachment." *Child & Family Social Work* 13(3): 329–37.

Bellamy, Jennifer L. 2008. "Behavioral Problems Following Reunification of Children in Long-term Foster Care." *Children and Youth Services Review* 30(2): 216–28.

Berne, Eric. 1973. *What Do You Say After You Say Hello?* New York: Bantam Books.

Berry, Marianne, Richard P. Barth, and Barbara Needell. 1996. "Preparation, Support and Satisfaction of Adoptive Families in Agency and Independent Adoptions." *Child and Adolescent Social Work Journal* 13(2): 157–83.

Bluebond-Langner, Myra. 1980. *The Private Worlds of Dying Children.* Princeton: Princeton University Press.

Bluebond-Langner, Myra, and Jill Korbin. 2007. "Challenges and Opportunities in the Anthropology of Childhood." *American Anthropologist* 109(2):241–46.

Boocock, Sarane Spence, and Kimberly A. Scott. 2005. *Kids in Context: The Sociological Study Of Children And Childhoods.* Lanham, MD: Rowman and Littlefield.

Boris, Neil W. 2003. "Attachment, Aggression and Holding: A Cautionary Tale." *Attachment and Human Development* 5(3): 245–47.

Bourdieu, Pierre. 1977 [1972]. *Outline of a Theory of Practice.* Transl. R. Nice. Cambridge: Cambridge University Press.

———. 1998. *Practical Reason: On the Theory of Action.* Stanford: Stanford University Press.

Bowen, Murray. 1978. *Family Therapy and Clinical Practice.* New York: J. Aronson.

Bowers, Karen. 1996. "Terrible Two." *Denver Westword News* (October 10). http://www.westword.com/1996-10-10/news/terrible-two/ (accessed May 18, 2000).

———. 2000. "Suffer the Children." *Denver Westword News* (July 27). http://www.westword.com/2000-07-27/news/suffer-the-children/1 (accessed October 25, 2008).

Bowlby, John. 1944. *Forty-four Juvenile Thieves: Their Characters and Home-Life.* London: Bailliere, Tindall and Cox.

———. 1952. *Maternal Care and Mental Health: A Report Prepared on Behalf of the World Health Organization as a Contribution to the United Nations Programme for the Welfare of Homeless Children.* Geneva: World Health Organization.

———. 1965. *Child Care and the Growth of Love.* Baltimore: Penguin Books.

Bretherton, Inge. 1992. "The Origins of Attachment Theory: John Bowlby and Mary Ainsworth." *Developmental Psychology* 28(5):759–75.

Brodzinsky, David, Daniel Smith, and Anne Brodzinsky. 1998. *Children's Adjustment to Adoption: Developmental and Clinical Issues.* Thousand Oaks, CA: Sage Publications.

Buttner, Carolyn, and William L. Fridley. 2007. "What Would Jim Do?: A Comparison of James Dobson's and Jim Fay's Philosophies of Parenting." *Ohio Valley Philosophy of Education Society Philosophical Studies in Education* 38:131–40.

Cadoret, Remi. 1990. "Biological Perspectives of Adoptee Adjustment." In *Psychology of Adoption,* ed. David Brodzinsky and Marshall Schechter, 25–41. London: Oxford University Press.

Cadoret, R. J., and A. Gath. 1980. "Biological Correlates of Hyperactivity: Evidence for a Genetic Factor." In *Human Functioning in Longitudinal Perspective,* ed. S. Sells, R. Crandall, and M. Roff. 103–14. Baltimore: William and Wilkins.

Cadoret, R. J., T. W. O'Gorman, and E. Heywood, 1985. "Genetic and Environmental Factors in Major Depression." *Journal of Affective Disorders* 9(2):155–64.

Cadoret, R. J., E. Troughton, and T. W. O'Gorman. 1986. "An Adoption Study of Genetic and Environmental Factors in Drug Abuse." *Archives of General Psychiatry* 43(12):1131–36.

Canellos, Peter S. 1997. "Adoption Ends in Death, Uproar over Mother's Murder Defense: Son, 2, Harmed Himself." *Boston Globe* (April 17), A1.

Capelletty, Gordon G., Melissa Mackie Brown, and Sarah E. Shumate. 2005. "Correlates of the Randolph Attachment Disorder Questionnaire (RADQ) in a Sample of Children in Foster Placement." *Child and Adolescent Social Work Journal* 22(1): 71–84.

Carlson, E. A. 1998. "A Prospective, Longitudinal Study of Disorganized/Disoriented Attachment." *Child Development* 69(4):1107–28.

Carnes, Patrick. 1997. *The Betrayal Bond: Breaking Free of Exploitive Relationships.* Deerfield Beach, FL: HCI.

Carter, Sue. 2005. "The Chemistry of Child Neglect: Do Oxytocin and Vasopressin Mediate the Effects of Early Experience?" *Proceedings of the National Academy of Sciences of the United States of America* 102(51): 18247–48.

Carter, C. S., and Eric B. Keverne. 2002. "The Neurobiology of Social Affiliation and Pair Bonding." In *Hormones, Brain, and Behavior,* ed. D. Pfaff, A. P. Arnold, A. M. Etgen, S. E. Fahrbach, and R. T. Rubin, 299–337. San Diego, CA: Academic Press.

Casper, Monica. 1998. *The Making of the Unborn Patient: A Social Anatomy of Fetal Surgery.* Camden, NJ: Rutgers University Press.

Cermak, Sharon, and Victor Groza. 1998. "Sensory Processing Problems in Post-Institutionalized Children: Implications for Social Work." *Child and Adolescent Social Work Journal* 15(1): 5–37.

Chaffin, Mark, Rochelle Hanson, Benjamin E. Saunders, Todd Nichols, Douglas Barnett, Charles Zeanah, Lucy Berliner, Byron Egeland, Elana Newman, Tom Lyon, Elizabeth LeTourneau, and Cindy Miller-Perrin. 2006. "Report of the APSAC Task Force on Attachment Therapy, Reactive Attachment Disorder, and Attachment Problems." *Child Maltreatment* 11(1): 76–89.

Choleris, E., J. A. Gustafsson, K. S. Korach, L. J. Muglia, D. W. Pfaff, and S. Ogawa. 2003. "An Estrogen-Dependent Four-Gene Micronet Regulating Social Recognition: A Study with Oxytocin and Estrogen Receptor-alpha and -beta Knockout Mice." *Proceedings of the National Academy of Sciences of the United States of America* 100(10): 6192–97.

Chugani, Harry T., Michael E. Behen, Otto Muzik, Csaba Juhász, Ferenc Nagy, and Diane C. Chugani. 2001. "Local Brain Functional Activity Following Early Deprivation: A Study of Postinstitutionalized Romanian Orphans." *Neuroimage* 14(6):1290–1301.

Cline, Foster W. 1979. *Understanding and Treating the Severely Disturbed Child.* Evergreen, CO: Youth Behavior Program.

——. 1991. *Parenting Kids with Love and Logic.* Colorado Springs, CO: NavPress.

Cocks, Alison J. 2006. "The Ethical Maze: Finding an Inclusive Path towards Gaining Children's Agreement to Research Participation." *Childhood* 13(2): 247–66.

Coco, Linda (researcher), and Ralph Nader (introduction). 1996. *Children First: A Parent's Guide to Fighting Corporate Predators.* Washington, DC: Acorn Institute.

Collins, M. E. 2001. "Transition to Adulthood for Vulnerable Youths: A Review of Research and Implications for Policy." *Social Service Review* June, 75(2): 271–79.

Colorado Health Institute. 2009. "Active Licensed Health Professionals, Jefferson County and Colorado, 2009 (Colorado Department of Regulatory Agencies and Colorado Demography Office)." Denver: Colorado Health Institute.

Council on Accreditation. 2009. "Introduction to Hague Accreditation and Approval." http://www.coanet.org/front3/page.cfm?sect=54 (accessed October 31, 2009).

Courtney, Mark E., and Darcy Hughes Heuring. 2005. "The Transition to Adulthood for Youth 'Aging Out' of the Foster Care System." In *On Your Own without a Net: The Transition to Adulthood for Vulnerable Populations,* ed. D. Osgood, E. M. Foster, C. Ranagan, and G. R. Ruth, 27–67. Chicago: University of Chicago Press.

Cradle of Hope. 2000. "Testimony of Rob and Marianne Rivinius." http://www.cradlehope.org/CHAC_families/Rivinius.html (accessed May 13, 2000).

De Mause, Lloyd. 1974. *The History of Childhood.* New York: Harper and Row.

Dementieva, N. F. 2000. *Social Orphanhood: Origins and Preventions.* Moscow: Institute of Family and Youth.

DeKlyen, M. 1996. "Disruptive Behavior Disorders and Intergenerational Attachment Patterns: A Comparison of Normal and Clinic-Referred Preschoolers and Their Mothers. *Journal of Consulting and Clinical Psychology* 64(2):357–65.

Delmore-Ko, Patricia, S. Mark Pancer, Bruce Hunsberger, and Michael Pratt. 2000. "Becoming a Parent: The Relation Between Prenatal Expectations and Postnatal Experience." *Journal of Family Psychology* 14(4).

Denver Department of Human Services. 2003a. "Our Mission." http://www.denvergov.org/Family_and_Children/AboutUs/tabid/387128/Default.aspx (accessed May 15, 2003).

——. 2003b. "Denver Children Available." http//: www.denvergov.org/DenverChildren/Images (accessed May 15, 2003).

Diener, Marissa L., Goldstein L. Heim, and S. C. Mangelsdorf. 1995. "The Role of Prenatal Expectations in Parents' Reports of Infant Temperament." Merrill-Palmer Quarterly, 41(2): 172–90

Donzelot, Jacques. 1979. *The Policing of Families*. New York: Pantheon Books.

Dorow, Sara. 2006. *Transnational Adoption: A Cultural Economy of Race, Gender, and Kinship*. New York: New York University Press.

Eidlitz-Markus, T., A. Shuper, and J. Amir. 2000. "Secondary Enuresis: Post-traumatic Stress Disorder in Children After Car Accidents." *Israeli Medical Association Journal* 2(2): 135–37.

Eisner, Donald. A. 2000. *The Death of Psychotherapy: From Freud to Alien Abductions*. New York: Praeger.

Eluvathingal, Thomas J., Harry T. Chugani, Michael E. Behen, Csaba Juhász, Otto Muzik, Mohsin Maqbool, Diane C. Chugani, and Malek Makki. 2006. "Abnormal Brain Connectivity in Children after Early Severe Socioemotional Deprivation: A Diffusion Tensor Imaging Study." *Pediatrics* 117(6): 2093–100.

Eng, David L. 2006. "Political Economics of Passion: Transnational Adoption and *Global Woman*—Roundtable on *Global Woman*." *Studies in Gender and Sexuality* 7(1): 49–59.

Englund, C. L. 1983. "Parenting and Parentage: Distinct Aspects of Children's Importance." *Family Relations* 32(1): 21–28.

Engels, Frederick. 1999 [1884]. "The Patriarchal Family." In *Social Theory: The Multicultural and Classic Readings*, ed. Charles Lemert. 66–69. Boulder, CO: Westview Press.

Evan B. Donaldson Adoption Institute. 2004. "What's Working for Children?: A Policy Study of Adoption Stability and Termination." http://www.adoptioninsti tute.org/publications/Disruption_Report.pdf (accessed November 15, 2004).

Family Service Association (FSA). 2004. http://cafca.net (accessed January 30, 2004).

Farmer, Paul. 2001. *Infections and Inequalities: The Modern Plagues*. Berkeley: University of California Press.

Fass, Paula. 2007. *Children of a New World: Society, Culture, and Globalization*. New York: New York University Press.

Festinger, Leon. 1957. *A Theory of Cognitive Dissonance*. Stanford: Stanford University Press.

Festinger, Trudy. 2002. "After Adoption: Dissolution or Permanence?" *Child Welfare* 81:515–25.

———. 2005. "Adoption Disruption: Rates, Correlates and Service Needs." In *Child Welfare for the Twenty-first Century: A Handbook of Children, Youth, and Family Services—Practices, Policies, and Programs*, ed. Gerald P. Mallon and Peg McCartt Hess, 22–43. New York: Columbia University Press.

Finn, Janet. 2009. "Child's Eye View." In *Childhood, Youth, and Social Work in Transformation: Implications for Policy and Practice*, ed. Lynn M. Nybell, Jeffrey J. Shook, and Janet L. Finn. 317–36. New York: Columbia University Press.

Fisher, Helen. 2004. *Why We Love: The Nature and Chemistry of Romantic Love*. New York: Henry Holt and Company.

Foucault, Michel. 1976 [1954]. *Mental Illness and Psychology*. New York: Harper Colophon Books.

———. 1991. "Governmentality." In *The Foucault Effect: Studies in Governmentality*, ed. Graham Burchell, Colin Gordon, and Peter Miller. 87–104. Chicago: University of Chicago Press.

Fries, A., B. Wismer, T. E. Zigler, J. R. Kurian, S. Jacoris, and S. D. Pollack. 2005. "Early Experience in Humans is Associated with Changes in Neuropeptides Critical for Regulating Social Behavior." *Proceedings of the National Academy of Sciences of the United States of America* 102(47): 17237–240. http://www.guardian.co.uk/g2/story/0,509588,00.html (accessed July 1, 2009).

Ghennie, Kerrie, and Charlie Wellenstein. 2009. "The Well-Being of Children and the Question of Attachment." In *Childhood, Youth, and Social Work in Transformation: Implications for Policy and Practice*, ed. Lynn M. Nybell, Jeffrey J. Shook, and Janet L. Finn. 145–70. New York: Columbia University Press.

Glick, Ira D., Ellen M. Berman, and John F. Clarkin. 2000. *Marital and Family Therapy*. 4th ed. Arlington, VA: American Psychiatric Publishing, Inc.

Goerge, R. M., E. C. Howard, D. Yu, and S. Radomsky. 1997. *Adoption, Disruption, and Displacement in the Child Welfare System, 1976–94*. Chicago: Chapin Hall Center for Children, University of Chicago.

Goldfarb, Walter. 1945. "Psychological Privation in Infancy and Subsequent Adjustment." *American Journal of Orthopsychiatry* 14:247–55.

Goodman, Mary Ellen. 1970. *The Culture of Childhood: Child's-Eye Views of Society and Culture*. New York: Teacher's College Press, Columbia University.

Greene, Melissa Faye. 2000. "The Orphan Ranger: Adopting a Damaged Child." *New Yorker* (July 17), 38–45.

Groza, Victor. 1996. *Successful Adoptive Families: A Longitudinal Study of Special Needs Adoption*. Westport, CT: Praeger.

Groza, V., and K. Rosenberg. 1998. *Clinical and Practice Issues in Adoption: Bridging the Gap between Adoptees Placed as Infants and as Older Children*. Westport, CT: Praeger.

Groza, Victor, Scott Ryan, and Sara Thomas. 2008. "Institutionalization, Romanian Adoptions, and Executive Functioning." *Child and Adolescent Social Work Journal* 25(3): 185–204.

Gubrium, J. F., and J. A. Holstein. 1990. *What Is Family?* Mountain View, CA: Mayfield.

Hall, S. E. K., and G. Geher. 2003. "Behavioral and Personality Characteristics of Children with Reactive Attachment Disorder." *Journal of Psychology: Interdisciplinary and Applied* 137(2): 145–62.

Hamabata, Matthews Masayuki. 1991. *Crested Kimono: Power and Love in the Japanese Business Family*. Ithaca: Cornell University Press.

Hanson, Rochelle F., and Eve G. Spratt. 2000. "Reactive Attachment Disorder: What We Know about the Disorder and Implications for Treatment." *Child Maltreatment* 5(2): 137–45.

Haugaard, J. J. 2004. "Recognizing and Treating Uncommon Behavioral and Emotional Disorders in Adolescents Who Have Been Severely Maltreated: Introduction." *Child Maltreatment* 9:123–30.

Hope's Promise. "About Us." http://www.hopespromise.com/about/ (accessed May 13, 2000).

Horn, Miriam. 1997. "A Dead Child, A Troubling Defense." *U.S. News and World Report* (July 14). http://web.archive.org/web/19970731005244/http://www.usnews.com/usnews/issue/970714/14atta.htm (accessed March 3, 1998).

Howell, Signe. 2007. *The Kinning of Foreigners: Transnational Adoption in a Global Perspective*. Oxford, UK: Berghahn Books.

Hussey, David L., and Shenyang Guo. 2005. "Characteristics and Trajectories of Treatment Foster Care Youth." *Child Welfare* 84(4): 485–506.

Iglehart, Alfreda P., and Rosina M. Becerra. 2002. "Hispanic and African-American Youth: Life after Foster Care Emancipation." *Journal of Ethnic and Cultural Diversity in Social Work* 11(1–2): 79–107.

Inden, Ronald, and Ralph Nicholas. 2005. *Kinship in Bengali Culture*. Andhra Pradesh, India: Orient Blackswan.

The Institute for Attachment and Child Development. n.d. "Protocol." http://www.attach.org/protocol/Instit%20Att%20&%20Chld%20Dev.pdf (accessed July 15, 2009).

Jacobson, Heather. 2008. *Culture Keeping: White Mothers, International Adoption, and the Negotiation of Family Difference*. Nashville: Vanderbilt University Press.

James, Allison, and Alan Prout, eds. 1997 [1990]. *Constructing and Reconstructing Childhood: Contemporary Issues in the Sociological Study of Childhood*. London: RoutledgeFalmer.

James, Beverly. 1994. *Handbook for Treatment of Attachment-Trauma Problems of Deeply Troubled Children*. Northvale, NJ: Jason Aronson.

Jenks, Chris. 1996. *Childhood*. London: Routledge.

Johnson, Daniel, and Edith Fein. 1991. "The Concept of Attachment: Applications to Adoption." *Children and Youth Services Review* 13(5–6): 397–412.

Jonson-Reid, M., and R. Barth. 2000. "From Placement to Prison: The Path to Adolescent Incarceration from Child Welfare Supervised Foster or Group Care." *Children and Youth Services Review* 22(7): 493–516.

Jonson-Reid, Melissa, Lionel D. Scott Jr., J. Curtis McMillen, and Tonya Edmond. 2007. "Dating Violence among Emancipating Foster Youth." *Children and Youth Services Review* 29(5): 557–71.

Karen, Robert. 1990. "Becoming Attached." *Atlantic Monthly* (February), 35–50, 63–70.

Karr-Morse, Robin, and Meredith S. Wiley. 1997. *Ghosts from the Nursery: Tracing the Roots of Violence*. New York: Atlantic Monthly Press.

Katz, Cindi. 2001. "Vagabond Capitalism and the Necessity of Social Reproduction." *Antipode* 33(4): 708–27.

———. 2005. *Growing Up Global: Economic Restructuring and Children's Everyday Lives*. Minneapolis: University of Minnesota Press.

Keverne, Eric B., and James P. Curley. 2004. "Vasopressin, Oxytocin, and Social Behaviour." *Current Opinion in Neurobiology* 14(6):777–83.

Kincheloe, Joe, and Shirley Steinberg. 1997. *Kinderculture: The Corporate Construction of Childhood*. Boulder, CO: Westview Press.

Kirmayer, Laurence, and Allan Young. 1999. "Culture and Context in the Evolutionary Concept of Mental Disorder." *Journal of Abnormal Psychology* 108(3): 446–52.

Kleinman, Arthur, Wen-Zhi Wang, and Shi-Chuo Li. 1995. "The Social Course of Epilepsy: Chronic Illness as a Social Experience in Interior China." *Social Science Medicine* 40(10): 1319–30.

Lakatos, K., Z. Nemoda, I. Toth, Z. Ronai, K. Ney, M. Sasvari-Szekely, and J. Gervai. 2003. "Further Evidence for the Role of the Dopamine D4 Receptor (DRD4) Gene in Attachment Disorganization: Interaction of the exon III 48-bp Repeat and -521 C/T Promoter Polymorphisms." *Molecular Psychiatry* 7(1): 27–31.

Lasch, Christopher. 1977. *Haven in a Heartless World: The Family Besieged.* New York: Basic Books.

Lash, Cindi. 2000. "Overwhelmed Families Dissolve Adoptions." *post-gazette.com*, August 14, www.post-gazette.com/headlines/20000814russiadaytwo1.asp (accessed July 15, 2009).

Latour, Bruno. 1987. *Science in Action: How to Follow Scientists and Engineers through Society.* Cambridge: Harvard University Press.

Leibenluft E., M. I. Gobbini, T. Harrison, and J. V. Haxby. 2004. "Mothers' Neural Activation in Response to Pictures of Their Children and Other Children." *Biological Psychiatry* 56(4):225–32.

Levy, Terry M., and Michael Orlans. 1998. *Attachment, Trauma, and Healing: Understanding and Treating Attachment Disorder in Children and Families.* Arlington, VA: Child Welfare League of America Press.

Lorberbaum, J. P., J. D. Newman, A. R. Horwitz, J. R. Dubno, R. B. Lydiard, and M. B. Hammer. 2002. "A Potential Role for Thalamocuingulate Circuitry in Human Maternal Behavior." *Biological Psychiatry* 51(6):431–45.

Lyons-Ruth, K. 1996. "Attachment Relationship among Children with Aggressive Behavior Problems: The Role of Disorganized Early Attachment Patterns." *Journal of Consulting and Clinical Psychology* 64(1):64–73.

Magid, Ken, and Carole A. McKelvey. 1989. *High Risk: Children without a Conscience.* New York: Bantam Books.

Main, M., and Carol George. 1979. "Social Interactions of Young Abused Children: Approach, Avoidance, and Aggression." *Child Development* 50(2):306–18.

Main, Mary, Nancy Kaplan, and Jude Cassidy. 1985. "Security in Infancy, Childhood, and Adulthood: A Move to the Level of Representation." *Monographs of the Society for Research in Child Development* 50(1–2): 66–104.

Mauss, Marcel. 1967. *The Gift: Forms and Functions of Exchange in Archaic Societies.* New York: Norton.

May, Elaine Tyler. 1988. *Homeward Bound: American Families in the Cold War Era.* New York: Basic Books.

Mayall, Berry. 2002. *Towards a Sociology for Childhood: Thinking from Children's Lives.* Buckingham, UK: Open University Press.

McGuinness, Teena M., Rebecca Ryan, and Cheryl Broadus Robinson. 2005. "Protective Influences of Families for Children Adopted from the Former Soviet Union." *Journal of Nursing Scholarship* 37(3): 216–21.

McGuinness, T., and L. Pallansch. 2007. "Problem Behavior of Children Adopted from the Former Soviet Union." *Journal of Pediatric Health Care* 21(3):71–179.

McMillen, Curtis J., W. Auslander, D. Elze, T. White, and R. Thompson. 2003. "Educational Experiences and Aspirations of Older Youth in Foster Care." *Child Welfare* 82(4): 475–95.

McMillen, Curtis J., B. Zima, L. Scott, W. Auslander, M. Munson, and M. Ollie. 2005. "Prevalence of Psychiatric Disorders among Older Youths in the Foster Care System." *Journal of the American Academy of Child and Adolescent Psychiatry* 44(1): 88–95.

Mennen, Ferol E., and Maura O'Keefe. 2005. "Informed Decisions in Child Welfare: The Use of Attachment Theory." *Children and Youth Services Review* 27(6): 577–93.

Mercer, Jean. n.d. "Research and Psychotherapy: Let the Buyer Beware." http://www.childrenintherapy.org/essays/research.html (accessed July 8, 2009).

Mercer, Jean, Larry Sarner, and Linda Rosa. 2003. *Attachment Therapy on Trial: The Torture and Death of Candace Newmaker.* Westport, CT: Praeger.

Miller, Laurie C. 2004. *The Handbook of International Adoption Medicine: A Guide for Physicians, Parents, and Providers.* New York: Oxford University Press.

Minde, K. 1999. "Assessment and Treatment of Attachment Disorders." *Current Opinion in Psychiatry* 16(4):377–81.

Minnis, Helen, and Gregory Keck. 2003. "A Clinical/Research Dialogue on Reactive Attachment Disorder." *Attachment and Human Development* 5(3): 297–301.

Minnis, Helen, Joanne Reekie, David Young, Tom O'Connor, Angelica Ronald, Alison Gray, and Robert Plomin. 2007. "Genetic, Environmental, and Gender Influences on Attachment Disorder Behaviors." *British Journal of Psychiatry* 190:490–95.

Modell, Judith. 1994. *Kinship with Strangers: Adoption and Interpretations of Kinship in American Culture.* Berkeley: University of California Press.

———. 2002. *A Sealed and Secret Kinship: Policies and Practices in American Adoption.* Oxford, UK: Berghahn Books.

Morrow, Jan, Catherine A. Yeager, and Dorothy Otnow Lewis. 1997. "Encopresis and Sexual Abuse in a Sample of Boys in Residential Treatment." *Child Abuse and Neglect* 21(2): 11–18.

Mosher, William D., and Christine A. Bachrach. 1996. "Understanding U.S. Fertility: Continuity and Change in the National Survey of Family Growth, 1988–1995." *Family Planning Perspectives* 27 (1): 4–12.

Myeroff, Rebecca, Gary Mertlich, and Jim Gross. 1999. "Comparative Effectiveness of Holding Therapy with Aggressive Children." *Child Psychiatry and Human Development* 29(4): 303–13.

Nader, Laura. 1980. "The Vertical Slice: Hierarchies and Children," In *Hierarchy and Society: Anthropological Perspectives on Bureaucracy,* ed. G. Britan and R. Cohen. 31–43. Philadelphia: Institute for the Study of Human Issues.

———. 1997. "Controlling Processes." *Current Anthropology* 38(5): 711–37.

Nader, Laura, and Roberto González. 2000. "The Framing of Teenage Health Care: Organizations, Culture, and Control." *Culture, Medicine, and Psychiatry* 24(2): 231–58.

NavPress. 2009. Homepage. http://www.navpress.com/ (accessed July 1, 2009).

Newberry, Ruth C., and Janice C. Swanson. 2008. "Implications of Breaking Mother-Young Social Bonds." *Applied Animal Behavior Science* 110(1–2): 3–23.

Newman, Louise, and Sarah Mares. 2007. "Recent Advances in the Theories of and Interventions with Attachment Disorders." *Current Opinions in Psychiatry* 20(4):343–48.

Nichols, M., M. D. Lacher, and J. May. 2004. *Parenting with Stories: Creating a Foundation of Attachment for Parenting Your Child*. Deephaven, MN: Family Attachment Counseling Center.

Nicholson, Kieran. 2008. "Therapist in 'Rebirthing' Death Leaves Prison." *Denver Post* (August 1). http://www.denverpost.com/news/ci_10068874 (accessed July 11, 2009).

Nitschke, J. B., E. E. Nelson, B. D. Rusch, A. S. Fox, T. R. Oakes, and R. J. Davidson. 2004. "Orbitofrontal Cortex Tracks Positive Mood in Mothers Viewing Pictures of Their Newborn Infants." *Neuroimage* 21(2):583–92.

Noriuchi, Madoka, Yoshiaki Kikuchi, and Atsushi Senoo. 2007. "The Functional Neuroanatomy of Maternal Love: Mother's Response to Infant's Attachment Behaviors." *Biological Psychiatry* 63(4): 415–23.

North American Council on Adoptable Children (NACAC). 2009. "Cost of Adopting." http://statistics.adoption.com/information/statistics-on-cost-of-adopting. html#public (accessed July 11, 2009).

Nybell, Lynn. 2001. "Meltdowns and Containments: Constructions of Children at Risk as Complex Systems." *Childhood* 8(2): 213–30.

Nybell, Lynn M., Jeffrey J. Shook, and Janet L. Finn. 2009. "Introduction and Conceptual Framework." In *Childhood, Youth, and Social Work in Transformation: Implications for Policy and Practice*, ed. Lynn M. Nybell, Jeffrey J. Shook, and Janet L. Finn. 1–36. New York: Columbia University Press.

O'Connor, T., and C. Zeanah. 2003. "Attachment Disorders: Assessment Strategies and Treatment Approaches." *Attachment and Human Development* 5(3):223–44.

Ortner, Sherry. 1973. "On Key Symbols." *American Anthropologist* 75(5): 1338–46.

Pfeffer, Naomi. 1987. "Artificial Insemination, in vitro Fertilization and the Stigma of Infertility." In *Reproductive Technologies: Gender, Motherhood, and Medicine*, ed. M. Stanworth. 81–97. Oxford, UK: Polity Press.

Porter, Roy. 1987. *Mind-forg'd Manacle*. Cambridge: Harvard University Press.

Prior, Vivien, and Danya Glaser. 2006. *Understanding Attachment and Attachment Disorders: Theory, Evidence and Practice*. London: Jessica Kingsley Publishers.

Randolph, Liz. 1994. *Children Who Shock and Surprise: A Guide to Attachment Disorders*. Evergreen, CO: RFR Publications.

———. 2002. "Broken Hearts; Wounded Minds: The Psychological Functioning of Severely Traumatized and Behavior Problem Children." Evergreen, CO: RFR Publications.

Rapp, Rayna. 1999. Foreword to *Transformative Motherhood: On Giving and Getting in a Consumer Culture*, ed. L. Layne. xi–xx. New York: New York University Press.

Reber, K. 1996. "Children at Risk for Reactive Attachment Disorder: Assessment, Diagnosis, and Treatment." *Progress: Family Systems Research and Therapy* 5:83–98.

Reece, Robert M. 2005. *Treatment of Child Abuse: Common Ground for Mental Health, Medical, and Legal Practitioners.* Baltimore: Johns Hopkins University Press.

Reed, Bill. 2008. "Attachment Disorder Treatments Wrapped in Controversy." *Colorado Springs Gazette* (March 31). http://www.gazette.com/articles/attachment_33829__article.html/therapy_colorado.html (accessed October 14, 2008).

Richters, Margot Moser, and Fred R. Volkmar. 1994. "Reactive Attachment Disorder of Infancy or Early Childhood." *Journal of the American Academy of Child and Adolescent Psychiatry* March–April, 33(3):328–32.

Rosenstein, D. S., and H. A. Horowitz. 1996. "Adolescent Attachment and Psychopathology." *Journal of Consulting and Clinical Psychology* 64(2):244–53.

Rutter, Michael. 2002. "Nature, Nurture, and Development: From Evangelism through Science toward Policy and Practice—2001 Presidential Address to the Society for Research in Child Development." *Child Development* 73(1): 1–21.

———. 2005. "Environmentally Mediated Risks for Psychopathology: Research Strategies and Findings." *Journal of American Academic Adolescent Psychiatry* 44(1): 3–18.

Ryan, Scott D., and Victor Groza. 2004. "Romanian Adoptees: A Cross-National Comparison." *International Social Work* 47(1): 53–79.

Scheper-Hughes, Nancy. 1993. *Death without Weeping: The Violence of Everyday Life in Brazil.* Berkeley: University of California Press.

Schiff, Jacqui Lee (with Beth Day). 1970. *All My Children.* Philadelphia: M. Evans and Company.

Seifritz, E., F. Esposito, J. G. Neuhoff, A. Luthi, H. Mustovic, and G. Dammann. 2003. "Differential Sex-Independent Amygdala Response to Infant Crying and Laughing in Parents versus Nonparents. *Biological Psychiatry* 54(12):1367–75.

Seymour, Susan C. 1999. *Women, Family, and Child Care in India: A World in Transition.* Cambridge: Cambridge University Press.

Shair, Harry N. 2007. "Acquisition and Expression of a Socially-Mediated Separation Response." *Behavioral Brain Research* 182(2):180–92.

Shang, Xiaoyuan. 2002. "Looking for a Better Way to Care for Children: Cooperation between the State and Civil Society in China." *Social Service Review* 76(2): 203–28.

Shechory, Mally. 2005. "Effects of the Holding Technique for Restraint of Aggression in Children in Residential Care." *International Journal of Adolescent Medicine and Health* 17(4): 355–65.

Shorter, Edward. 1977. *The Making of the Modern Family.* London: Fontana.

Showalter, Elaine. 1997. *Hystories: Hysteria Epidemics and Modern Media.* New York: Columbia University Press.

Siegel, Bryna, 1996. *The World of the Autistic Child.* Oxford, UK: Oxford University Press.

Simon, Christian. 1999. "Images and Image: Technology and the Politics of Revealing Disorder in a North American Hospital." *Medical Anthropology Quarterly* 13(2): 141–62.

Smith, C., and T. P. Thornberry. 1995. "The Relationship between Childhood Maltreatment and Adolescent Involvement in Delinquency." *Criminology* 33(4): 451–81.

Southerland, Dannia, Cecilia E. Casanueva, and Heather Ringeisen. 2009. "Young Adult Outcomes and Mental Health Problems among Transition Age Youth Investigated for Maltreatment during Adolescence." *Children and Youth Services Review* 31(9): 947–56.

Speltz, Matthew L. 2002. "Description, History, and Critique of Corrective Attachment Therapy." *APSAC Advisor* 14(3): 4–8.

Spitz, René A. 1945. "Hospitalism: An Enquiry into the Genesis of Psychiatric Conditions in Early Childhood." *Psychoanalytic Study of the Child* 1:53–74.

———. 1962. *A Genetic Field Theory of Ego Formation: Its Implication for Pathology.* New York: International Universities Press.

———. 1965. *The First Year of Life: A Psychoanalytic Study of Normal and Deviant Development of Object Relations.* New York: International Universities Press.

Spradley, James, David McCurdy, and Dianna Shandy. 2005. *The Cultural Experience: Ethnography in Complex Society,* 2nd. ed. Long Grove, IL: Waveland Press.

Stein, Howard. 1985. "Alcoholism as Metaphor in American Culture: Ritual Desecration as Social Integration." *Ethos* 13(3): 195–235.

Steiner, Claude. 1994. *Scripts People Live: Transactional Analysis of Life Scripts.* Grove Press.

Stephens, Sharon. 1995. *Children and the Politics of Culture.* Princeton: Princeton University Press.

Strathern, Marilyn. 1992. *Reproducing the Future: Anthropology, Kinship, and the New Reproductive Technologies.* New York: Routledge.

Stryker, Rachael. 2000. "Ethnographic Solutions to the Problems of Russian Adoptees." *Anthropology of East Europe Review* 18(2): 79–84.

———. 2002. "Baby Brokering or Saving the Children?: The Moral Ambiguity of Exchange in Russian State-Run Orphanages." Paper presented at the Distinguished Lecture Series, November 12, at Haverford College, Pennsylvania.

———. In press. "The War at Home: Affective Economies in the American Transnationally Adoptive Family." *International Migration.*

Talbot, Margaret. 1998. "Attachment Theory: The Ultimate Experiment." *New York Times Magazine* (May 24), 24–30, 38, 46, 50, 54.

Thomas, Nancy. n.d. "Wagging Tails and Kids Who Kill." http://attachment.org/pages_parents_articles23.php (accessed June 1, 2009).

———. 2005. *When Love Is Not Enough: A Guide to Parenting Children with RAD.* Glenwood Springs, CO: Families by Design Publishing.

Thomas, Nancy, Terena Thomas, and Beth Thomas. 2002. *Dandelion on My Pillow, Butcher Knife Beneath.* Glenwood Springs, CO: Families by Design Publishing.

Trawick, Margaret. 1992. *Notes on Love in a Tamil Family.* Berkeley: University of California Press.

Tunina, Olga, and Rachael Stryker. 2001. "When Local Myths Meet Global Reality: Preparing Russia's Abandoned Children for International Adoption." *Kroeber Anthropological Society Papers* 89:143–52.

Tyejbee, Tyzoon. 2003. "Attitude, Interest, and *Motivation* for *Adoption* and Foster Care." *Child Welfare.*" 82 (6): 685–706.

United States Department of Health and Human Services. 2008. "Adoption and Foster Care Analysis and Reporting System (AFCARS) Trends in Foster Care and Adoption—FY 2002-FY 2007." http://www.acf.hhs.gov/programs/cb/stats_research/afcars/trends.htm (accessed July 10, 2009).

United States Department of State. 2008. "Total Adoptions to the United States, 1998–2008." http://adoption.state.gov/news/total_chart.html (accessed July 11, 2009).

——. 2009. "Accredited, Temporarily Accredited, and Approved Hague Adoption Service Providers, September 15, 2009." http://adoption.state.gov/pdf/Accred ited_and_Approved_list_%2009-15-2009.pdf (accessed October 31, 2009)

Van Ausdale, Debra, and Joe Feagin. 2002. *The First R: How Children Learn Race and Racism*. Lanham, MD: Rowman and Littlefield.

Volkman, Toby Alice. 2005. *Cultures of Transnational Adoption*. Durham: Duke University Press.

Wall, A. E., and P. L. Kohl. 2007. "Substance Use in Maltreated Youth: Findings from the National Survey of Child and Adolescent Well-being." *Child Maltreatment* 12(1): 20.

Warren, S. L., L. Huston, B. Egeland, and L. A. Sroufe. 1997. "Child and Adolescent Anxiety Disorders and Early Attachment." *Journal of the American Academy of Child and Adolescent Psychiatry* 36(5):637–44.

Waters, Everett, Leah Matas, and Alan Sroufe. 1975. "Infants' Reactions to an Approaching Stranger: Description, Validation, and Functional Significance of Wariness." *Child Development* 46(2): 348–56.

Welch, Martha. 1989. *Holding Time*. New York: Simon and Schuster.

Welsh, Janet A., Andres G. Viana, Stephen A. Petrill, and Matthew D. Mathias. 2008. "Ready to Adopt: Characteristics and Expectations of Preadoptive Families Pursuing International Adoptions." *Adoption Quarterly* 11(3): 176–203.

Wenegrat, Brant. 2001. *Theater of Disorder: Patients, Doctors, and the Construction of Illness*. New York: Oxford University Press.

Wingert, Pat. 2008. "Wanted: A Bundle of Joy, Why Fewer Americans Are Adopting Overseas." *Newsweek* (Oct 13), 152(15): 12.

Winslow, J. T., and T. R. Insel. 2002. "The Social Deficits of the Oxytocin Knockout Mouse." *Neuropeptides* 36(2–3): 221–29.

Wolkind, S. N. 1974. "The Components of 'Affectionless Psychopathy' in Institutionalized Children." *Journal of Child Psychology and Psychiatry* 15(3):215–20.

Wood, Robert. 1968. *Children 1772–1890*. London: Evans.

Worthington, Rebecca. 2009. "The Road to Parentless Children is Paved with Good Intentions: How the Hague Convention and Recent Intercountry Adoption Rules are Affecting Potential Parents and the Best Interests of Children." *Duke Journal of Comparative and International Law* 19:559–86.

Young, Allan. 1995. *The Harmony of Illusions: Inventing Post-Traumatic Stress Disorder*. Princeton: Princeton University Press.

Yngvesson, Barbara. 2002. "Placing the 'Gift Child' in Transnational Adoption." *Law and Society Review* 36(2): 227–55.

Zak, Paul J. 2008. "The Neurobiology of Trust." *Scientific American* 298(6): 88–95.

Zak, Paul J., Robert Kurzban, and Robert Matzner. 2004. "The Neurobiology of Trust." *New York Academy of Sciences* 1032:224–27.

——. 2005. "Oxytocin is Associated with Human Trustworthiness." *Hormones and Behavior* 48(5):522–27.

Zaretsky, Eli. 1973. "Capitalism, the Family, and Personal Life: Part 2." *Socialist Revolution* 3(3): 19–70.

Zaslow, Robert W., and Marilyn Menta. 1975. *The Psychology of the Z-Process: Attachment and Activity.* San Jose, CA: San Jose State University Press.

Zeanah, C. 1996. "Beyond Insecurity: A Reconceptualization of Attachment Disorders of Infancy." *Journal of Consulting and Clinical Psychology* 64(1):42–52.

Zeanah, Charles H., Anna T. Smyke, and Alina Dumitrescu. 2002. "Attachment Disturbances in Young Children, Part 2: Indiscriminate Behavior and Institutional Care." *Journal of the American Academy of Child and Adolescent Psychiatry* 41(8): 983.

Zeanah, Charles H., Anna T. Smyke, Sebastian F. Koga, and Elizabeth Carlson. 2005. "Attachment in Institutionalized and Community Children in Romania." *Child Development* 76(5): 1015–28.

Zeanah, Charles H., and Anna T. Smyke. 2008. "Attachment Disorders in Family and Social Context." *Infant Mental Health Journal* 29(3): 219–33.

Zelizer, Viviana. 1985. *Pricing the Priceless Child: The Changing Social Value of Children.* Princeton: Princeton University Press.

Zilberstein, Karen. 2006. "Clarifying Core Characteristics of Attachment Disorders: A Review of Current Research and Theory." *American Journal of Orthopsychiatry* 76(1): 55–64.

Index